Samuel Graham Wilson

Persian Life and Customs

Samuel Graham Wilson

Persian Life and Customs

ISBN/EAN: 9783337293949

Printed in Europe, USA, Canada, Australia, Japan

Cover: Foto ©ninafisch / pixelio.de

More available books at **www.hansebooks.com**

PERSIAN LIFE AND CUSTOMS

WITH SCENES AND INCIDENTS OF RESIDENCE AND TRAVEL IN THE LAND OF THE LION AND THE SUN

BY THE

REV. S. G. WILSON, M. A.

FIFTEEN YEARS A MISSIONARY IN PERSIA

With Map and Illustrations

FLEMING H. REVELL COMPANY

NEW YORK   CHICAGO   TORONTO

1895

CONTENTS

5

CHAPTER XI

CHAPTER XII

CHAPTER XIII

CHAPTER XIV

CHAPTER XV

CHAPTER XVI

CHAPTER XVII

LIST OF ILLUSTRATIONS

7

PERSIAN LIFE AND CUSTOMS

INTRODUCTION

THE pleasing satire, "The Last Mekrikan," pictures the arrival in America, in the year 2990, of Professor Noz-yt-al, of the University of Ispahan, in company with the curator of the Royal Museum of Teheran. At that time art and science are supposed to be flourishing in those ancient cities. The voyage of the wanderers brought them to an unknown harbor, where, amid uninhabited ruins and the debris of a mighty past, the archæologists discover inscriptions which reveal the site as that of the once famous New York. Penetrating to the interior of the country, they enter a building whose splendid dome and grand pillars, even though dilapidated, tell of its former magnificence. Protruding over the railing of the rotunda a pair of boots comes into view, a sign of the presence of a man—the last inhabitant of the vast continent—who defends himself with shoulder-strokes so straight and powerful as to fell the astonished Persians. Thus habit and custom persist even to the latest generation. According to this accepted principle a present-day wanderer amid the ruins of the palaces of Darius and Xerxes, and their cuneiform inscriptions of twenty-five centuries ago, thinks that he is observing the same

9

life and customs as those described by Herodotus and Xenophon. His supposition has a considerable element of error in it, for Oriental customs, though in great degree immutable, are no more unalterable than the laws of the Medes and Persians. Further modifications are continually taking place. The Persians are not averse to change. The tea-drinking habit, now almost universal, is an introduction of the present century. Ballet-dancer skirts have superseded the long full ones which were depicted in art a few decades ago as the indoor costume of the women. The tall *kula* or rimless hat of lambskin has undergone various modifications in style and material. The official and largely the mercantile classes have abandoned their long flowing robes and multifold girdle for a frock-coat and leather belt. The short roundabout tunic of the Austrian uniform is worn by military officers, though some don it with reluctance, regarding it as immodestly exposing the manly form. The long beards of a former generation, which followed the fashion set by Fath Ali Shah, are, in accordance with present royal example, reduced to mustaches.

Persian customs are not only not stereotyped, they are not even uniform in different parts of the country or even of the same province. It is constantly necessary to guard against sweeping statements, and one finds the use of limiting phrases, which are required for accuracy, a hindrance to the succinct expression of main facts.

Great interest continues to be taken in Persia as an historic land, even though it does not occupy as large a space in the public view as do some other countries of Asia. The glimpses of Persian life, as seen in the Greek classics and Holy Writ, have given the country a definite place in the mind of the Christian public. Cyrus and Daniel, Esther and Alexander, are living characters to many people. To a more limited number the Zoroastrian faith and the fire-altars of Persia, its mystic sufism, its portrayal in the " Arabian Nights," the fame of its poets,

Fardusi, Hâfiz, and Saadi, its loyalty to and heroic struggle for the house of Ali, are deeply attractive, and prepare the modern reader for an acquaintance with the Persia of to-day.

Increased attention was directed to Persia by the reports of the ambassadors of the East India Company and of Napoleon in the earlier part of this century. This was augmented by the work of a corps of able travelers and discoverers, such as Rawlinson, Morier, Ker Porter, and Fraser, and has lately been increased by the successive visits of his Majesty the Shah to Europe. The relations between America and Persia, and the knowledge of each other's conditions, are becoming more intimate. America is known as the New World. An American traveler in Persia heard repeatedly the phrase in Turki, " Yanki-dun-ya dan di" ("He is from the New World "), which he was fond of interpreting as "Yankee-Doodle dandy." Perhaps some one may yet cite this as a legitimate etymology.

Knowledge of America is still very limited. Few now refer to it, however, as the place where gold grows on trees, and which is inhabited by the descendants of Columbus and the red men. It is to them a strange country without a king, whose power they have never felt and scarcely recognize. The shah is said to have asked, " How many soldiers have the United States?" When told fifty thousand he replied, "It is not much of a country." General Upton, when on a tour of the world, knew better how to impress his Majesty. To the same question he replied, "Ten million." The establishment of diplomatic relations between the two countries is tending to foster commerce and develop more intimate international acquaintance. The Chicago Exposition increased their knowledge of each other.

The need in America of information regarding Persia is often shown. Some new arrivals at Castle Garden were once pelted with snowballs by street urchins, and complaint of this was made. A great newspaper, in giving an account of the affray, remarked, in entire ignorance of the climate of Persia, that the Persians had never seen this strange white substance, and wondered what it was.

The literature relating to Persia is increasing. Nothing along historical lines has yet equaled the "History of Persia," by Sir John Malcolm. Markham's history is a faithful chronicle from the earliest times. Watson's "History of Persia under the Kajar Dynasty" is essential to a good understanding of the present political conditions. An interesting episode in recent Persian history is the rise, persecution, and progress of Babism. This new religion is exhaustively treated by Professor Browne, of Oxford, in "The New History," "The Episode of the Bab," and "A Year in Persia," in which he gives their history and doctrinal tenets in such detail as to leave little to be desired. The recent publication of these volumes makes it unnecessary here to detail my experiences with this sect. A volume on "Persian Literature" by Miss Reed, lately issued in America, is an admirable popular treatise on this attractive subject. Translations of the chief Persian poets are accessible in English. Some of them have been rendered into verse.

Books of travel in Persia are not lacking in number, chiefly by English authors. Some travelers seem to record the length of their slumbers, the time of their arrival at a *menzil*, the sickness of their horse, or their own personal discomforts, as more important than the life of the people about them. The most exhaustive treatise on the country, in its geographical, commercial, and political aspects, is "Persia and the Persian Question," by the Hon. George N. Curzon, M.P. Ex-Minister S. G. W. Benjamin's chapters on "Persian Art" and "The Royal Family," in his "Persia and the Persians," are unsurpassed. The volume, moreover, has a fine literary flavor. Rev. James Bassett, in "The Land of the Imam," has given specially accurate and detailed accounts of places along the principal routes of travel. A good work on the social customs is "The Land of the Lion and the Sun," by Dr. Wills, of the Indo-European Telegraph service, though it has been condemned by some as inaccurate. I presume no one, even with the best intentions in the way of fidelity to truth, can avoid falling into errors in treating of such a country as Persia, or fail to be misinformed by the deceitful Persians.

The preparation for writing the present volume was a residence of fourteen years in Tabriz, Persia, as a missionary under the Presbyterian Board of (American) Foreign Missions. The prosecution of mission work in its usual departments as preacher and evangelist, principal of the Memorial Training and Theological School, mission treasurer, superintendent of buildings and of legal affairs, has brought me into contact with Persian life and character among those of low and high degree alike. Itinerancies and mission business have led me to visit many localities, and given me wide opportunities to observe the manners and customs of the people. I have read nearly every work in English on Persia and Mohammedanism, yet have recorded for the most part only my own observations and experiences, and what I have heard from the people regarding themselves. My residence at Tabriz has been among the dominant race of Persia, the Turkis or Tartars, to whom the royal Kajars belong, and who have supplanted the ancient races in the northwest provinces as far south as Teheran and Hamadan. It is one of the ironies of fate that the old contest so long waged, according to legend and poetry, between Iran and Turan should end at last in the supremacy of Turan, even after the Iranians had regained their beloved land from the Semitic Arabs. The life portrayed here is that modified by the mixture of these races.

The present volume has been a gradual growth. Some portions, in a different form, were contributed to the religious and secular press and to periodicals. A furlough in America has given me the opportunity to arrange the notes of previous

years, and throw them into permanent form. The work aims to
be popular in its presentation, and is committed to the public
with no thought that it is exhaustive. It is hoped that it will
add something to the real knowledge of Persian life, and may
help in forming a just estimate of an interesting people. The
early chapters are devoted to a description of scenes and places
visited *en route* to Persia and during successive journeys, with
their accompanying incidents. Where several journeys have
been made over the same ground, their attendant experiences
have been combined in one narrative. The succeeding chapters describe the civil, religious, social, domestic, and commercial life of the people in cities, villages, and tents. The clos-
ing chapter gives, briefly, some of the methods and the results
of missionary work among different races in Persia.

The volume, it is proper to say, is not intended as a direct
contribution to missionary literature; but I trust that its exposition of the moral, intellectual, and religious condition of the
Persians will appeal to Christian people and quicken an interest in missions among them. The cities and provinces described are those in which mission work is now carried on by
both Protestants and Catholics.

Discussion of the political situation has been avoided,
partly because the writer's residence has been in the commercial metropolis, and not in Teheran, the center of political intrigues for Central Asia, and partly from prudential reasons, as
well as because politics are a favorite theme, thoroughly can-
vassed by most writers on Persia, and concerning which the
facts and possible solutions have often been stated. All writers seem to reach the same conclusion, namely, that the future
of Persia politically depends upon Russia. They regard it as
a ripe apple within reach of that power whenever it shall put
forth its hand to pluck it. As far as has been thought necessary this subject is treated in the chapter on "The Condition
and Needs of Persia." Facts of geography and history such

as may be found in the ordinary encyclopedias are generally excluded.

Persia has not yet awakened to a sense of its need of modern civilization or of Christian enlightenment. Many of its intelligent people recognize the backwardness of their country, and would gladly welcome an era of substantial progress, the opening up of the country to the advancements of the age, the amelioration of the people, socially and economically, the introduction of science and the mechanical arts, together with a greater degree of liberty. The present outlook is not favorable to a speedy reception of nineteenth-century ideas in the way of commercial exploitation, or to any marked change in the religious beliefs of the people. Foreign commercial enterprises are, in an especial degree, in a state of stagnation, owing to the collapse of many projects, among which was the tobacco monopoly, whose overthrow seemed to shake even the throne itself. The administration of the country is weakened by the antagonism of the priestly orders. The shah, with a progressive spirit and an earnest purpose for the advancement and enlightenment of his people, seems powerless to effect his purpose against official corruption on the one hand and the conservatism of the mollas on the other. But in spite of murky clouds and a sullen outlook I have hope with regard both to the future of the people and to the capabilities of the land.

SAMUEL GRAHAM WILSON.

" THE cultivated imagination kindles at the mention of Persia. The names of Cyrus and Darius and Xerxes are household words. Every school-boy has pored over the narrative of the invasion of Greece by the mighty hosts of Persia; but it is difficult for one who has not been actually in Persia to realize that the nation founded and ruled by these sovereigns centuries before Christ is still a living power, with a continuous vitality that may preserve her national integrity for ages to come. She had already developed a distinct civilization and an extraordinary genius for political organization before the star of Rome had begun to cast its rays above the horizon of history. The immortal colonnades of Persepolis were reared before those of the Parthenon, and are still the greatest rivals of the architectural triumphs of Greek civilization. Although shorn of some of her vast territories, which with various fluctuations have at times extended from the Ganges to the Nile, and from the Don to the Indian Ocean, Persia is yet by no means an insignificant power, with her well-defined limits more than twice the area of France; while the intellectual vigor of her people, after the lapse of twenty-five hundred years, shows few signs of degeneracy."—Ex-Minister BENJAMIN's " Persia and the Persians."

CHAPTER I

COASTING THE BLACK SEA

THE most direct route to Persia is across Europe to Odessa, thence by the Black Sea and Transcaucasia. During our five days' voyage the Black Sea belied its reputation. Not only did the reports of rats holding high carnival at night on the steamer, and taking liberties with the passengers' ears, and the tales of other unmentionable discomforts, find no verification in our experience, but the Euxine itself was, except for a few hours, calm and glassy. On the decks European and Oriental life were strangely commingled. While the saloons bespoke the civilization of the West, the lower deck was a kaleidoscope of the East. Among the passengers one met the Russian general, with long Wellington boots and glittering epaulets, ready to converse in almost any language; the Polish nobleman, muttering his discontent over fallen Sarmatia; the dread Cossack officer, strutting proudly about in his long and graceful uniform; the Georgian prince, satisfied with promotion in the service of the czar, in lieu of the crown of former days; and the scion of the Kajars, a refugee from Persia, enjoying a liberal pension as the guest of the Romanoffs. Besides soldiers of various ranks, there were the German merchant, the Scotch exporter of lumber, the Swiss governess bound for Tiflis, the Russian gentleman, wrapping his big fur coat about him and then holding up his

17

umbrella to keep off the sunshine, and his wife, smoking her cigarette with the unconcern of established custom.

On the lower deck was a strange mixture alike of physiognomies and dress: the Russian peasants, cutting large slices from a ten-pound loaf of black bread; the Georgians, dipping the sop from a common dish; the Turkish family, with the baby strapped, papoose-like, on the mother's back, puffing the narghile or water-pipe; Tartars, Armenians, Greeks, Mingrelians, and people of unknown name, with all sorts and shapes of hats, lounging on their bags and bedding—a motley crowd, never lacking in novelty and interest.

The pleasure of the voyage was heightened by the calls which the steamer made along the coast. The first morning (a Wednesday in October, 1880) we and our party * entered the Bay of Sebastopol, famous in the history of the Crimean War. No one point presents the city in full view. Stretching over the hills, it so nestles between the trees and in the slopes of the town that at a little distance it is almost invisible. Two large forts frown upon the left, ready to pour forth fire and desolation. A large crumbling inclosure seen from the steamer, with high walls and three rows of empty windows, is the ruin of extensive barracks. The walls and mounds of earth stretching far away are in an equally dilapidated condition. The different groupings of white stone buildings with red roofs, the dome of the new Russian church, the palace and Grand Hotel, the fine flight of stone steps, flanked by crouching lions, reaching down to the landing, attracted attention. At the wharf there was an opportunity to go ashore and visit the War Museum, which has many relics of the memorable conflict in the fifties. Great amusement was afforded by the naked urchins who came alongside the ship to dive for copecks. The passenger throws a shining coin into the water;

* Our party consisted of the Misses Mary Jewett, Mary A. Clarke, and Agnes Carey, the Rev. James W. Hawkes, and the writer.

down dives the boy, and in a few seconds comes up with it in his hand. The Muscovite gamin then throws the coin into his mouth, and continues the sport until that purse would seem unable to hold any more. As we steamed out of the harbor, its size and security were specially observable.

We next rounded the Crimean peninsula, the Chersonesus, associated with ancient colonization and modern warfare. Balaclava called to mind "the charge of the Light Brigade." The Crimea is a great resort for wealthy Russians. Yalta rivals Bath or Newport. It is beautiful for situation, and the hour spent in strolling past its handsome residences and in examining the shells collected from its beach was delightful. Near by is Livadia, the country-seat of the czar, and Orianda, the property of the Grand Duke Constantine, with other charming villas. The palace of Livadia, among the trees on the sloping mountain-side, is now memorable as the scene of the death of Alexander III. Theodosia, our next stopping-place, led us back to the days of Greek prowess and of the Genoese navigators. We stood off here during the night un-loading cargo into small boats which came alongside for it. Much grain, wine, and raisins are exported from the hill-country beyond.

Thursday morning we passed into the Strait of Yenikale, connecting with the Sea of Azof, which is yearly becoming shallower, owing to the deposits of the Don and to the ballast thrown from steamers. At noon we anchored at Kertch, the harbor not yet being frozen over. This is the ancient Greek Panticapeum, where the great Mithridates, king of Pontus, driven from Asia Minor by Pompey, established his power for a brief time, and whence he planned to unite all the Sarmatian tribes for a descent on Italy. The steamer stopped here for some hours, and we had time to climb the Hill of Mithridates, which rises back of the town to the height of three hundred feet. Its sides are covered with pieces of old pottery, some of

it said to belong to the best age of Grecian fictile art.   Most
of the better specimens have been transferred to the museum
at St. Petersburg, and some are collected in the city museum ;
but many curious relics can yet be picked up, even of the more
valuable colored ware.   Passing through an arched gateway,
the ascent is by a broad flight of steps of uncertain age.   They
look old, and have had very little repairing ; but the critics are
certainly right in refusing to credit the tradition that they are
the remains of a palace of Mithridates.   We seated ourselves
on the topmost rock, covered with dry, yellow moss, some of
it almost petrified with age.   On the brow of the hill is a hermitage of monks.   Encircling it, at some distance down, are
the remains of earthworks, forming a circumvallation, and
higher up a concentric circle, so perfectly preserved that it
would still serve the purpose of breastworks.   Here Mithridates, two thousand years ago, forsaken by his near followers,
and driven to despair, ended his life.   Directly in front, and
overlooking the city, is a tomb of white stone, surmounted
by a wooden cross, and covered with the names of those who
must in some fashion make their mark in the world.   This is
said to be the tomb of the king ; but history records that he
was entombed with high military honors by Pompey at Sinope.
The investigators who broke open the tomb found that nothing had been left by the vandals who had preceded them.

From the summit there is a splendid view of the surrounding country.   Below lies the city, for the most part quiet and
silent, like a country town, the activity and business of the open
square being in strong contrast ; while the scores of ships and
small craft which dot the bay show its high commercial standing.   The hill-range beyond, sloping to the sea in a gradual
descent, reaches to the boundary of Europe ; and in dim outline
through the haze was discernible the low coast-line of Asia,
the first extended view we had of that vast continent.

We paid for our excursion by unfortunately missing our

dinner. Our discomfort was increased by the sea becoming
slightly boisterous, causing the vessel to toss and reel, and by
a drizzle driving us in from the deck. This change in the
state of affairs made an early exit to the deck on Friday
morning very convenient, and thus gave us a view of Novoroshisk. The lower deck now presented a sorry spectacle. The
third-class passengers were huddled together in great disarray,
curled up indiscriminately with bags and bundles. Every now
and then a wave would come dashing up, giving them a full
immersion.

Novoroshisk, at the time of our visit, we found had an oil
boom. A one-thousand-barrel well was owned by an American. Its boom has since somewhat collapsed; but the town
has developed, with the swiftness of an American city, into a
thriving commercial center. It is, moreover, a railway terminus. Splendid wharves and fortifications are being erected,
and every sign of prosperity is now visible.

All of the next day we skirted the now desolate Abkasian
coast, covered with low forests and a thick undergrowth of
brambles. From the forests considerable ash, oak, walnut,
and boxwood timber is exported. The land is fertile and
very productive, and before the Russian conquest was thickly
populated. After the subjugation of the various tribes of the
Cherkess or Circassians in 1864, four hundred thousand of the
inhabitants, prompted by religious fanaticism and a laudable
spirit of liberty, expatriated themselves and took refuge with
their co-religionists of Turkey.

Along this coast are at least a dozen forts, while towns are
also gradually being built. One of these we noticed growing
up around the monastery of New Athos. It is near the ruins
of a Genoese fort, on a wild tract of forest given by the government to a colony of three hundred monks. It is already
taking on the appearance of civilization, for an ancient Byzan-
tine church has been repaired and put to use; while around it

and the monastery fruitful fields and vineyards are being cultivated.   An extensive hospice for pilgrims has been erected.*

Passing on, we caught a glimpse of the snow-cap of Elburz at a considerable distance inland, stopped at Sukum Kala, and arrived off Poti on Saturday afternoon.   Here we were transferred to a flat-bottomed steamer so as to cross the bar.   The channel is very shallow, and sometimes fills up within three feet of the surface, delaying ships at anchor outside or captive within, for several months at a time.   Miserable as the harbor is, it was at that time the port for the trade of the Caucasus and for many of the exportations of Persia.

In our flat-bottom we steamed into the river Rion or Phasis, following the course of Jason and his followers when they went in search of the golden fleece.   We landed not at all pleased with the prospect of spending Sunday in that unpromising and unhealthy place.

When a cook went to make her engagement she laid down as a condition that she should have the F's.   The lady inquired what these were, and was told, " Why, fat, fur, and feather, of course."   So when we stopped at Poti we supposed we should enjoy "the F's of Poti—fleas, flies, fevers, fogs, frogs, and

* When we were returning at Easter (1894) a band of pilgrims came out in little boats rowed by the monks, and were put on board.   They were of the ignorant peasantry, uncouthly clothed, with hoods over their disheveled locks, and the dirt of the pilgrimage clinging to them.   It was a sight to see them climb the ladders at the sides of the boat and throw themselves, beds, bundles, and babies, on the lower deck.   The monks rowed back and forth until four hundred pilgrims were packed in as thick as sardines.   Shortly afterward rain began to fall, and the saloon passengers retired below to give the protection of the covered deck to this motley crowd of men and women, priests and nuns.   In the morning a nun passed around and took up a collection.   Among the deck-passengers were a crowd of Mingrelian boys and girls returning to school, whose songs in their own tongue were highly interesting to hear.   The performance of some strolling musicians on their native instruments with falsetto songs earned some copecks, which a monkey collected in his miniature fez.

filth." These and other advantages give it the unenviable reputation of being one of the worst places in all civilization, in climate and accommodations for travelers. Not long ago the place was a huge marsh, and even now the ground is only about one foot above sea-level, and liable to disaster from floods by land and storms by sea. When the snow-floods come pouring down the rapid Rion the waters overflow the streets, and for a time the inhabitants become amphibious. The ladies then don their high boots with long leggings, and their promenades undergo no interruption. Most of the houses are one story, set up on posts, allowing free course to the water, and affording good berths to the millions of frogs, which, being in such close proximity to the bedroom window, offer abundant music without putting their bowstrings under too great tension. The miasma which necessarily arises from low lands under such circumstances, and from the immense swamps in the neighborhood, renders the sanitary condition bad in the extreme. Murray advises one by no means to pass the night there, and it is confidently affirmed that no European has ever lodged there and escaped the fever. English sailors are prohibited by government regulation from landing at the place. Either liberal doses of quinine saved us, or the slight chill and fever which one of our party had three weeks afterward proved the universality of the rule.

Happily, when we arrived, the frogs had gone into winter quarters. If some enterprising Frenchman wishes to branch out in a new line of trade he might start an establishment for canning this delicacy. There we abstained from water and became tea-drinkers or, like the Malokans, milk-drinkers. But by no ingenuity of the traveler or change of season can the last F on the list be subdued. Filth abounded more than they all.

In spite of these various plagues, real and imaginary, our stay in Poti was quite comfortable. The Hôtel de Jaquot afforded

passable accommodation; but from the way in which the proprietor sought the golden fleece it deserved the surname " Hôtel
de Jason."

Our stay was made pleasant by the kindness of Mr. Gardner, H. B. M. consul at Poti.   In finding the consul we had
our first experience of Oriental hotel porters.   A Georgian,
in a long gray wrapper-coat, with an air of confidence which
showed that he understood the situation, took us around by a
circuit of two miles, stopped at half a dozen wrong places,
and finally landed us before the lion and the unicorn, just two
doors from the hotel where we started.   He was the most
crestfallen Oriental we have ever met, and the only one who
was in too great haste to wait for his bakshish.

Mr. Gardner was the only Englishman in Poti.   His wife
and an aunt had been snatched from him by the fever.   Prior
to the late war the departure of his three children to England
became necessary; yet there he remained, bound by political
and financial interests.

The commerce of Poti demanded that the consulates of
European governments should be there.   It was the emporium
of an immense trade, reaching even to America.   Regular
lines of steamers ply between it and Marseilles, as well as between it and Constantinople and Odessa.   Hence went the
corn of the Mingrelian plains for the English market, and boxwood and walnut from the slopes of the Caucasus.   The latter is said to be of better quality than American walnut, hard
enough to admit of the finest polish, and so knotted and
twisted that it veneers beautifully.   A considerable trade is
carried on in Persian flowers, from which insect-powder and
other drugs are made.   Tons of these dried flowers are exported.   Formerly they were powdered previous to exportation; but the natives had become so adept in adulteration that
the flowers are now shipped in an unprepared state.   Quantities of cotton, tobacco, silks, and carpets also find exit through

Poti via Tiflis. The high revenue and protective tariff of
Russia now drives a great deal of Persian trade to Trebizond
via Erzrum.

Aside from its commerce, Poti has little worthy of mention.
The Botanical Gardens are quite extensive, and tropical plants
flourish luxuriantly without the fostering nurture of the hot-
house. This is possible on account of the mild character of
the winter. An old Turkish fort stands by the seaside, a relic
of a time anterior to Russian occupation. The changed character of the dress, the strange faces, the bazaars, and the peculiar conveyances we saw about told us that we were in a new
civilization. We kept a sharp lookout for the world-renowned
Georgian women. We were soon able to look upon princes
and princesses with undazed vision, for they are as numerous
in this region as generals and colonels among American poli-
ticians. Many of the women had adopted as their Sunday
dress the long trains of their Western sisters; but, like most
Orientals when they don European costume, they retain the
native head-dress. The bonnet is a kind of diadem of bright
color, adorned with tinsel, or sometimes with gold and precious stones, and covered with a white veil, gaily ornamented,
hanging down at some length, though not so as to conceal the
features.

Baron Thielmann informed us that Poti owed its prosperity
to a slip of the pen; that when Turkey ceded to Russia, by
the treaty of Adrianople, the territory between Kars and the
sea, the boundary-line was drawn to run down the river
Tschorock, which would have conceded to Russia the fine
harbor of Batum. It was discovered, however, after the rati-
fication of the treaty, that the river Tscholoch, which runs
eighteen miles to the north of Batum, had been inserted as the
boundary-line. Thus, in lieu of a better, Poti became the port
for a flourishing trade.

By the treaty of Berlin, Batum was transferred to Russia,

and soon after our passing through, the railroad was completed to Batum; so Poti's prosperity and commerce were
transferred to the latter port.   When we returned we found
Batum a lively young city, grown from two thousand to
twelve thousand, with scarcely a mark of the Turk upon it.
Its paved streets, wharves, improved harbor, and Prospect Park
on the seaside, the bustle and activity of its stores, the large
petroleum refineries and export trade, all show that it has
fallen into energetic hands.   It is being fortified, contrary to
the treaty of Berlin, and has been declared a naval port, liable
to be closed to commerce.   Here Mr. Chambers resides, as
vice-consul for the United States, and representative of the
Standard Oil Company, to watch the Russian oil-trade.   The
refineries of the Rothschilds, Nobel, and others were closed,
and negotiations had been going on between them and the
Standard Oil Company to form a syndicate and divide the
trade of the world.

The principal Russian oil-field is at Baku, on the Caspian.
For ages the gas arising there through the fissures in the rocks
has fed the perpetual flame of the fire-worshipers, and an old
priest still remains, a witness of modern industry.   When the
well of the Kalafy Company was first opened, the oil burst up
in a fountain nine feet in diameter and forty feet high into the
air—at least so Arthur Arnold says.   The average depth of
the wells is one hundred and fifty feet.   Some time ago a pipe-
line was projected to be laid from Baku to Poti, over the Caucasus, in order to give the field an outlet on the Black Sea.
Interested in this were three American gentlemen who wished
to prosecute the undertaking.   In pursuance of their object they
called on the governor-general of the province, a pompous
man, with a very high opinion of his own importance.   They
were introduced, but not invited to be seated, nor shown
proper civilities.   To the question, "What is your business,
gentlemen?" they answered by explaining their object and the

manner of its intended execution. He replied, "This is an enormous project and requires an immense amount of capital; where is it to come from?" On their informing him that they represented thirty million dollars and could get thirty millions more, the weight of the almighty dollar was felt. It was, "Please be seated, gentlemen," and all other civilities were shown them. The project for a pipe-line, however, came to nothing.

The railroad from Poti to Tiflis, the first in Transcaucasia, was completed in 1873. It was subsidized by the government, but the engineering was largely done by foreigners. The bridges were brought from England in pieces ready to erect. The Vladikavkaz terminus is to be extended across the Caucasus to Tiflis. The cost was estimated at twenty-five million dollars, with twenty-eight versts (twenty-one miles) of tunnel. If any one will consider the energy and enterprise of Russia since 1880 he will be convinced that she has immense national possibilities. Not only has she pushed her conquests in Asia, but cities and towns have sprung up as on the American prairies; new life has been infused into regions dead for ages; the appliances of modern civilization, the railroad, telegraph, improved irrigation, higher education, and many of the amenities of life, have followed in the train of these enterprises. To deny that Russia is a great civilizing agency in central Asia is to shut one's eyes to the facts. It was only in 1880 that Shobeloff took Geogtapa. Merv, an oasis practically unknown before O'Donovan's journey in 1881, surrendered in 1884. It has been rebuilt in good style. Colonization has been encouraged; town lots have been given away on condition of being built upon immediately. The railway was extended to Baku in 1882, to Askabad in 1883, thus commanding the commerce of north Khorassan, to Merv in 1886, and has already reached Samarcand, and by rapid stages is being extended also from Vladivostok, on the Pacific; it is fast

spanning the wide stretch of Asia.   Difficulties of drifting sand
have been obviated by planting trees; artesian wells have been
dug, a canal for the Murghab constructed, the dike of Sultan
Band is to be rebuilt, and four hundred thousand acres of land
reclaimed.   Everywhere throughout Transcaucasia, too, the
marks of enterprise are evident.   Russia has a great future
before her—doubly great when she shall have learned certain
sound lessons of civil and religious freedom.   Other nations
which have taken centuries to learn them, and the pages of
whose histories are dark with records of civil oppression and
religious persecution, must not be impatient with the development of this young and lusty race.   There are indications that
the reign of Czar Nicholas II. may show as great advance in
civil and religious liberty as that of his predecessor has shown
in material progress and territorial expansion.

There was no danger of our getting dizzy or missing the
beauties of the landscape on a Russian railway.   The express
on the Transcaucasian Railway went at a speed of fifteen miles
an hour.   The mail-train made the distance of some two hundred miles in seventeen hours.   Accommodations are good
and time for meals abundant, if one remembers that three
bells ring before a Russian train starts.   It is very common
for the traveling Russian to take his bed and tea-urn along
with him on the train, and run out and get the urn filled with
hot water at the station.   A missionary party once sent one
of their number out with a pitcher to get some tea.   He
returned and said that "there was nothing but hot beer."
He did not recognize the tea in large glasses and without
cream.

The first part of our course from Poti lay along the Rion.
We failed to notice the place where the maniac came out to
greet the Argonauts.   The marshy lowlands were covered
with shrubbery and low forests.   They were large compared
with those of the Circassian coast or with the bushes of the

swamps, but puny compared with the trees of the Alleghanies. Quite a curiosity was an extensive forest of dead trees near Poti, looking like melancholy types of death. Stripped of all foliage, and even of their bark, they seemed like pillars of despair. This was caused by the embankments of the railroad stopping the natural drainage and forming a swamp. On the sloping ascent the country was well cultivated, considering the careless manner of the East. Field after field of Indian corn extended on either side. Hedges of willows were quite frequent, but the common fence was of twigs and branches of trees placed upright, with others interlaced diagonally. The beech and pine trees, the elder with ripe berries, the thistle and ferns, all reminded us of home and the common latitude of the districts.

The scenery could not be called grand, but it was quite beautiful. Winding and irregular vales, covered with forests variegated with many-tinted autumn leaves, lay between steep cliffs jutting out from the main chain. When through the midst rolled the rock-bedded stream, with the castles and fortress of bygone days crowning the jutting hills, the military road winding around the base, and the snowy peaks afar in the background, the scene became truly picturesque. The tortuous course of the Rion led us up the sides of the Suram Mountains, which connect the upper and lower ranges of the Caucasus. It was at times a hard struggle to proceed, and several times the engines halted. The grade is in places equal to that of St. Gothard's,* and even with the power of three large engines progress was very slow. At last we reached the Pass of Suram, at the height of thirty-two hundred feet above the sea. The Rion here became a dried rivulet-bed, and, crossing the narrow watershed, the fountains of the Kura appear wending their way toward the Caspian. It was not yet dark when we reached the old city of Gori, from the heights

* Since then a tunnel has been cut and the grade improved.

back of which frown the ruins of a Georgian fort, and in the sides of whose cliffs are the cave-dwellings of an old race. When we alighted at Tiflis we bade formal adieu to railroad-trains, and Melchizedek met us—a Christian from Urumia—who conducted us to the Hôtel de l'Europe.

CHAPTER II

WE were detained in Tiflis for some days, and had an opportunity to see this ancient capital of Georgia—ancient, indeed, but so modernized, as the capital of the Russian provinces of Transcaucasia, that it would scarcely recognize its former self. The population of the city is said to be two hundred thousand, and is rapidly increasing. It has many of the advantages of European life, including railroad communication, wide, finely paved streets, a well-regulated system of cabs or phaëtons, an organized police, good postal facilities, and other benefits of a paternal and municipal government.

Tiflis has been compared to Constantinople in respect of its mongrel population. Certainly few cities can equal it in this regard. Here are representatives of all the native tribes of the mountains and plains—Georgians, Mingrelians, Kastalians, and Chewsurs, as well as former dwellers in Circassia, Daghestan, and the regions of Azerbijan about Urumia, strangers from the far East, Jews, and Arabians. We meet the high fur *kulah* of the Persians, the brown sheepskin conical hat of the Tartars, the pointed cap of the Grusinians, the fez of the Turks, as well as the varied-colored turbans of other races. Armenians, too, in their semi-European dress, are thickly scattered through the crowd, and occupy prominent positions in the bazaars. Europeans are many, and of multiform names. The French chiefly own and conduct the hotels, the English have the Indo-European telegraph, and both are engaged in

31

the importation and sale of European merchandise. An American store with American manufactures also claims a place. The Russian section of the city contrasts strongly with the Oriental quarters. Its large stone blocks, its museum, theater, and ducal palace, its broad avenues, look strange in close proximity to the low flat houses and narrow lanes of the city. Directly across the Kura from the Russian quarter is the Colony. This takes its name from a colony of Germans from Würtemberg who settled here in the early part of the century. Germans, indeed, are settled all over Russia, and are scattered here and there over all this region of country; but the Tiflis colony has a peculiar history. About 1805–10 two colonies started eastward from Würtemberg. One went off because of a new hymn-book which the prince was trying to introduce against their conscientious scruples. Arrived here, they were assigned land by the government. The other colony was a party of second-adventists going to Jerusalem to await the second coming of Christ, under the lead of a bold and enthusiastic woman. They were stopped here by the Cossacks, and settled down with the others. Their hopes of the imminence of Christ's coming have diminished, and their objections to new hymn-books have been succeeded by indifference; but their approval of beer knows no wavering, and the product of their breweries is renowned throughout the Caucasus.

The best full view of this heterogeneous and, in a true sense, cosmopolitan center is obtained from the summit of the lofty hill on the southeast. Starting out one morning, we were kindly guided by Mr. M. A. Morrison, A.M., the agent of the British and Foreign Bible Society, through some of the most interesting parts of the city to the summit. Our course lay through the old quarter and the crowded bazaars of the Armenians and the Tartars. The latter is familiarly called Sha-

tan or Satan bazaar, the jangling and wrangling of the Tartars,
dickering in regard to the price of their wares, seeming to deserve this sinister epithet. We passed the cathedral, an ancient
Georgian edifice, renovated since the Georgian church has
been embraced in the Orthodox fold. Next we came upon
the warm sulphur-baths, famed for their curative properties.
They are situated underground, their dome-like roofs, with
skylights, being on a level with the ground, because of the low
source of the springs. Tiflis is said to signify "hot." No
doubt the reason the city occupies this site is the presence of
the springs, for the situation has little else to recommend it.
We wended our way around the hillside until we reached the
Botanical Garden, an oasis in the midst of the dreary, barren,
and desolate hills on either side and around the city. In the
early spring these hills are covered with a beautiful verdure,
and when the snow melts from the mountains the Kura swells
into an impetuous stream and rushes through the rocky gorge
like a torrent. But the dry, sultry summer comes on apace,
and vegetation on the hills decays, and the gardens and parks
require special irrigation and care, and appear all the more refreshing and delightful on account of the surrounding desolate-
ness. Then many leave the city for the mountains, and return
with the coolness of autumn. The garden is a favored spot.
Kept ever verdant by the perennial spring which, gushing up
far above, sends its cooling stream rushing in little cascades
down the hillside, it abounds in flowers and foliage and shady
bowers. On the opposite hillside a company of Tartar mourners were burying their dead. How rude and uncouth their
monuments look ! How dreary in all respects, without a
flower, a blade of grass, or a solitary shade-tree ! There is
no beauty in their city of the dead.

Far above us was the old wall and line of fortifications, with
strong buttresses and high circular turrets, and the massive

ruins of the old tower, memorials of the times of the mighty
Bagratides, and later the defense against the Persian * invad-
ers, prior to the coming forth of the Russian bear from the
North. We mounted up, resting awhile at the fountain-head.
Arriving at the summit, we found the large gates shut and
our way blocked. We climbed the old walls, imagining for a
moment the spear of the enemy might pierce us, and stood
upon the breastworks of former greatness. While standing
here some Mussulman women ascended the hill. Mr. Morrison offered his hand to assist them over the wall, but no !
they drew back and refused. Their hands might be soiled
and their clothes torn, but to touch the hand of an infidel was
contamination.

From this elevation the full panorama of the city lay in
view. In the midst of the valley, dividing the city into two
equal parts, runs the rapid Kura, on whose banks Pompey and
his legions celebrated the Saturnalia. In the center of the
city the river itself divides, forming an island which supports
the piers for the bridge. A strange mixture of various styles of
architecture is presented—the minaret and mosque, the Greek
cross and the Latin, the weather-vanes of the German church,
as well as the Armenian domes. Just below us appeared the
garden and palace of the Grand Duke Michael, vacant half
the year, while his Highness retreats to his summer residence
at Borshom. Directly opposite it is a fine museum of the
zoölogy and mineralogy of the Caucasus. To the left, flank-
ing the city on the west, rises the hill which tradition says is
the Mount Gilboa on which Saul was slain. When it is settled whether Mark Twain discovered the grave of Adam it
will be time enough to discuss the accuracy of this tradition.
On the side of this hill stands a Latin monastery, and near

* Aga Mohammed, Kajar, in 1795 sacked Tiflis, leveled its churches,
cast the priests into the river, and carried off twenty-five thousand female
captives.

by a Catholic cemetery, green even amid its parched surroundings.

Turning our eyes to the right, we had before us, on the opposite hill, a collection of fine stone buildings, forming almost
a town. This is the Russian arsenal, frowning down upon the
city, and reminding any of the inhabitants who may have a
longing for independence, that hope is futile. Tiflis is the
military headquarters of Transcaucasia, and has accommodations for many of the one hundred and fifty thousand soldiers
who are stationed within its bounds for the protection and
awing of the inhabitants. Transcaucasia, from the outpost
stations all along the Turkish frontier to the mountain fastnesses, is one huge garrison, and everywhere one meets the
gay uniforms of the Cossacks. Straight before our eyes the
other slope was dotted thickly with tents, the camping-ground
of thousands. They believe in the star of Russia, and that
she, of all nations, is the greatest and best.

Taking a long look at the curiously interesting picture before us, and turning our eyes away beyond to Mount Kasbek,
towering to the height of sixteen thousand five hundred feet,
we descended reluctantly on the other side of the hill. On its
brow we met an anti-Talmudic Jew, dressed in black-and-
red striped robes reaching to the ground. The hostility to
the Jews who accept the Talmud is very bitter. The seat of
their strength is in the Crimea, where they have in their possession some valuable manuscripts. At the foot of the hill we
entered the Armenian caravansary, a "grand depot" full of
the curious and beautiful manufactures of the East.

The museum is an unique and interesting exhibit. It contains wax figures of the numerous tribes of the Caucasus and
Transcaucasus, dressed in their native costumes, with their
old armor and utensils. The seats and walls are covered with
embroideries, the floors with carpets, the windows with curtains, and the doors with portières of the double-faced carpets

(*ghelims*)—all the handiwork of women of its various races.
Here are the woods, shells, rocks, birds, and beasts of the
mountains, valleys, and shores. Ancient ruins, too, and tombs
have given up their implements and antiquities to enrich the
museum.

From Tiflis to Tabriz the distance is less than three hundred and eighty miles. Three hundred miles of the course is
through Russian territory, and the remainder in Persian. But
we had no long and wearisome horseback ride at a caravan
pace over the whole of the distance. Such was the manner
of travel formerly in vogue when Dr. Perkins and Miss Fiske
climbed the mountains of Kurdistan, and it required eight
months to reach their destination from the United States.
Even much later this was the mode of travel, and going via
Erzrum the only safety from the dangers of the way is to join
a caravan and come at the slow, jogging gait of a camel or a
mule.

We were agreeably surprised to find the best mode of
traveling, where steam-power cannot be utilized, to be the
Russian post system, which is now completely organized.
About every ten miles along the principal highways there is a
post-station, with relays of horses kept in waiting, so that the
mail is sent forward with great rapidity. In case of necessity
or great haste the traveler can go by this means on a flying
gallop, though it would rightly be supposed not to minister
much to his comfort. The government maintains an efficient
system of livery, with conveyances of many varieties, shapes,
and conditions, from the two-wheeled drosky or cart and the
four-wheeled troika—a rough wooden bed set on the axles
without springs, and drawn by three horses—to the well-up-
holstered and easy carriage.

Of course, before our arrangements could be made, the
governmental red tape must be unwound. No one could
travel with the use of post-horses, nor have accommodations

at the post-houses along the road, without a license regularly drawn up and certified after the examination of his passport. This document goes by the name of *padarozhuna*. The passport system of Russia says to every man, "To spy out the land are you come," until he can show his credentials to the contrary. When we entered from Austria, whenever we stayed overnight at a hotel, when we wished to leave, and again when we crossed into Persia, our passports were demanded. A hotel proprietor who will give you lodging without obtaining your passport and having you registered at the prefecture of police is liable to a fine of five hundred rubles, to be suspected of disloyalty, as well as to be subjected to profuse financial bleeding by the officials.*

There are three kinds of padarozhuna—the single-sealed or common license, given to travelers indiscriminately, and the double-sealed, and the triple crown license. The latter are given to officials and representatives of foreign governments.

* During my journey to Persia in 1886, on giving my passports to the proprietor of a hotel, he read the names " Samuel " and "Anna," and exclaimed, " Why, these names indicate that you are Jews ! " His suspicions were further confirmed by a visit I received from a wandering Nestorian, who looked like a Jew, and with whom I spoke an unknown tongue. My passport was sent to the police station, and the next day I was summoned to appear there at nine o'clock at night. I went, accompanied by a Scotch gentleman, who interpreted for me. The officer asked, " Are you not Moseanski? " I affirmed, with a smile, that I was far from it ; that I was a Christian, *en route* for Persia. I was told to come the next day and sign a document declaring, " I am a Christian of the Presbyterian Church of the United States." Then my passport was given me with a permit to reside in Russia for twelve months, whereas all I wanted was to get over the frosty Caucasus and into Persia before the snow of winter. The reason for this care was that so many Russian Jews have gone to America, become naturalized, and returned to reside in Russia, to the annoyance of the government. The latter prefers to exclude them. In all my dealings with the officials of Russia, I have found them most affable and polite, giving no trouble at custom-houses or on post-roads, nor scrutinizing passports closely, with the above exception.

They afford them prior privileges and right to horses at the
stations, and give notice to postmasters to show them regard
and to expedite them on their way. We were fortunate
enough to obtain the second kind; for it happened that
M. Audebert, secretary of the French consulate at Tabriz,
and Mrs. Abbot, wife of the English consul, were leaving for
Tabriz at that time, and joined our party for the journey.
Our carriage was quite a complex affair, with a closed apartment for the ladies, and a covered section open in front, divided into two parts, one of which was occupied by passengers and the other by the conductor. A box yet farther in
front was for the driver. We drove out in fine style, recalling
the days of tally-ho, the driver flourishing his long whip over
the six horses, and the conductor sounding the bugle-call to
clear the way.

For some time after leaving Tiflis our course lay along the
valley of the Kura. A river-valley naturally suggests verdure
and fertility, but this seemed like "a dry and thirsty land,
where no water is." Far and near the fields presented a most
desolate appearance, and fortunate was the farm-house which
was surrounded by a few trees. The irrigation from the river
is little able to withstand the scorching heat of summer. The
river-banks were dotted with water-mills for raising the water
to a higher level. The plowmen were at work with the oxen
and the primeval wooden plow. As neither the roadside nor
the bleak hills around afforded us interest, our attention became confined to the attractions of the road. Now it was a
caravan of camels marching patiently and meekly in long
line, with only a connecting rope, the leader preceding with
a jingling bell on its big neck. Then in contrast with these
huge creatures would come the Lilliputian donkeys, with immense pack-saddles and burdens larger than themselves—a
never-ending source of amusement. Again a mingling group
of buffaloes and oxen drawing carts and rude wagons would

appear, and then covered wagons drawn by horses, suggesting the old emigrant-trains of America.

As our constant companions we had the two lines of telegraph-poles, one of wood and the other of iron. The wooden ones are the Russian government line, which goes as far as Julfa. The iron ones are the great Indo-European line, which, proceeding via Tabriz, connects at Teheran with the Indian government line. The line was built by Messrs. Siemens, who are retained by contract to keep it in repair, and have their agents for that purpose all along the route. The iron posts were brought from England ready-made. By means of this line the foreigners in Tabriz and Teheran get the most important news of the world every morning, written out and sent around to them.

For two hundred and fifty miles the magnificent military, postal, and commercial thoroughfare continues, certainly, next to a railroad, the best thing on which to hasten the Cossacks to the front. While we were proceeding our progress was quite rapid and satisfactory; but at many of the stations there were stoppages for new relays of horses, so that much of the time in going was lost in waiting. We had to content ourselves with a progress of thirty miles for what of Saturday remained after our late start; and we rested over Sunday at a post-house, which, together with a watermelon stand and a caravansary, made up the place. The chief sights to be seen without were a company of Cossacks bivouacking, and some swine which seemed to merit the disdain of the Jew and the Mohammedan. The typical post-house has two rooms free for travelers, furnished with a stand for the omnipresent samovar, and two bedsteads, whose mattresses are hard boards. This is amply sufficient for a Russian, who may be said to take the command of Christ to the impotent man as of perpetual and universal obligation. The old-school Russian is not himself unless accompanied by his bed. On the principle of doing as Rome

does when you are in Rome, we had provided for the emergency. So in true Oriental style, seven in a room, the other one
being in like manner occupied, we passed two happily fleeting
nights.

Monday morning, at three o'clock, found us again on the
way; and after being kept waiting most of the afternoon we
determined to try an all-night trip. From Dilijan the character of the country suddenly changed. We began to ascend the
valley of the Akstafa, covered with forests of beech and pine,
and pronounced by all very beautiful. The road ascends with
many tortuous windings, guarded by posts, until at the summit the altitude of seventy-three hundred feet is reached. We
had, however, little opportunity of enjoying the scenery, not
only on account of the darkness, but because the bitter, icy
coldness compelled us to envelop ourselves in all our wraps.

Morning brought us alongside of Lake Goktcha or Sivan,
a beautiful mountain lake, equal in extent to the largest lakes
of Switzerland. The gray morning light cast a pleasing glare
on its crystalline waters, but the barren volcanic hills by
which it is surrounded make its appearance far less attractive
than if it were bordered with grassy and wooded shores. It
is noted for its fine trout, though we had to bear the disappointment of being unable to obtain any at the Malaka villages along the road. One of their mountain villages—a little
off from the lake—named Seminofka, excited our lively interest. The houses, contrasting well with the prevailing style of
mud-houses, were built of wood, one story high, the roofs of
many being covered with huge haystacks, oftentimes higher
than the houses, of symmetrical conical shape, so as readily to
shed the rain. The people of the place raise great numbers
of cattle and horses, which seemed in better condition than any
we observed elsewhere. The cattle as well as the horses are
raised for draft-work, for it is a tenet of their faith not to eat
flesh. They have control of most of the freightage of Trans-

caucasia, while the drosky or phaëton system of Tiflis is in their hands. The village was alive with activity at this early hour, and the hurrying to and fro to bring water from the mountain spring at one end of the village—each woman carrying two buckets suspended on a pole across her shoulders—the patter of milk in the pails coming from groups of cowherds, and the general appearance of things, showed that industry was their motto.

Here we witnessed a most beautiful sunrise, which in the brilliancy, harmony, and perfection of its colors could scarcely be surpassed.

> " Lo, in the East
> Flamed the first fires of beauteous day, poured forth
> Through fleeting folds of night's black drapery.
> High in the widening blue the herald star
> Faded to paler silver as there shot
> Brighter and brighter bars of rosy gleam
> Across the gray.
> A white verge, clear, a widening, brightening white
> Caught
> By topmost clouds, and flaming on their rims
> To fervent, golden glow, flushed from the brink
> With saffron, scarlet, crimson, amethyst ;
> Whereat the sky burned splendid to the blue,
> And, robed in raiment of glad light, the King
> Of life and glory came.
>
> " So in the East the miracle of day
> Gathered and grew. The pleasured gaze
> Roamed o'er the feast of beauty." *

Its bright shining was, however, unable to dispel the chilliness of the atmosphere. The region, we were not surprised to learn, is becoming a popular summer resort for the wealthier denizens of the Erivan plain during the heated term.

All day we proceeded, descending from this height through

---

* Sir Edwin Arnold, " The Light of Asia."

a monotonous region.   Delays for horses gave us full time to
forage for milk, eggs, and fruit in the villages, to add to the
picnic stock which we had laid in at Tiflis.   Restaurants there
were none, and all the provision the post-houses could furnish
was tea in the samovar—the constant beverage of the millions
of Asia.   When the darkness of night grew upon us, the rain
drove us to shelter, and we eagerly sought repose again after
forty hours' intermission.   The ladies, preferring the carriage
to the post-house accommodations, turned it into a Pullman
sleeper.

In the first stages of Wednesday some interesting sights
appeared.   Mount Alogos, whose height is thirteen thousand
five hundred feet, presented its snowy crest, and far away lay
Etchmiadzin, the seat of the Armenian catholicos, whence
he exercises supremacy over his followers in Russia, Turkey,
Persia, and other Asiatic countries.   Beyond was Turkey itself,
and our conductor pointed out the situation of Bayazid, the
scene of the terrible brutalities in the late war.

Farther on Mount Ararat came grandly into view, fully sixty
miles away.   We had been anticipating with extreme pleasure
the sight of the wonderful mount as the dessert of our Asiatic
repast.   Our first view fully realized our expectations, though
not as satisfactorily as did later and closer views.   The peak
of the great Ararat was encircled by the clouds which enveloped its summit.   These themselves appeared very beautiful
in the glistening sunlight, and now and then the hoary white
head would pierce its environment and lift itself loftily, as if
scorning things terrestrial.

Before long we neared Erivan, the capital of the government of the same name.   The brow of the hill, overlooking
the valley, is occupied by a Russian fort and arsenal, and
with the ruins of the fortifications of the Persians during their
former occupation of the region.   The valley, as we looked
down upon it, was certainly charming.   It is an oasis in a

parched land, and a delight to the eyes after so much desolation. Orchards and vineyards, cultivated forests and green fields, with farms, bearing marks of steady culture, and the town nestling among the shade-trees, were a treat and refreshment. Nature has favored this valley highly, and art has not lagged in coming to her assistance. Unlike Lake Van and Lake Urumia, Lake Goktcha or Sivan is fresh water and has an outlet. The river Zenghi flows from it, and bears its refreshing and fructifying stream down through the valley, finally emptying into the Aras. By artificial irrigation this stream becomes the constant and inexhaustible source of blessing, causing the wilderness to be glad, and the desert to blossom as the rose.

Erivan, a progressive and thriving city, is remarkable for little except as having been, as we are told, the antediluvian residence of Noah. The fort and mosque are said to be worth a visit; but what time we had was spent at the only hotel testing the culinary art of the place, in a department other than that of architecture, and in the bazaars, laying in a supply for future experiment in underwear in a cognate branch of industry.

Proceeding farther, almost the only object which could draw our attention was Ararat, which for three days was almost constantly in view. It was the last sight at night and the first in the morning. There it stood, silent, solitary, awe-inspiring, mysterious, grand. The clouds had rolled away and left it distinct in all its majestic outline and massiveness. The ages, like the clouds, have come and gone, but it remains immovable. Since the ark rested on its heights there have been movements in heaven above and on the earth beneath—earthquake, storm, and flood—but it remains, presumably, substantially the same. Like the old ocean, a thousand years sweep over it in vain. It reminded one of Napoleon's address under the shadow of the pyramids. In forty centuries what has it not seen of the rise and fall of empires and the wonderful

movements of the race of Noah ?   He sits a king, wrapped in
his snowy robes, and with a perennial crown upon his brow.
Though the puppet kings of men may include him in their
dominion, he scorns subjection to their sway, and even bids
defiance to the king of day.   However near and furiously
Apollo may drive his chariot and let his horses blow their
warm breath upon him, neither the fire from his eye, the heat
from the wheels, nor the warm breath of the horses can cause
the whiteness of his countenance to color, or tan his fair com-
plexion.   His foot may become scorched and burned, his
twin brother, the Little Ararat, may lay aside his crown, but
the Great Ararat, unsubdued, lifts his proud head nearer to the
throne in the sky and acknowledges no allegiance.   The Little
Ararat is like an earthly dynasty, which for a season wears the
insignia of supremacy and then must surrender them; but the
Great Ararat is like God himself, whose dominion is everlasting.

Ararat is not now the mysterious and unknown mountain,
the center of myths and legends and of superstitious awe
among the natives, and of vague admiration and reverence
from the Christian world.   It is true, the popular associations
still cling around it.   Bryce, in his work * describing his ascent,
gives an extended notice of these traditions.   It was supposed
to be the center of the earth.   It was connected with the
Chaldean worship of the stars.   Upon it stood a pillar with
the figure of a star.   Before the birth of Christ twelve wise
men were stationed by the pillar to watch for the appearing
of the star in the east, which three of them followed, when it
appeared, to Bethlehem.

Its summit was declared to be inaccessible, and it became
almost an article of faith with the Armenians, and a firm belief among all the natives, that God would not permit it to be
ascended; nor are they yet convinced that this has ever been
done.   So much stronger, observes a traveler, is prejudice than

* " Transcaucasia and Ararat in 1876," by James Bryce, M.P.

evidence. On its top were said to be the remains of the ark. Far in the distant past the monk Jacob attempted its ascent, to obtain some of the precious relics. In the midst of each attempt he was overcome with sleep, and found himself on awakening at the same point where he started. The third time an angel told him that it was forbidden man to touch the vessel in which the race had been preserved, but he gave him a piece of the ark as a reward for his perseverance. The relic is said to be still preserved in the treasury of the monastery of Etchmiadzin.

All these myths have been rudely shattered and cast into the vortex in which the legendary lore of the nations is fast disappearing. Modern adventure and scientific investigation, which compass sea and land in the search for truth, have dispelled all these fancies, and have given us much information about this Koh-i-Nuh. Daring travelers, from Parrot, in 1835, to Allen and Sachtleben, the bicyclists, who waved the American flag on it July 4, 1890, have scaled its glaciers and crossed its ravines and stood upon its summit. Its altitude has been measured. Its geological structure has been critically treated by the celebrated Hermann Abich. Its great chasm on the north and east sides has a perpendicular height of four thousand feet. Its fissures and its glaciers have been described. I will not repeat the description. Its solitary position adds much to its grandeur. At Karmalou, a station directly east of the mount, we ascended to the flat roof of one of the native houses and took a long and meditative view of Ararat. Though thirty miles away, the levelness of the country and the lack of intervening objects made this appear scarcely credible. From the plain the Great Ararat rises in irregular form to the height of seventeen thousand feet above sea-level. Its line of perpetual snow is thirteen thousand four hundred feet. The Little Ararat is almost a perfect cone, thirteen thousand feet high, and, though below the level of perpetual snow, was for a considerable distance down covered with the white winding-sheet, owing to the rigorous season. Its summit is the boundary-line of the empires of the czar, the sultan, and the shah.

In 1883 the Levant " Herald " published a detailed account of an alleged discovery of the ark on Mount Ararat. In 1893, Dr. Honri, a Chaldean archdeacon, claimed to have seen the ancient " houseboat." It would be interesting to know what it is that has apparently deceived these worthy and no doubt veracious chroniclers.

Any doubt that existed as to the volcanic nature of the mountain was dispelled by the earthquake in 1840, which, accompanied by a loud subterranean roar and a great blast of wind, shook the giant mass to its center. Old Agghuri, a pastoral village of the Armenians at the foot of the chasm, was overwhelmed with instant and total destruction. The vine from which Noah is said to have made his wine, the willow which sprang from a plank of the ark, and the old monastery of St. Jacob, in which Christian service had continued undisturbed for a thousand years, were blotted from the face of the earth.

We were favored with a sight of a gorgeous sunset behind its lofty summit, contrasting with, yet similar in its perfect beauty to, the sunrise of the previous morning. Nature put on her best attire and decked herself, as in evening dress, in robes of Oriental splendor and magnificence. The sky formed a background of superb loveliness. The light reflecting on the snow gave it the brilliancy of crystal. The lights and shadows played on the landscape. The red, golden sky cast a purple hue over the fields and gave a pleasing tinge even to the bleak hills in the east. The divine Architect, whose handiwork had excited in us awe and reverence, seemed to remind us that in the mixing of colors, and in painting the outspread curtain of the heavens and the firmament below, there is no artist like the divine. Soon the evening shade deepened and the darkness brought our delightful day to a close, bringing us to a halt for the night.

From Ararat we proceeded in a southeasterly direction. We had made but one stage on Thursday morning when we were stopped at Sadarak for want of horses. The reason was that they had been stolen by the Kurds. The story was told that a band of Kurds had come along a few days before in need of horses, and had appropriated those belonging to the station. A Russian official, who had stopped for the night, resisting them, they had stripped him of his clothing and effects, including his watch and three hundred rubles, and in the scuffle stabbed him in the arm. In this condition he sought shelter in the house of the telegraph-operator. After five of the best hours of the day had passed we were able to get on our way again. Not long afterward we met some of these wild knights of the mountains, and observed a Kurdish village—a collection of tents, always easily recognized from their black covers. About four or five thousand Kurds roam incessantly around the base of Ararat.

From Erivan onward the road was not in good condition. Often we waded through deep sand and over rough and stony places. Once we stuck in the bed of the Arpa-Chai; on another occasion the driver fell asleep in his box and nearly precipitated us over the hillside. Again, in passing between two cliffs, trying overmuch to avoid Scylla, he almost dashed us against the rocky Charybdis. Then it was that our conductor showed his metal, brandishing his sword and hurling invectives at the driver's defenseless pate in jaw-breaking Russian, more terrifying to an Anglo-Saxon than the sight of a drawn sword.

On Friday morning we reached Nakhejevan, a considerable town of great antiquity. The name means "he descended first," and it is reputed to be the permanent settlement of Noah, and here his grave and monument are shown. As we were informed that horses could not be obtained until the morrow, we gladly seized the opportunity to see its sights, and strolled through the public gardens. At one corner we came across a neat little chapel embowered among the trees. The fine new Armenian church of brownstone, so rare a thing in these lands, excited our surprise. The bazaars presented some interesting features. Having finished our stroll through these, we came to a grand ruin. It was the remains of an ancient mosque, a reminder, also, of the former dominion of the Persians. The outer gateway was entered between two large cylindrical columns, reaching to the height of one hundred and fifty feet, surmounted by a curious arch. The mosque was of equal height, and magnificent even in its dilapidated condition. The dome was gone, but the walls were embossed and ornamented with taste and art.

The chief sight of interest was the supposed tomb of Noah. A ten minutes' ride brought us to it. It is in an Armenian cemetery which, aside from this, presents nothing but miserable-looking, rough headstones and mud-mounds. The monument which a grateful posterity has erected to the memory of our common father is not an imposing one. The form is that of a regular octagonal prism, whose perimeter is eighty feet, and the height of which above-ground is three feet, and underground ten feet. Hence it may rather be considered a vault. It is built of common stone and sun-dried brick, and plastered over with gypsum, which, when hardened, withstands the influence of the weather. Two flights of stairs lead down on opposite sides, and the entrance is made through low wooden doors. The interior presents little attraction. The floor is dirty and uncared for. The roof is formed by sixteen half-arches, joining in the center on a pillar. The pillar is hollow, and serves the purpose of a flue for the altar of incense at its base. The appearance of the altar, black and begrimed with smoke and ashes, would seem to betoken frequent offer-

TYPES SEEN IN THE CAUCASUS.

ings from the faithful. The ceiling was stuck over with stones, for when the worshiper comes to pray he believes that his prayer will be answered if a stone, pressed by him, sticks to the ceiling. The tomb is said to be held in great veneration by both Armenians and Mussulmans. Notwithstanding this the walls are defaced and marked with names, showing that our Occidental habits are not confined to the West.

From Nakhejevan a short drive brought us to Julfa, on the Aras River, the boundary between Russia and Persia. We crossed the Aras by an old-fashioned wire-rope ferry in the same place and manner that Henry Martyn and Justin Perkins crossed the river. At low water the boat could not reach the opposite bank, but obliging porters stood ready to receive the ladies on their backs and carry them to land.*

* When we were returning, the river was high and the rope-ferry would not work. Flat diamond-shaped boats, each side about ten feet long and two and one-half feet high, were made ready. Our baggage was placed as a seat for us in one end near the oarsman. Some chickens and a donkey or two were brought on; and a crowd of Mohammedan fellahs, hundreds of whom were going to Russia to get work, filled the rest of the space. Collecting the fares from them caused a great hubbub. The ropes were then loosed. We were pushed off from the bank with the long poles, which were used as oars, and started diagonally down the stream. Then, in beseeching tones, the passengers exclaimed, "Allah akbar !" ("God is great !") "In the name of God the compassionate, the merciful !" Next they shouted in unison, "Ya ali, ya ali !" ("Help us, help us !") The pilot answered, "It is enough ; we are safe," and soon they were all tumbling out on the other side far down the stream, where a row of camels were waiting to convey our baggage to the custom-house.

When I had presented our passport to the Persian official, he looked it over and affixed his visé and seal. After a short time he asked, "Are you a Persian subject ? " I said, " No." He said, " A German ? " I looked surprised and said, "An American." He said, "Oh, I can't read the passport." I asked him, "What is the charge ? " "Whatever you favor me with." "But certainly you have a regular charge ? " "No; with such honorable persons as you, we are content with whatever favor you confer."

From Julfa one road leads directly, via Salmas, to Urumia, five days' travel by caravan; another to Tabriz, in four days. Horses and a gig had been sent from Tabriz to meet us. We had nothing to do but to go forward. When the baggage was loaded on the pack-saddles, with the *charvadars* or muleteers keeping pace alongside, and the others of our party had mounted or surrounded the rickety gig, we made a presentable caravan. The day was bright and cheerful, and we started off in fine spirits. But alas for our progress ! The sun looks upon few worse roads. Not to speak of the sand-bars, or the embankments for irrigation, or the bridges built with acute angles, our windings through the valley of the Dizzi will be sufficient to describe.

During the season of freshets a torrent had come raging through the defile, washing away the earth and loosening the rocks; but in the dry season only a rivulet preserved the identity of the Dizzi. The river-bed was the road. Rocks were everywhere, often one or two feet square. Two horses were hitched tandem, and Moses was mounted on the leader. His main achievement seemed to be to conduct his horse around an obstacle and then pull up the gig against it. After vain attempts at guiding, he dismounted and showed his good-will by walking in the water behind the gig. A score of times we alighted and became quarrymen, or put our shoulders to the wheel. The springs snapped and the whip became a stump. The latent balking capacity of the horses was developed. No wonder that the shades of night overtook us before we got to the first station. During the succeeding days the road was not so bad. The landscape was monotonous and uninteresting, varied by an occasional village, a caravansary, or a watermill. The first night we halted at Galin Kaiya, where a colony from Talish were settled in Nadir Shah's time, who still speak the Talish dialect of the Persian tongue. We took possession of its best guest-room. Its walls were of dark mud. There was a large range at one end, a *tandur* in the center for baking bread, and a pile of loose grain at the other end. In this confusion we managed to stretch our curtains and put up our camp-beds. Our other *menzils* (stations) were Marend and Sofian. The former is a district capital of eight thousand inhabitants, with sixty villages surrounding it on a beautiful plain, fertile and noted for its melons. Sofian was the scene of the defeat of the Turks, in 1585, by Hamza Mirza. In these places the walls of our lodgings were covered with grotesque frescos of all the inmates of Noah's ark, and of the products of the Botanical Gardens.

On November 4th we started in full expectation of soon reaching our destination. It is a beautiful custom in the East, followed since the time of Melchizedek, to go out some distance to meet a coming guest, and, when he departs, to conduct him on his way. This custom has been adopted by foreign residents. During the morning some little speck in the distance would often cause us to gallop forward, eager to greet our friends, but only to be disappointed. At last, when we were eating lunch, Yacob came flying up, having supplanted his brethren, and announced their coming. We mounted quickly. Soon one and another of the missionaries and the brethren came riding up with many salaams and Eastern salutations. The natives were mounted on their gay saddles, in holiday attire, and with bright faces. As they turned for the three hours' ride yet before us, we formed together quite a cavalcade. There were khans, hadjis, barons, mirzas, and shameshas. There were Persians and Turks, Armenians and Nestorians, Jews and Kurds, as well as representatives of seven or eight States of America. We were glad that so many tongues spoke us welcome, and that so many hearts were open to receive us. Proceeding thus, before we were aware of it, the city of Tabriz, with its gardens, lay stretched before our eyes, with the snow-covered Sahend beyond. Soon we passed through the old walls of the city and reached the houses of the missionaries in the Armenian quarter.

CHAPTER III

TABRIZ is the metropolis of Persia, the first city in commercial importance, and the capital of Azerbijan, the finest province of the kingdom. Its political title is Dar-il-Sultaneh, the "door of the kingdom"; and its religious title the "pinnacle of Islam." Like many Oriental cities, it has witnessed the vicissitudes of fortune, at one time borne on the high tide of prosperity, and anon overwhelmed with earthquake and despoiled by war and pestilence. In the time of Chardin (seventeenth century) it could boast its half a million inhabitants, three hundred caravansaries, and two hundred and fifty mosques. A century ago a terrible earthquake shook its houses into dust-heaps. In 1810 it was estimated by Kinnier to have a population of thirty thousand in the midst of its ruins. In 1830 Dr. Eli Smith reported it as having a population of sixty thousand. Now it is estimated at from one hundred and fifty thousand to two hundred thousand, of whom three thousand are Armenians. There are about one hundred Europeans in various occupations.

The city fills the arena and spreads over the slopes of an amphitheater, formed by red and yellow hills, at the head of a plain, thirty-six miles in length, which reaches down to Lake Urumia. These hills are barren and at first sight unattractive; but as one gets accustomed to Persian scenery they impress one with a beauty of their own. The plain on the other side affords both a similarity and a contrast to the bleak hills. In

52

part of it the soil is so sandy and impregnated with salt and sulphur as to be unproductive. Sulphur can be picked up on the surface of the ground, and salt is often so plentiful as to whiten the earth. The other part presents a pleasing contrast, especially in the opening spring. There is a wide extent of well-cultivated vineyards, orchards, and gardens. The length of the city, including the suburbs, is about twelve miles.

A bird's-eye view of Tabriz is disappointing to one who has formed conceptions of Oriental magnificence and splendor. The half-mythic, half-poetic ideals of Persian grandeur are rudely shattered by a glimpse of the realities. The accumulated romance of the ages, concentrated into a picture, presents to the mind a city with lofty domes and minarets and splendid palaces, with brilliance and light and beauty. To sober sight the gold is sordid dust. The cities of Persia—Tabriz among them—are for the most part a mass of mud-walls, differing but little in color from the surrounding hills or plains. The flat roofs of the houses, the arched roofs of the bazaars, the walls of the gardens, covered with a mud-plaster, look common and unattractive, and give the whole a dingy appearance. The style of architecture is mean and inartistic. The houses are for the most part only one story high. A strange appearance, as of a conflagration, is presented when the sun is reflected from the tin and oiled paper in the windows. The streets are narrow, many of them being only eight or ten feet wide, and the *darbands* or alleys only half that width. Those leading out to the king's highways are broader, the one to Teheran being a fine avenue lined with trees, called the Kheaban. A few streets have paving and sidewalks of cobblestones. Those of the Kala were paved, in 1879, by famished laborers, who were thus furnished with bread by the Manchester Fund.

Strolling through the streets gave me many real impressions of Oriental life. Walls rise on either side to the height of from ten to twenty-five feet, and exclude all view of the yards or of the harems. Entrance to the yards is through strong wooden doors in the walls. Surrounding the gate, and forming an arch over it, are checkered or various-colored pilasters of brick. Formerly the gateways were low and unornamented, because fear of oppression prevented a display of wealth.

The crooks and bends of the streets are innumerable; even the Rasta Koocha, or Straight Street, is like the street in Damascus of which Mark Twain remarked that the Acts showed its accuracy in saying "the street that is called Straight," and not affirming its straightness. The *darbands* are like New-Year's resolutions—they start out all right, but soon change and come to a sudden end. Attempts to take a short cut frequently led me against a door at the end of an alley. Many times I have found myself tripping into the steps which go down to the yards and take up much of the narrow sidewalk. More often I collided with a drove of donkeys. Oh, how many caravans of donkeys are we not familiar with!—donkeys with provision-baskets filled with grapes or other fruits, with garden-truck or firewood; donkeys with butchered animals strapped on their backs; donkeys loaded with two mountains of straw in rope netting larger than the beast itself; donkeys with all sorts of building-material, the brick falling off, the poles dragging behind and ready to hit an unwary passer-by on the shins; white donkeys, mounted by white-turbaned high priests of Islam or veiled khanums of the harems; wee gray donkeys, with the rider dangling his bare feet within a few inches of the ground; donkeys returning at double-quick time, their loads having been disposed of; donkeys braying, and drivers uh-uh-uhing—yes, donkeys are the sight *par excellence* of the streets of Tabriz. Without halter or bridle, they crowd on one another and over all the sidewalks, leaving no room for the pedestrian. Some may try to maintain their right of way against these street caravans by the free use of a cane; but I found that the easiest manner to get them out of one's way was to go around them. Soon it became a matter of indifference to me whether I was on the sidewalk or in the middle of the street. The latter is just as popular. But in that I had a new danger to guard against, namely, of tripping into the holes * which at every few rods open into the waterways. Above these holes a *sakka* or water-carrier was once standing, dipping his leathern bucket into the water and filling his bag of skin, which he carried slung over his hip. Coming past the place I met a mounted official with two rows of attendants behind and before him. They cried " Khabar-dar !" ("Take notice !") and the crowd at this slunk against the walls to let the great man pass. Again, a carriage—a late innovation—passed, occupied by a nobleman. His outriders galloped ahead and cried out, "Make way; the prince is com-ing!" and enforced the warning with blows of their batons. When they reached a place where carpets had been spread in the street, and men, women, and children were seated listening to the eulogies of the martyrs, the carriage drove over the rugs, while the pulpit was hustled out of the way, and the audience pressed one another against the walls. Deference is paid to the man only who has a great retinue.

In strolling around I encountered a variety of beggars, ragged, dirty, and miserable; some of them half-witted, some blind. One was without arms, another a dumb man, who could only say " Huk, huk!" An old hag was squatting in the street, shivering in the cold wind, and crying, piteously, "Give me bread-money! May God bless your children ! For the Prophet's sake give me a black money! For the sake of Jesus † look upon me !" Some little ragamuffins, like

---

* General Von Wagner, among other reforms he tried to introduce, procured an order for the stopping up of these holes. To bring the project into ridicule, the opposers blocked up the skylights in the bazaars.

† Mohammedan beggars ask alms from Christians in the name of Jesus.

Ali and Gooli,* ran after me for squares and pestered the peace
out of me, until I said, "Because these youngsters trouble me,
I will give them, lest by their continual following they shame
me !" Farther on I heard the sound of dogs fighting, and saw
a group of children gathered on a roof looking down upon the
scene. What was my surprise on reaching the place to see
simply a boy imitating a dog-fight, mimicing the barks and
snarls of the supposed canines in a marvelous manner, and
reaping his reward of shahis! On passing around the corner
I came to the genuine curs. They are the scavengers of the
street, and have two or three kennels in every ward. They are
large and fierce, and bark at a Christian's heels as they do at
any strange dogs who go by. The shopkeepers, too, seemed
to enjoy the sport of hissing them on and of watching the dis-
comfiture of Christians.†

I next came to a *bazaarcha*, a group of shops such as are
located here and there throughout the city. This *bazaarcha*
consisted of a couple of bakeries, with the *sangak* (sheets of

---

* Ali and Gooli were two little waifs, whom every foreigner knew.
They grew up in the streets. On every festival day they were in their
element. " Sahib, may your festival be blessed!" At every arrival or
departure of guests, they were there, their swift little feet carrying them
along with the cavalcade of horsemen, until, if setting out, a long distance
was traversed and they received their bakshish, and gave their blessing on
the journey.

† The street dogs almost created an international difficulty on one occasion. An Armenian, having imbibed too freely at the cemetery grog-
shop, was passing along. The dogs were hissed on at him. He drew
his revolver and shot a dog. The sayids attacked him, declaring that he
had shot a man. He was severely dealt with and taken to the police station
half dead. Because he was the servant of the Armenian lady teacher, the
teachers all came to his rescue. They also were beaten by the crowd.
The sufferers being Russian subjects, the consul demanded that the sayids
be punished. The sayids appealed to the mujtchid, and asked his kind
permission to loot the Armenian quarter, one of them saying that his father
was one of the " lootees " formerly. The Armenian vartabed wrote the

bread) spread out on a plastered incline, or flung over a rod ; a butcher's shop, with some sheep dressed and hung up, a steer and buffalo lying in the street on their hides, ready to be cut up, other sheep tied by ropes and eating watermelon rinds. There were also the greengrocer and the attar or spice seller, who dealt also in tobacco, and had bags of it standing before his shop. The blacksmith occupied half the street, and every passer-by dodged behind the horse's heels, fearing a kick, especially when the smith was twisting its ears with a knotted rope. The *bazaarcha* contained also a *bakkal* or dealer in fuel and horse-feed, dealers in lime and in petroleum, and a carpenter ; and, since the corner is of some importance, it had its *chai-khana* or tea-house, the Persian loafing-place, corresponding to the saloon of civilized (?) lands. The beverage which cheers but does not inebriate was dispensed in tiny glasses all the day long. I saw a fellow strutting hither and thither, and calling out like an auctioneer ; but no, he was not a crier. He was a dervish, who, in his long flowing robes and uncut, unkempt locks, was telling tales of faith and devotion, mingled with war and love ; growing fervid with the progress of his plot, his strange eyes flashed with excitement as the climax was reached and the "black" money began to pour down upon his outspread aba or cloak, and into his *kashgul* or Indian nut-shell, which his pupil carried around to the shopkeepers. Beyond the *bazaarcha* was another dervish, standing before a highly colored canvas, several yards square, on which some sacred scene was pictured, which added inter-

mujtehid a letter, in which he threatened that he would telegraph to Teheran. The mujtehid was offended. The Armenian merchants feared for the consequences. They went to the mujtehid, told him their vartabed was an ignoramus, and apologized for his letter. An Armenian subject of Turkey, a few days afterward, was attacked by the same dogs. He appealed to his consul, but was answered, " I came here to deal with men, not with dogs !"

est to his narrative and kept the attention of the eager crowd.
In the open space not far distant a snake-charmer was to be
seen.   He had gone to the Elan Dagh ("Snake Mountain"),
ten miles north of the city, whose reputed myriads of reptiles
make the people shun it.   He had thrown his spell over some
of these enemies of man, and brought them here to delight
the crowd.   How was it that the same snake, as it seemed,
bit a hen and it toppled over and died, with visible evidence
of pain, yet its bite had no terror for the charmer who toyed
with it?   Let those answer who know.   The charmer turned
additional pennies into his pocket by selling written prayers
guaranteeing safety from snake-bites.   Vying with him was a
trickster with imported jacks and aces, playing three-card
monte, and inveigling the youth to stake their shahis.   It
was a continual surprise to see how many things the people
were unconcernedly doing in the confined streets.   At one
place was a group of villagers, with their huge sheepskin hats,
sitting smoking their pipes.   One was sprawling at full length
in the sun, asleep, his head pillowed on a cobblestone.   At
another place a huge pile of earth had been thrown from a lot,
and the moulder of sun-dried bricks was filling up most of the
street with his layers of brick.   Another was mixing a bed of
mud and cut-straw mortar, so large that barely room for passing remained.   The bath-house had its towels hung on the
walls to dry; the weaver was using the same place to arrange
his long warp.   Dyers and others were standing in the *gaziran*
or fuller's tank, with pantaloons rolled up above their knees,
and washing dyed cotton cloth, and kidskins to be salted
down for exportation.   Women, too, had brought their quilts
and carpets to clean, and with faces carefully veiled, but
limbs bare, they were standing in the water.   Even the children were able to make the narrow street their playground.
Boys, more than half naked, were running about, making
mud-balls, or playing marbles with sheep's knuckle-bones.   I

looked to see them trampled upon by the strings of camels or prancing horses which passed so close to them, but they escaped without injury. When a Christian passed, the urchins yelled after him, " Armeni, Armeni!" and sometimes followed and hooted him.*

But of all the street scenes it struck me as most ludicrous to see was a perambulating barber, his implements of trade inserted in his girdle, present his hand-mirror before the face of a laborer, and the latter, taking the hint, squat down in the street to submit himself to the operation. His head was soon shaved—all except the locks behind the ears—and his beard trimmed in the sight of all.

The city of Tabriz is divided into twenty-four wards. The oldest and principal one is the Kala, or fortified portion, which still retains the name, though the walls have for the most part disappeared, the moat is filled, and the space used for buildings. The center of the Kala is occupied by the bazaars, the eastern side by the government buildings, and the southwest corner by the Armenians and Europeans.

The bazaars are among the finest in the East. "The Mirror of Cities," a Persian work, says that there are five thousand shops in the main bazaars, and fifteen hundred in other parts of the city. General Schindler, in 1886, reported thirty-nine hundred and twenty-two shops and one hundred and sixty-six caravansaries. From the time of the last earthquake until about twenty-five years ago many of them were rude structures, roofed with timbers. These were removed by Tamash Mirza Mujid-ud-Doulah, and extensive brick structures with high-vaulted roofs have replaced them. The arches often span the breadth of thirty feet, and show well the pecu-

---

* In distant wards it is not uncommon for the gamins to sling stones at Christians ; but when we remember that Washington City arabs called " Bah, bah!" after the Persian minister, because of his lambskin hat, we have little reason to complain.

liar skill of the Persian in constructing the arch. The best idea of these bazaars can be formed, by one who has never seen them, from the arcades of a European or American city. Light and air are admitted through small skylights. The shops, ranging along between the piers, have about ten or twelve feet frontage, and even less depth. Some have additional rooms for storage. Movable shutters inclose them at night.

The bazaars excited my curiosity as much as anything in Persia. They possessed a never-failing interest. To take a view of them I entered the Amir Bazaar, one of the finest of its kind. What a throng there was! City and village were mingling and rubbing against each other amid great confusion, with a continual cry of " Khabar-dar!" and excited dickerings.*

The Amir Bazaar presented first to the view a long line of dealers in prints and dress-goods, displaying all the gaudy colors that Manchester can mix for the Oriental taste. The dealers were sitting on rugs on the floor, quietly waiting for customers. Their stock of merchandise was placed in full view and within easy reach of them ; the abacus and account-books were lying beside them. One was smoking his *kalean*, another reading the Koran or saying his prayers, keeping an eye squinted all the while on the passers-by, and interrupting his devotions to detain a customer. Between the shops, on spaces four feet square in front of the piers, sat Armenian silversmiths. Each one had a show-case for displaying his wares, and room enough behind it for the motion of his elbows.†

From the Amir Bazaar I passed into the Amir caravansary,

---

* Foreign ladies can scarcely visit the bazaars, except in Armenian costume, because a curious and gaping crowd gathers around, making it inconvenient and possibly dangerous to thread their labyrinths.

† In the winter they sit with their abas or cloaks closely wrapped around them, and pans of charcoals under their hands. Habit has inured them to withstand severe cold.

so called from a former Amir-i-Nizam, who built it and the
bazaar.   In the center of this caravansary is an open square,
two or three hundred feet in dimension, and a fountain.
Broad pavements surround the square and divide it into sections, which are planted with trees.   The pavements were
occupied, as usual, by cases of merchandise, which were quite
safe, as the outer doors, as well as those of the bazaars, are
locked at sundown, and watchmen patrol on the arched roofs.
The entrances are *dālāns* or arcades, lined with shops.   The
sides of the squares are built up two stories high and divided
into shops and offices.   They are occupied by Messrs. Ziegler
& Co., the Imperial Bank, and other European and Armenian
merchants, and by the Book Depository of the American Bible
Society.

Thence I passed to the Geurgi or Georgian *timcha*, a circular or octagonal structure, covered by a dome.   Around its
interior were shops where Armenians were displaying the goods
of Nijni-Novgorod—knickknacks of various kinds.   Farther
on was the Rasta Bazaar, which glittered with glass and
chinaware, vases and lamps, most of them elaborately decorated.   There, too, were dealers in leather, carpets, tea, sugar,
notions, drugs, and a hundred other articles.   The bazaars
continued on both sides of the bridge over the Kuri Chai—a
Rialto without fame—and opened into the Madan-i-Sahib-il-
Amr.   In this square or market-place, under sheds and booths,
meats and fruits in abundance and variety were being sold.
The place was crowded and dirty.   I retraced my steps by a
parallel street, passing row after row of shops.   My attention
was especially arrested by the *dallal* or peddlers' bazaar—a
curiosity-shop where the old work of Shiraz, Ispahan, Kerman,
and Resht was shown.   The exhibitions of Persian goods interested me most, but imported articles were largely taking
their places.

To the east of the bazaars are the public buildings.   On one side are the government school, the post-office, and the custom-house. On another side is the *jabah-khana* or armory, a large square, surrounded by shops, in which muskets, swords, kalamdans, and other articles are manufactured. It was near its entrance that the Bab was executed. Thielmann, Curzon, and even Browne make the mistake of placing that event in the ark. The Bab's body was afterward thrown to the dogs near the Kheaban gate, whence Hadji Suleiman Khan, with two other Babis, took it for burial. To the right of the *jabah-khana* are the royal stables, and farther on the arsenal court-yard, where a few old cannon and other arms are kept. On the south of this courtyard is a high arched gateway, called the *Ala Gapi* or Sublime Porte; on the east is the crown prince's prison for the worst criminals, while through an entrance to the north is a court where the "Takia," or Persian play of Muharam, is acted. Here are the *divan-khana* or court-house, the new palace of the prince, and his *anderoon*, with extensive flower-gardens attached. A few squares beyond is the Madan-i-Mashk, the soldiers' headquarters and drill-ground, with a flaring lion and sun over its portal.

The most striking government building is the summer pal-ace of the crown prince. It is situated in what is called the Baghi Shamal (the "Northern Garden"), to the south of the city. This misnomer is caused by the garden taking the place of one on the other side of the city. It is a park of one hundred and seventy acres. The entrance-gate is a handsome brick arch, from which a long double avenue leads to the palace. Immediately in front of it is a circular fountain, fifty feet in diameter, in which swans are disporting. The reception-room, built by Abbas Mirza, is a small saloon adorned with paintings of envoys who have come to Persia, of Napoleon and other celebrities, the work of a Persian artist who had studied in Europe. The walls and ceilings are covered with minute pieces of mirror wrought into artistic forms. The large interior court has a fountain through its whole length and flower-beds on both sides. At its farther end is the palace, built by the present Vali Ahd. It is a circular building, with a marble fountain in the center, overlooking which are five or six tiers of balustrades or galleries, arched over and crowned with a cupola. Around the sides of the court are rooms for the harem. In its environment, and compared with the city, it may be deemed palatial. We had been admitted by the guards, and on walking up to the fountain the crown prince unexpectedly appeared from his tent, inquired for our health and of what nationality we were, and treated us most graciously. Usually when the prince is resident visitors are not admitted. In one part of the garden was a menagerie, which consisted of a deer, a wolf, a stuffed bear, and a few small animals.

Another sight of Tabriz is the Blue Mosque, or Goeg Mesjid, which stands on the Kheaban. It was built by Jehan Shah, of the Black Sheep dynasty, in A.D. 1464, though some—Markham, to wit—mistakenly attribute it to Ghazan Khan. Though ruined by earthquakes, the magnificence of it when new and perfect is yet evident. "The Mirror of Cities" says, "The like of it there was not on earth." Texier made numerous plates of it. He is quoted by Curzon as saying that "it is the chief work of Persian, perhaps of all Oriental, architecture." It is an imposing arched structure, covered inside and out with glazed tiles of various colors—blue and white prevailing—wrought into symmetrical figures. Over the arched doorway, and along the base of the arches in the interior, verses from the Koran in arabesque figures are written in the tiles. The dado of the apse is composed of immense slabs of alabaster, inscribed with verses from the Koran, and larger than any at present mined in Persia. As it is a Sunni mosque, it is neglected by the Shiahs. A few years ago it was a dog-kennel, but later a door was put up. It is kept locked, probably as much to obtain bakshish from travelers as for any other purpose.

A relic of still greater antiquity is the ark or citadel, a conspicuous landmark from every approach to the city. It was originally built as a mosque by Ali Shah Jelan, Taj-i-Din, a successor of Ghazan Khan Mongol. Its court was two hundred and fifty arshins square, and its porches were of great size. Innumerable slabs of marble were used, and the walls were covered with *kashee* or tiles. " It surpassed in size all buildings in Persia." Through the court a watercourse flowed, and many kinds of trees grew around the mosque. In settling, much of the structure fell. The present ark is probably a part of that mosque. It is popularly called Tagh-i-Ali Shah (the "Arch of Ali Shah "). It is one hundred and twenty feet high; its walls at the base are twenty-five feet thick, and slanting slightly inward as they ascend. Steps ascend to the top, where there is a corridor around three sides, and a small room, on the walls of which travelers have registered their names. From it a wide prospect of the province is obtained. Lake Urumia appears as a streak of white in the distance, and beyond the Zagros show their pale outline. One tradition of its building is that the bricks were thrown to the mason on the wall, even for the topmost layers, by a black slave of great strength, who was liberated when the work was finished. Another story relates that an aspiring youth once climbed to its top with his back to the wall, by putting his fingers into the interstices between the bricks, and was rewarded for his deed of daring by being promptly executed, on the ground that if he grew to manhood he would be the world's greatest thief. Casting criminals from its summit was once a mode of execution, and it is told how a woman was saved by her skirts spreading and so sustaining her in the air that she alighted on the ground easily and without injury. In later times this structure was turned into a fort and surrounded by a wall with bastions

and moat. Abbas Mirza established in it a foundry for mould-
ing cannon, and also an armory, which was erected under the
superintendence of Mr. Armstrong, an Englishman.

Tabriz is a very religious city, and a description of it is in-
complete without some account of its existing mosques and
shrines. It is said to have three hundred and eighteen
mosques, and eight tombs of imamzadas. Most of the
mosques are low, with roofs supported by posts, and unceiled.
One ancient mosque is the Ustad-i-Shagird, near the timber-
market. It was built by Amir Sheik Hasan Chupani, over
five hundred years ago. Another is the Sayid Hamza, built
by a vizier of Ghazan Khan, who was executed by him, and
is regarded as a martyr by the Shiahs. Here Kajar princes
and prominent men are buried. It is a sacred refuge.

The two most important centers of religious life are the
Talabiya and the Măgâm-i-Sahib-il-Amr. The Talabiya contains a large theological school and three mosques. Hadji
Mirza Javat Agha, mujtehid of the Mutasharis, has two of
these, one for summer and one for winter. The former was
built by Sultan Ahmed during Osmanli occupation. It is one
lofty arch, forty-four feet wide and three hundred feet long,
with side-rooms and galleries for the women. Another in the
same inclosure is the " Mosque of Forty Pillars," in which the
Hujat-il-Islam leads prayers for the sheiks. The capitals of
the pillars are ornamented with verses from the Koran, written
with white color upon a dark-blue background. The Măgâm-
i-Sahib-il-Amr (the " Palace of the Master of the Command-
ment") is so called because the twelfth imam appeared there
in a dream. A dome has been built over the place, and the
stones of the shrine have been worn smooth by the kisses of
worshipers. Around it are the Mosque of Sahib-il-Amr,
which has two blue glazed tile minarets and is in charge of
the Sigat-il-Islam, the school of the Sadikiya, and the Mosque
and Madressa of Hassan Padishah.

A special shrine is Ainali-Zainali. It is on the range of that name, just north of the city, and so designated from two descendants of Ali who were wounded in the Arab conquest and died on this mountain. A visit to it repays one with a fine view of the city and the plains around. The people consider a pilgrimage to it very meritorious, and climb the steep hill on the warmest days of summer—especially on Fridays— to obtain the intercession of the buried martyrs. To go on seven successive Fridays is said to be equivalent to a pilgrimage to Kerbela. When the Hujat-il-Islam died his body was borne with a long procession to Ainali-Zainali, where service was held. When we went the attendant allowed us to enter with our shoes on, probably in the hope of receiving a larger fee. The monuments are rude structures, covered with green cloth, the color which is sacred to the sayids. At one end of the shrine is a pulpit where lamentations for the dead are repeated. On the walls are pictures of the shrines of Kerbela and Meshed.

Let us now take a glance at Persian municipal life. The government of Tabriz may serve as a sample of that of other cities of Persia. A provincial or district governor (hakim) is ruler in each city; but he is often transferred from one place to another, and has few local attachments. The city government proper consists of officers who are rarely changed. These are the beglar-begi or mayor, and the kand-khudas or aldermen, of different wards of the city. These officials are subject to removal at the pleasure of the king; yet as they are hereditary nobles, men of means, and steady supporters of the throne, they often hold their positions through life and transmit them to their descendants. They hold court in their own houses, have their own prisons, decide cases, and punish with fines, the bastinado, or imprisonment in chains. Great criminals are transferred to the governor-general and punished by him. The salary of such an official is derived from various sources. In the first place, the revenue of some crown villages is assigned to him. Then he receives fines, fees for certifying deeds and other documents, ten per cent. for collecting debts, fees from illegal traffic, such as liquor-selling, with presents at festivals and on various occasions.

One of the most influential aldermen of Tabriz was the Kala-Begi-Hadji Agha Khan, who filled this position for many years, and who was a man of intelligence, a reader of books not only in Persian, but in Osmanli Turkish, and was specially interested in all matters of information regarding the politics, races, and religions of the world. With a retentive memory and a power of pleasing conversation, he was most entertaining and well versed in the traditions and past associations of the city.

The police are the personal retainers of the mayor and aldermen, and are employed and dismissed by them at their pleasure. They are called *farash*, a name signifying sweeper, which originated from the servants who swept the mosque and palace of the caliphs. Each group is under the charge of a chief of police. They receive no salary, but are required to pay to the aldermen a certain amount each month. To assure a daily income to themselves, and to collect this extra amount, they are alert and active in ferreting out offenders. But as their object is to make the greatest cash profit out of every case, they are ready to overlook a crime for a liberal donation, or to torture the one who refuses to pay. A person who is falsely accused has little hope of easy and speedy escape except by a bribe of money, unless he has a powerful friend to mediate for him. Wine-sellers, thieves, and lewd men and women are levied upon for hush-money, *à la* Tammany. Looties or rogues often become policemen or servants of a khan, in order to be unmolested in their rascality, as a nobleman deems it his prerogative to protect his retainers. One night the officers of the mayor arrested twenty thieves, locked them up, and threatened to beat several of them. The latter said, "You had better not molest us; we are the prince's servants." The officers were about to punish others of them. They said, "We are the governor's men." Others announced themselves as under the protection of the commander of the guards. At one time looties became so numerous and troublesome that the governor put a price on each head, and they set to killing one another for the reward. Some of them even transgressed so far as to pilfer the crown prince's dinner as it was being taken to his summer palace. His Highness's indignation was aroused, and the luckless official who should have prevented such a mishap was severely bastinadoed and banished from the city.

Another institution for the protection of the city is a series of guard-houses, placed here and there through the streets. They are small, filthy, dark rooms, with porches in front, where the guards can stand or sleep. The guards are soldiers detailed in squads from whatever regiment is on duty. They are poorly clad and fed, and try to eke out a living by money-changing or lending at usurious interest, and by levying on the loads of wood, brick, and provisions which pass by. In 1881, after the Kurdish raid, the governor ordered these guard-houses repaired, and reintroduced the *ismi-shab*—the night watchword. Every one found on the streets later than three hours after sundown was liable to arrest and detention until morning, unless he could give the countersign. Those designing to be out later could procure the word from their consul or the aldermen. Occasionally we would neglect to procure the countersign, and the guards would present arms and block our way in the street and threaten us with incarceration. A slight bakshish would open the way as effectually as the *ismi-shab*. The use of a watchword has since been abolished.

As the streets are not lighted, every one going about at night carries, or has carried before him, a lantern. These resemble Chinese lanterns, except that the "shirt," as it is called,

A Nobleman and his Retainers.

is of oiled muslin, and the top and bottom of tinned copper. They vary in size according to the dignity of the person. A consul or nobleman will have several lanterns carried before him, two feet in diameter and three feet long. The foreigner and the well-to-do Persian are content with one a foot in diameter, while the poor have very small ones.

Several attempts have been made to light the streets. When the shah came to Tabriz, in 1889, an order was issued that every man should put a street-lamp before his door and keep it lighted. After a few weeks the effort was abandoned and darkness prevailed as before.

Street-cleaning is very spasmodic. Dust, piles of rubbish, earth, brick, or snow fill the width of the street for weeks at a time, so that men and donkeys must go over mounds from three to five feet high. Then a fortunate accident overturns a governor's carriage, or a pestilence threatens, and a peremptory order is issued for cleaning up. One governor in Maragha never went out riding in summer without first sending orders to have the streets along his course sprinkled and swept.

The water-supply of cities is from two sources, the rivers and *karises*. Some cities, such as Urumia, Khoi, Maragha, and Ispahan, have a sufficient supply from streams running by, and its distribution is the only problem. Tabriz and Teheran are without abundant water-supply. The river running by Tabriz, the Aji Chai, is so brackish that it is scarcely suitable even for irrigation. Two creeks, the Kuri Chai and Madan Chai, are completely dried up in summer before they enter the city. One reservoir, called Shah Gyol, built by Naib-i-Sultanah in the early part of this century, retains a partial supply of water for summer use; but the main supply comes through *karises* or *kanauts*, underground channels, which are described in the chapter on village life. At least twenty or thirty of these *karises* reach the city. Sometimes they run open in the streets, bordered by trees; but usually they are several feet below the surface, in cemented channels or clay pipes. The level of the yards is lower than the streets, that the water may flow over them. To turn the water into a yard the *mirab* or waterman lies down in the street, inserts his arm, and moves about the lump of clay or clot of rags which is used as a stopper. When one place has been watered a certain number of hours, according to contract, the stream is turned to the next house, not to return for ten or twenty days, and sometimes in winter for several months, if the channel is frozen up. Hence almost every house has an *ab-ambar* or tank in the cellar, which holds from six hundred to two thousand cubic feet of water. A neighborhood of poor people have one in common, and it is considered a meritorious act for a rich man to build public tanks for them. The water in these tanks often becomes putrid, not only from long stagnation, but because clothes are washed in the open waterways, and a good deal of surface filth flows into them, as the city has no system of drainage. Only a marvelous natural climate prevents an excessive mortality from this impure water-supply.

CHAPTER IV

MARAGHA, THE SEAT OF THE MONGOLS

ONE of the cities of Azerbijan, of medieval fame, is Maragha, once a capital of the Mongols. It is situated thirty-five miles southwest of Tabriz, and in midsummer is accessible by a road over the snowy Sahend; but at other times a circuit of the mountains is necessary, by the shore of Lake Urumia, making the distance eighty miles.

As we rode out of Tabriz it may have seemed as if, like the Israelites, we had borrowed of our neighbors, from the volume and bulk of our baggage. If we could have done without eating and sleeping we might have dispensed with traveling-beds, galvanized plates, cooking-utensils, and the cook; but we found it true that "sound sleep at night made the day bright, and good food made a merry mood." The beggars evidently thought that our train needed a blessing, for they followed us with persistent beseechings for alms. How could we refuse? Would not our journey be a failure unless we obtained favor by a safety-offering? We thought the exertion of getting the *charvadar* or muleteer was enough, without having to wait hungry for the arrival of the horses in the evening. If you read of the fleet Arabian steed and the strong and fiery Turkoman, believe it; but do not imagine the common horse of Persia is of any such stock. His market-value is appraised at from four to thirty dollars. Among Persian steeds the *charvadar* horses carry off the prize, for a more balky, bony, bruised, sore-backed, stumbling set was never

seen. Our original equipment of them had to be dismissed at
the first station.

We lodged at Sardarud, a village of some note in connection with the holy wars of Islam. Fallen battlements and
other ruins are yet to be seen about the place. Passing into
a caravansary, we found ourselves surrounded by quadrupeds
of numberless sorts, and all the arrangements for their accommodation. Above, however, were small *balakhanas* * or upper
rooms, with gray mud-walls and an entire absence of furniture. A few strips of carpet were hastily spread, the oiled-
paper windows thrown open, and we were soon comfortable.

The road during the next day had little to interest one.
Numerous caravans of camels met us, loaded with the products
of Kurdistan, the animals trudging along single file, chained
to one another, the drivers sprawling on the camels' backs, doz-
ing away, reclining in all sorts of comical and ridiculous pos-
tures, their heads dangling in the air, their feet keeping time
to the slow and solemn procession. Though our course was
over a sandy plain, splendid mountains were continually in
sight—on the one side Sahend, on the other Shahi, and, beyond Lake Urumia, the mountains of Kurdistan, the home of
the untamed Chief Josephs and Captain Jacks of Asia. Soon
rounding the " nose " of the mountain, the lake itself came in
view, and later the plain of Goigan, separated by a slight rise
from that of Ducargan. Ducargan is the seat of the district
governor, who has a difficult time of it with the turbulent
population. Goigan contains the telegraph station and post-
office. The two towns have a population of ten to fifteen thousand. This was one of the pleasantest pictures I had yet seen
in Persia. In the autumn everything presented a parched,
dreary appearance. Winter but added to the barrenness of the
landscape. In contrast with the winter desolation, nature, in
her festive attire, looked charming, and her spring suit was

* From this term our word " balcony " is derived.

most becoming. There were undulating fields covered with the sprouting grain, wide stretches of orchards and gardens budding heavily, the almond and apricot blossoms with their delicate tints showing full on the background of green, while Goigan and Ducargan were almost hidden beneath the foliage; the river, swollen by the melting snows, rushing along like a torrent, with its overflowing stream refreshing the fields through a thousand willow and poplar bordered watercourses. Only an inhabitant of the East can appreciate the epithet "well-watered," as it was applied to the goodly land of Israel.

In the market-place we were for the time being the center of an intensely interested group. Our spectacles, our hats, and a score of things about us excited remark, frequently laughter, though rarely admiration. Ducargan has an Armenian church, a relic of the Armenians whom the fanaticism of the people had forced to abandon their homes. The glebes are still a source of revenue to the Tabriz priests.

The next morning, on pursuing our journey, the character of the landscape changed. We passed through a rough and mountainous region, at times on a mere beaten path, and through defiles infested with robbers. Whether robbers always infest places near good springs, or the guards have found it convenient to give it out that they do so, it is difficult precisely to say; at all events, the latter are usually to be found at such places waiting for their *anams*. Some travelers, indeed, hold that the terms "robber" and "guard" are interchangeable.

Geologically the region is intensely interesting. Sulphur-springs deposit their incrustations on the hillsides; layers of limestone and marble form the paving of the highway. The tramping of the horses' hoofs gave back a hollow echo. For half a mile we seemed to be treading over the roofs of caverns. Our imagination pictured subterranean halls, adorned with pendent stalactites, and having winding labyrinths, intricate and endless. Soon we reached a point where we had an

opportunity of entering these caves. There were several
stories of them, each about twenty feet high, opening one
above the other on the hillside. The first was used for stables
and sheepfolds, with mangers cut into the rocks, reminding
one of the story of Bethlehem. The next had several large
divisions, inhabited by birds. On the vaulted roofs and sides
were many curious formations, caused by the oozing of the
mineral water through the porous rock. The third was held
in dread by the natives, being a den of monstrous snakes.
Only the terror awakened by the approach of the Balbas, as
they called the Kurds, pointing with a frenzy of fear to their
distant mountains, had led them to conceal their household
gods and other treasure in the depths of these caves.

Near by the caves are some quarries of famous alabaster,
fine specimens of which are conspicuous in the Blue Mosque
at Tabriz. It is cream-colored, finely veined, and prettily
spotted with red and other hues. It is translucent, and is
used for skylights of baths and street-windows. The thickest
layers are eight inches. The sayid, who has the monopoly of
the mines, helped us to select specimens. He has a shop in
Tabriz for making tombstones. Several workmen were chisel-
ing away after a primitive manner. The marble is used for
lithographic purposes, but the difficulty and cost of transportation interfere with its general use for buildings. It was taken
as far as Samarcand by Genghis Khan, and to Ispahan for the
Safavean palaces; Nadir Shah also took immense quantities
of it to ornament his palaces at Kelat and Meshed. In 1894
I sent some samples to the Smithsonian Institution.

The alabaster or onyx-marble is continually being formed.
Here and there mineral springs come gushing forth. The
water flows but a few rods, when by exposure to the air the
mineral deposit settles, and becomes stone before one's
eyes. Alongside one of the springs we lunched, and drank of
the foaming, bubbling stream. It seemed to contain salts,

lime, soda, iron, and carbonic-acid gas. It was moderately
cool and pleasant to the taste. The near village of Dashkasan
uses the mineral water constantly, and regards it as very healthful. Around us here were many sweet and delicate flowers,
and in front a green and fruitful plain, leading down to the lake.

For a good part of that day the lake continued in view.
A beautiful mirage produced the effect of an extension of
the lake. The impression was so vivid, so true to nature, the
water seeming to dance in the sun, obscuring the real shore
and producing such an artificial semblance of it, that only posi-
tive knowledge prevented the jury of our senses from deciding
in favor of its reality. Nature had conspired to remind us that
it was the day for April fools. The natives living in sight of
the place declared it to be the lake. At our last glimpse of
it, as we passed over the defiles, it had broadened and spread
until it apparently covered the whole plateau with a glassy
sheet of water, immersing the villages and plain through which
we had passed but a few hours before.

Night found us at Ajab Shahr (" Wonderful City "), so named
by a Tabriz man who receives the revenue of the town for his
salary. Among our visitors was a dervish. His long, curly
black locks and robe of untanned kidskin, with the hoofs
dangling at his sides, made a striking picture. If salvation
could come by mortification of the flesh, surely he would earn
it! "What," said he, "can be worse than my condition? I
am homeless and a wanderer; I abandon my body a prey to
filth and a habitation for vermin, giving it up to the gnawings
of hunger and the biting of fierce, cold winds. Surely my flesh
will one day be conquered, and my spirit be free to rise and
dwell where I long to be." In the winter he eats opium, be-
numbing himself to the exposure and neglect.

On leaving Ajab Shahr we noticed a man lying by the roadside. It was said that he had died of starvation, and the on-
lookers asked money to bury him. On the supposition that

the story was true, some money was given them, but likely enough it was a hoax.

Our next day brought us to the region desolated by the Kurds. The deserted villages and blackened walls enabled us to conceive of the ruthless completeness of their ravages. So entirely had the "terror of the Canaanites" fallen upon the inhabitants that our coming created considerable anxiety among them. The villagers of Dush, who had returned from their retreat in the mountains, plied us with no end of questions. They watched us with fear, as they might a band of gipsies, whom we partly resembled, as we tied our horses to the trees and sat down on the grassy bank to our lunch. A short afternoon's ride brought us to our destination, the ancient city of Maragha.

Maragha is situated about ten miles from Lake Urumia, at the head of the plain which slopes down to the lake. The plain, watered by the Sufi River, is fertile and populous. The valley, with its indented border of hills, resembles a scorpion. The city has a reputation for being beautiful; but either our eyes were blinded or the season was unpropitious, for it did not impress us as such. The broad river-banks, covered with willow and sycamore trees, have a pleasing park-like appearance, suited to make them a summer rendezvous for the tea-loving inhabitants. A wall, twenty feet high—repaired in anticipation of an attack from the Kurds—with ponderous gates sheeted with iron, gives it an ancient appearance.

Filth was obtrusively apparent. In the course of a walk one day, we took the trouble to notice all the extraneous matter in a principal street, and obtained a surprising catalogue: strings and rags of all colors and sizes; pieces of pottery, glass, and carpet; ashes, wood, refuse, and offal; loose stones and boulders of millstone size; gravestones; bones, carcasses, and skeletons of animals; with dogs, men, women, and children lying prostrate and almost naked amid the filth.

It may not be elegant to particularize so about the filth of an Oriental city, but it will not look blacker in printers' ink than it did in reality.

Maragha has its glory from a former epoch, and the relics remaining from that time claim our interest. In the thirteenth century Hulaku Khan, the grandson of Genghis Khan, issued from Tartary, exterminated the Assassins, overthrew the caliphs of Bagdad, and finally settled down as a civilized and enlightened monarch. He is said to have chosen Maragha for his capital because the scorpion shape of the valley was a propitious omen. He and his Christian queen gathered around them the philosophers, poets, and wise men of the age. He was the special patron of Nasir-i-Din, the celebrated astronomer, whose " Tables of the Ilkhany " remain as a lasting contribution to science. The crown of the hill near the city was leveled for his observatory, and the foundations of it still remain. He is also said to have had a deep hole dug in the ground, from which in daytime he could observe the stars.

We very much enjoyed the examination of the remains of Mongol supremacy. The architecture was of that solid kind which seems to have been long abandoned, if not a lost art— well-burnt brick, huge stones, firmly set arches, and colored tiling of great beauty. Nothing new has any probability of being preserved as long as these have been. Two of these ancient structures are the tower-tombs of Hulaku and his queen. In the form of decagons, twenty-five feet in diameter, they rise to the height of seventy feet, surmounted by domes. The tower of the king is ornamented with blue, green, and black tiling in mosaic, and with arabesque inscriptions. The coloring remains as perfect as it was seven centuries ago, and the surface is as smooth and glossy. The interior is unornamented, save by a marble slab, in the shape of a Grecian shield, inscribed on the under side. The tower is occupied as a stable. The storks' nests on the top of the dome are probably more valued now, as omens of good luck to the city, than the towers themselves. There are several other monuments of the same style and age in the city. One, with a remarkable arched foundation, was evidently a fort. Some of the cut stones are fourteen feet long. Nasir-i-Din, the astronomer, is said to have been the architect of these various structures.

The designation Mar-Agha, the name of a bishop among the Nestorians, bespeaks a more ancient period of Christian influence in the place. A rock-hewn hermitage in the hill overlooking the city was, according to Mussulman and Christian tradition, the dwelling of Christian monks. Ker Porter supposed that it belonged to the fire-worshipers. The Nestorians claim that it was theirs. We learned from other sources that the Nestorians had a school in Maragha before the time of Tamerlane.* I explored one of the largest of these rock-hewn abodes. The first room was about forty feet by fifteen. At one end was a rock platform, and on it a large altar, carved out of the everlasting hills. This was evidently the chapel of the hermitage. At the side of the chapel were various rooms, and from some of them underground ways led into cells. Through one of these passages, winding downward to a distance of sixty feet, I crept on my hands and knees. It opened into a small chamber, doubtless a place of solitary meditation for the old monks.

In the mountains beyond Maragha are found the remains of animals of remote geological ages. Immense skeletons have been excavated, and an Austrian scientist has exported a large quantity of these remains. A false report, however, at the Khoi custom-house, that the cases were full of gold-dust, led to their detention, and further export was prohibited. Near Maragha are caves which none can enter on account of poisonous gas. There are also iron springs. One of these springs is called the ox-head. The water is blood-red, and

---

* Anderson, "Oriental Missions," vol. i., p. 168, note.

comes gurgling out with puffs of gas, with a sound resembling, as the natives say, the blood flowing from a decapitated ox. The rocks are in layers like a pile of native bread. A folk-tale relates that once there was a wedding-party sacrificing an ox and making preparations for a feast, when an enemy came upon them and cursed them, so that the baked meats of the festival were turned into stone. The petrified bread, there-fore, remains uneaten, and the blood of the ox still continues to flow.

Maragha has now a population of twenty thousand, with one hundred and fifty families of Armenians. Its greatest trade is in raisins. The district abounds in vineyards; but though the grapes are superior, little wine is made. Grape-molasses is manufactured in considerable quantity, but the chief product of the vineyard consists of raisins. From the Urumia, Ducar-gan, and Maragha regions nine hundred and ninety tons of raisins were exported via Astara in 1894. They were sent by caravan on fifty-four thousand animals. All the boxes were made by hand, and gave employment for fourteen thousand days to carpenters. The raisins are of two kinds—the *kish-mish* and the *sabza*. The kishmish are dried by being placed in the sun, frequently on a plastered surface on the hillside. The sabza are dipped in a kettle of boiling lye-water, made from the ashes of a thorn-bush or of the vine. They are laid on the ground to dry for a week. All of them fall from their stems. The best kind is from the seedless grape. It is inter-esting to watch the packing process: the cleaning, sifting, pressing into boxes by stamping them with the bare feet, and the covering of the boxes with sheepskin to protect the fruit from the rain.

In Maragha we called on the chief mujtehids, two tall and jovial brothers, whose long robes and immense white turbans became them greatly. Their reception-room was crowded with those who had come to catch words of wisdom. After discussing the Trinity, the subject was turned to the nature and origin of Christ's spirit. One claimed that Jesus was a creature, and therefore it is a sin to worship him; another affirmed that in his preëxistence he was in no whit superior, for all spirit is eternal; another advanced the idea that Moses, Christ, and Mohammed were all manifestations of the same spirit; while still another asserted that there is no creature, but all is creator.

When we desired to return from Maragha we were made acquainted with an interesting Persian custom. All the district governors had been summoned to a grand council at Tabriz. For the large retinue of the governor many horses were necessary. According to custom, he sent an order levying on every available liveryman and stable-keeper. It so happened that his draft of one hundred horses included those we had engaged. When requested, the governor politely released them; but we found that after all they were of no use, and we sent to another city for horses. When we arrived near Tabriz we found the governor waiting. He had sent forward word, and was tarrying until a procession proportionate to his rank should be sent to meet him.

CHAPTER V

A CIRCUIT OF LAKE URUMIA

THE basin of Lake Urumia is the most populous and best-cultivated region in Persia. It drains twenty-one thousand two hundred and fifty square miles. The lake was anciently known as Lake Matiana, and in Armenia as Kabuta (the "Blue Sea"); but it is now called the Sea of Shaki or Urumia. It is forty-three hundred and twenty feet above the sea-level, extends eighty miles from north to south, averages twenty-five miles in wid h, and has a surface of fifteen hundred square miles. It has no outlet; is intensely salt, dense, and heavy. The specific gravity of the water is 11.55. It is strongly impregnated with sulphureted hydrogen. A swimmer floats upon it without effort. The brine forms a coating on the skin, and, if the bather is not careful, gives intense pain to the eyes. Its average depth is from twelve to sixteen feet; its greatest depth forty-six feet. The northern part is very shallow, and is becoming shallower year by year. A tradition among the Nestorians narrates that the Apostle Thomas, when departing for India, crossed the lake, walking on the water. In commemoration of this event they keep a festival day, on which they go to bathe in the lake. Some small islands are situated in its midst, on which game and sea-gulls are found; but in the lake itself there is no life.

The privilege of navigating the lake is granted by the government as a monopoly to Prince Iman Guli Mirza for one thousand tomans a year. His father, Melek Kazim Mirza, pro-

cured a small steamer for it, but it soon got out of order. Another nobleman had some vessels built to engage in the trade;
but the holder of the monopoly made good his right, and the
vessels rotted unused. Dr. Lobdell and the Rev. J. G. Cochran,
M.D., visited Melek Kazim Mirza at Shishevan, and embarked
in the private sail-boat of the prince to go to Urumia. Its cabin
was quite sumptuously furnished. On the third day out they
were becalmed. They cast anchor at an uninhabited island
and resorted to a boat with oars. They were overtaken by a
storm, which dashed the waves into the boat. Drenched by
the briny water, and bailing the boat with the energy of despair, they momentarily expected to be submerged. Finally
they were driven ashore twenty miles below the harbor. Car-
goes in flat sail-boats, manned by a dozen men, are now often
delayed for days by contrary winds. With a small steamer the
city of Urumia could be reached from Tabriz in a day or two,
while the journey around the lake on horseback requires five
or six days. An American gentleman offered, through Dr.
Cochran, to provide a steamer for its traffic, but the business
could not be arranged. Traffic in passengers, grain, raisins,
and general merchandise would make such an enterprise
profitable. Some Europeans in Teheran, it is said, purpose,
sooner or later, to acquire the concession.

The journey around Lake Urumia is one which few travelers make, yet it leads through some of the pleasantest regions
of Persia. In going northward one sets out over the great
caravan route from Tabriz to Trebizond. The telegraph and
post routes go to Marend, thence over the mountains to Khoi.
The caravan route lies over the Myan plain—the difficult part
of the journey. In spring it is muddy and slippery; in winter
it is flooded over and frozen, with a deep covering of snow.
The ice breaks under the horses' hoofs. The sky is sometimes
cloudy, and the cold penetrates even through an overcoat and a
Persian aba. Often, too, the river is impassable. In summer

the heat and glare of the sun are reflected from the glistening sand, and make it extremely uncomfortable for the traveler. For hours of the journey, moreover, only brackish water can be obtained. No place shows better than this the contrast between summer and winter in Azerbijan.

The first station is Ali Shah. Here we lodged in the house of the Rev. Samuel A. Rhea and were shown the room to which he was borne in a dying condition twenty-five years before. After leaving the village we passed through the fertile district of Guneh, having in view all the while the blue waters of the lake, and finding fanciful resemblances in its islands to reclining calves and baby elephants. On the third day we crossed the Pass of Sayid-Taj-i-Din. It is steep and rocky, and the road bears the marks of so energetic a hand that one is led to suspect the work of the Roman. For a long distance a path has been cut in the solid rock, and there the horse must walk with wary foot. From the other side the Khoi plain opened up before us. It is well watered by the Kutur and Aland rivers, both of which rise on the Turkish border and, uniting, flow into the Aras. The approach to the city is through a wide avenue, two miles in length, bordered by watercourses and double rows of willows, fenceless gardens extending on both sides. At its farther end the walls and battlements of the city frown upon us. A double wall, with towers (having picket-holes for cannon and musketry), eleven feet thick, built of sun-dried brick, and encircled by a moat twenty feet deep, surrounds the city. Five large and ponderous gates of wood, sheeted with iron, lead out to the chief highways. Across the moat are slight bridges, easily removed on the approach of an enemy. It is a frontier fortress, but the time is long past when such breastworks could withstand the cannon of either Russia or Turkey. Against Kurds, however, the fortress would still afford protection. Many of the streets of the city are of unusual width for the Orient, with rows of trees and running water in

the center. Low garden walls give glimpses of the interior.
The bazaars are poor, though caravansaries are numerous.
There are several noted mosques and an armory.   Considerable copperware is manufactured in the town. The population
of twenty thousand within the walls is entirely Mussulman.
The latter were formerly noted for their bigotry, but of late
they have become much freer from prejudice.   Sects abound.
A curious illustration of perversion was lately exhibited.   A
number of Mussulmans, taught by a cobbler who is a disciple
of a strolling dervish, had adopted a Hindu Pantheism, and,
holding that the divine Spirit only exists as manifested in
man, deny all responsibility for sin.

Mussulman superstition in Khoi is in no way more strikingly
manifested than in the reverence shown to the mosque over the
tomb of the Hadji Mir Yacob. This man, a descendant of the
Prophet, was a meek villager, to whom doors were supposed to
open of their own accord, and by whose blessing bandages
received power to dispel fever. When he died, not in the
olden times of legend, but just forty years ago, they erected a
mosque on his grave, which has become a shrine and a refuge.
I was permitted to look into the interior. The mausoleum was
decorated with shawls, embroideries, mirrors, chandeliers, and
other offerings of the faithful. The sick are brought and laid
within its precincts for the operation of the faith-cure. A
hundred swords and dirks were hung around, consecrated by
criminals fleeing to the shrine with vows of repentance. The
governor, however, noticed that it was only discovered criminals who professed repentance, so he abolished its privilege
as a sanctuary. Here, they say, the Imam Husain manifested himself when the Turks forbade access to Kerbela. A
deformed and lame boy was healed, though unbelievers say
there was a collusion between a surgeon and the mollas. Once
a camel, mistaking it for a caravansary, entered the place.
The faithful immediately exclaimed, " Even the dumb beast

recognizes the presence of the Prophet !" Decked in gorgeous array, they paraded it through the streets, each one
taking some of the hair of the animal as a blessed talisman.
The camel became an attaché of the mosque.

At Khoi there is a curious structure called the Tower of Shan
Ismiel, he who fought with Sultan Selim I. on this historic plain
in 1514. The tower is circular, and is about sixty feet high,
with innumerable horns of wild goats worked into the masonry,
the points projecting outward. Some say that the horns were
the spoils of one day's hunting by the royal party. This story
not being marvelous enough, another has been invented to the
effect that a holy man from Tabriz, a miracle-worker, called
all the gazelles together from the country round about. These
were slain and consumed in a single feast, and the horns were
then built into a tower as a memorial.

The Armenians of Khoi live in three wards outside of the
walls and in the surrounding villages. They are shopkeepers,
farmers, and carpenters. They are financially prosperous, but
intellectually and spiritually destitute. The church is said to
be six hundred years old. The windows are very high up and
small, like port-holes. In one corner is a small stone basin for
the immersion of infants. One of the pictures is of Constantine and Helena, with Greek inscriptions. Another Armenian
church stands in a Mohammedan village. Many sick ones are
brought to its shrine, and for two days in the year pilgrimages
are made to it from the Armenian villages. Superstition preserves the church from destruction. One Mohammedan took
a stone from it for his stable. The same day he ran the tongs
into his eye. He brought back the stone and made an offering to the offended saint.

From Khoi northward to Maku is about seventy miles.
The district is mountainous. Much of it is *dame*, that is, not
artificially irrigated. Its inhabitants are of the tribe of Kara-
Goyunlis, or the "Black Sheep," who once ruled Azerbijan.

Most of them are Ali-Allahis. If our experience is a criterion, they are very quarrelsome. The family with whom we lodged at Kasian had a free fight, in which the neighbors, including the women, joined with clubs and stones and fierce revilings. The women came off victorious. The village master and his servants illustrated the dishonesty of Persian life. The servants, it seems, had taken wheat to market, and claimed that it had come out short weight. They had exchanged the wheat for fruit, and this was also light in weight. They said they had paid sixteen shahis a batman, while the Khoi price was ten. At every point they wished to "eat." The master made them "eat sticks," that is, suffer the bastinado.

In the mountain fastnesses one's imagination is free to picture Kurds and robbers behind the rocks and in the recesses of the valleys. Our traveling without sword or gun excited continual wonder. Our chance companion was armed with a Martini-Henry, two carbines, a sword, a dirk, and a great display of ammunition. His fear was proportionate to his armor. The Persian proverb is, " A man bitten by a snake fears a rope." So the people are on the outlook for Kurds, and in constant alarm. Once, on coming down the mountain, we saw a caravan fleeing before us, and on giving them our "peace" we found that "half of their life had escaped" from fear of us.

The air of the region makes it a perfect sanatorium, invigorating and bracing, even in midsummer. The lordly Ararat, veiled in white and wreathed in cloud, was visible in front of us. Beyond Shoat is a warm spring, much frequented by bathers. As we approached Maku our course wound in and out of a narrow valley, through which the river of the same name flows, and frequently descends in rapids. In one of the turns of the confined rocky gorge Maku suddenly came into view, and presented a wonderful sight. The bare rocky mountain rose abruptly on both sides to a height which seemed at least a thousand feet. The mountain on the right, in the course of its ascent, turns outward, and jutting far forward hangs like a canopy over the city. In the recess at the angle the fortress is built, presenting a formidable front, and flanked with walls. Here are stored ammunition and much treasure, and above, high on the ledge of the rock, reached only by scaling a rope hand over hand, are provisions, and by removing a plug a spring of water flows out, which in ordinary times finds exit below. Nature and man have combined to make a stronghold for old-time warfare. Beneath this overhanging mountain, the first sight of which fills one with awe, the city of five thousand carries on its business without a feeling of uneasiness, though we were shown houses destroyed by the falling rocks and by destructive torrents flowing down upon them. Boulders lie about in the streets. Some houses are built on a single rock. The echo in the recess gives to the thousand sounds from below a confused reverberation. The houses, which are built of rough stone and mud, are one story high, and bear a striking resemblance to the old houses of New Mexico. Many are erected on such a declivity, like those in Quebec, that the roof is on a level with the street above. The homes of the khans stand as palaces in the midst of hovels. The house of Isaac Pasha is built on a prominent rock, with a pentagonal front, and having one continuous window, with panes of plain and colored glass; it presents a unique and fantastic appearance. Tamur Pasha has a palace near the gardens by the river-bank. He is a feudal lord, and the hereditary chief of the region. He and the khans of his family hold the title in fee simple to hundreds of villages, with their attached lands—a territory of many square miles. He has an army of retainers, generally quartered on the villagers, and also a considerable Kurdish following. His personal property, we were told, is immense. People made no estimate of it. They simply pointed to the fortress and spoke of its chests of uncounted gold and silver. This chief once raised his head against the shah. But the

shah's forces, under the Sipah Silar, humbled him and led him
captive to Teheran.   A present of twenty thousand dollars
secured his pardon.

The district is full of murder and rapine.   Nearly every
man carries a sword and owns a musket.   One of my visitors
had just recovered from a fight, and had a terrible gash on his
brow.   Another was dumb, his tongue having been pulled
loose by a young khan.   As I passed through the pasha's
grounds to visit him, a molla was seated on the ground trying
a case of murder, in which a village of Ali-Allahis were accu-
sers of some Kurds.   The oath of neither party was credible,
but a payment of blood-money of three hundred dollars was
fixed upon the Kurds.   This was a high price, for frequently
a man's life is not valued at more than twenty-five dollars.

The room in which I was received by the pasha was in
mixed Persian style.   The windows were formed of ten thousand pieces of stained glass, while the walls and ceiling were
covered with innumerable mirrors, large and small, set in plaster.   The carpets were of superior quality, though chairs and
tables from Europe stood about and completed the furnishings
of the apartment.   The representative of the Vali Ahd, several
khans and mollas were present, and in the halls and adjoining
rooms were numerous retainers and some Kurds.   After showing me to a seat of honor, and making some general inquiries,
the pasha questioned me pointedly on matters of religion,
entering with me into controversy.   First they desired to know
why I did not receive Mohammed and the Koran.   Then they
discussed the subject of the Trinity, with the incarnation and
divinity of Christ.   I explained the doctrines and offered
proofs from the Scriptures.   The pasha said, " Oh, away with
your books!   Give us something that commends itself to the
reason."

Europeans rarely find their way to Maku.   I had my lodging in the Isaac Pasha caravansary.   It had about forty shops,

the lower story being for mechanics, the upper for merchants and travelers. Opposite my windows were a tea-house and the shops of a couple of rival tailors—one with the Howe, the other with the Singer, sewing-machine! I opened a stock of Scriptures and exposed them for sale, curiosity drawing the people in a continuous stream to my booth during the five days I was there. There are many hundred Armenians in the community, most of them living, however, outside of the town. The monastery of Thaddeus is not far distant.

Around Maku are many curious sights. There are undeciphered inscriptions, some in Cufic and some in ancient Georgian, carved crosses on the rocks, rooms cut in the solid mountain, buried treasures, old churches, and a bottomless pit, whose gas extinguishes a light and reduces a man to unconsciousness, from which he is revived with difficulty if speedily withdrawn.

Retracing our way, and passing through Khoi, one day's march west of the latter brought us to Salmas.

Salmas is a well-watered and fruitful plain, surrounded on three sides by mountains, and on the fourth by Lake Urumia. Through its center flows the Zolah River, rising in the Zagros. Its surface, of about one hundred square miles, contains fourscore villages. Dilman and Kuhna Shahr, or "Old City," are the chief towns, which are of five thousand inhabitants each. The former is the capital, and contains the court-house, custom-house, post and telegraph offices, and chief bazaars. The markets are open two days in each place. Sunday is a special market-day, and is called here, as in Turkey, "bazaar-day." Back of the plain is Chahari, the seat of the Shakoik Kurds. It has a natural fortification, from which issues an immense fountain of water. The mountains contain curious petrifications of fish, snakes, and other animals. Near the foot of the plain, on a rocky hill called Surat Daghi, is a Sassanian sculpture in bas-relief. It represents two horsemen and a figure

on foot, of mammoth size, supposed to be Ardeshir and Shapur I. receiving the submission of the Armenians. Ker Porter
(vol. ii., p. 597) reproduced the inscription and describes it
fully. He supposes one horseman to be the Emperor Galerius,
the other Narsi, king of Persia, and the one on foot Tiridates,
king of Armenia. The spot where the eyes of the figures are
focused has been dug up in search of treasure, just as Washington Irving narrates regarding the Alhambra.

The inhabitants of the plain are mostly Turks, with some
Kurds, six thousand Armenians, three thousand Chaldeans and
Assyrians, and five hundred Jews. The Jews reside in Kuhna
Shahr, the Christians in a score or more villages. The Armenians are thrifty and prosperous. They were free from oppression until of late years, when quarrels with other Christians
—especially Catholics—and political agitations have given occasion to some Persian officials to fine and maltreat some of
them. The Armenian villages of Salmas are the best built of
any in Persia, and farmers and tradesmen alike have a comparatively high standard of living. The chief Armenian merchant had an electric bell to ring at his gate; one of his sons
was an amateur photographer, another dabbled in telegraphy.
At Haftdewan is a curious old church built of stone, with
arched dome and large altar. As usual, it was without seats,
and the back gallery was assigned to the women. Its walls we
found frescoed and hung with old pictures, representing scenes
in the life of Christ and the apostles, the canvas almost falling
to pieces from age. One fresco represents the judgment. A
male angel, with black hair, holds a pair of balances. The
one scale is filled with light, the other with darkness, which is
overweighted, though the devil and a group of imps are pulling with all their might on the side of darkness. On the side
of light are groups sitting peaceably in Paradise; on the other
is hell's gate, and behind it souls in misery. In the church is
a dark well, in which many sick persons, and especially luna-

tics, are confined in the hope of being healed. Mussulmans, while rejecting much of the good they might see in the Armenians, are fully ready to adopt this superstition. I met a straggling procession of about thirty women, with their babies sniffling and coughing. They were Mussulmans from Dilman coming to the Christian shrine for the healing of their children. Above the Old City is a monastery, to which pilgrimages are made, and where sacrifices are offered. It also has a crazy-pit for the faith-cure. The monastery walls were lately strengthened and heightened. The government, hearing that a fortification was being built, ordered the walls to be razed. Afterward permission was given to build low walls. The shrine and supposed grave of the Apostle Bartholomew is a short distance off in Turkey, at Albak (Arebanes). A numerous caravan of merit-seeking pilgrims yearly visits the shrine with great feasting. The estimated expense for one year of the congregated Salmas pilgrims was thirty thousand days' wages.

The American Presbyterian missionaries reside in Haftdewan; the French Lazarists have for many years had the headquarters of their work at Khosrova.

From the plain of Salmas we passed on toward the south, crossing the Gadik, or Pass of Werkewiz. Near the foot of the pass, in the waters of the lake, are the ruins of Gugerchin Kala, a fortress. The fortress dominates a rock about eight hundred feet high, but now made an island by the disintegration of its land side. There are caves under the fortress, with reservoirs of fresh water. Here, it is said, the treasures of Hulaku Khan, Mongol, were concealed.

Our station for the night was Gavlan, the village of Mar Yokannan, who visited America with Dr. Perkins. Here the American Mission has a building, combining chapel, school, and summer residence. The next day brought us to Urumia. Fortunate is he who visits this region in the springtime. Sir Ker Porter thought the Khoi plain the finest he had seen in

Persia. He would have awarded this praise to Urumia had he seen it at its best. An excursion to Mount Seir, seventy-three hundred and thirty-four feet above sea-level, gave us the finest view of the district. Dr. Cochran, the physician of the mission, invited Mr. Whipple and me to be his guests at the Seir house. A little off the road as we ascend is an ancient church of Mar Sergis (St. Sergis), another of the shrines and crazy-dens patronized alike by Christians and Mohammedans. The interior of the church was dark and dingy; its walls were adorned with numerous handkerchiefs, the offerings of the pilgrims. The great number of handkerchiefs—we counted as many as one hundred and forty, and these are a recent collection, for the Kurds stripped the shrine when they overran the country—leads one to suppose that this article is especially necessary to the worthy saint.

We spent the night at Seir, in the house where a generation of American missionaries have lived and labored. Here were the college and seminary of former days; and these poorly lighted mud-rooms are hallowed by the associations of glorious revivals of religion, and are looked back to by the old pastors with most sacred memories. Here, too, is the cemetery in which rests all that was mortal of Wright, Stoddard, Cochran, Breath, Thomson, Rhea, and others, who, being dead, yet speak to two continents. In the same picket inclosure are many little mounds—of Judith Perkins, the " Flower of Persia," and other childlike forms—which tell the story of bereaved hearts. Over thirty stones bear silent witness to the consecration by America of her sons and daughters for the evangelization of this people. Here, too, is the sparkling perennial spring from which a generation of missionaries and their children have been refreshed. Seir is now used merely as a summer retreat from the heat and malaria of the plain; but its annals of past work for God have hallowed it in the hearts of many.

In the morning we passed up the mountain-side, which was

clothed in the rich verdure of spring. The floral attire, too, was bright-tinted and varied. Tulips, hyacinths, irises, blue-bells, buttercups, and, higher up, crocuses just springing from the melted snow, and some almost growing in it, and fragrant herbs of unknown name, made a pleasing variety. The air was filled with the sweet perfume, the horses' hoofs found a flowery path, and our anticipations were more than realized. Reaching one of the highest points of Seir, we surveyed the scene both from the front and from the rear.

Farther on lay Mergawar and Tergawar, the valleys in the mountains, and the roads leading to Gawar, and to the home of the sheik of the Kurds, up the snow-capped range which separates Persia from Turkey. The view to the rear, looking out upon the plain, though not so fine, was more interesting. At the foot of the undulating, grassy hills stretched to the southward Baranduz plain, with its river of the same name; in the center the city, with the meandering Shahr Chai; and to the north the Nazlu plain and river. The whole scene was well watered, green with grain and grass, and bright with rice-fields, with innumerable rows of willows and poplars along a thousand life-giving arteries, fed from the main streams, and giving fertility to numberless orchards and vineyards—a stretch of verdure fifty miles long and twenty wide, having in its center the compact city of Urumia, and seven hundred villages scattered about in every fitting spot. The ash-mounds of the fire-worshipers, Geogtapa, Sheikhtapa, and Degala, arrested the eye. Prominent, too, was Bakhsh Kala, whose fort is said to have been built of stones passed from a distant mountain by a row of men from hand to hand, like water-buckets at a fire. On the north and south the plain is fringed by bleak, barren hills, the whole terminating in the blue waters of the lake, dotted here and there with islands. Across the lake the range of Ainal-Zainal appears beyond Tabriz, and southward the snowy Sahend and the regions of Maragha and Mianduab. It is a splendid panoramic view, showing the plains in all their beauty, the positions of the villages and the geography of the lake region in striking clearness. Picnicking on these beautiful mountains was a pastime long to be remembered.

Quite near the center of this fertile plain is the city of Urumia. It is built in the usual Persian style, with narrow, crooked streets, some of them paved with cobblestones. The population is twenty-five thousand. A few hundred Christians reside in the city, and in the villages are about twenty-five thousand Nestorians and five thousand Armenians. The bazaars are inferior. The city is surrounded by an adobe wall, which was repaired after the attack of the Kurds, but is now crumbling and dilapidated in many places. Urumia is entered by seven gates, leading from five avenues of trees. The wall, three miles in length, is surrounded by a moat, a receptacle for the offal of the slaughter and bath houses, and for the drainage of the city, and is, of course, a fertile breeding-spot for malaria. Formerly the moat was full of trees ; but during the Kurdish raid they interfered with the firing, so the Nestorians were sent out to cut them down. The enemy not caring to waste their ammunition on the unarmed Christians, they worked away during the thickest of the firing, and remained unharmed. The fortress of the beglar-begi has walls of much greater strength than the city itself. It was the stronghold of the khans when Urumia was independent.

Two wards of the city are inhabited principally by Christians, most of them Assyrians. In the quarter of Gyol Fath Ali Khan the Lazarist Mission has its headquarters; in the other the American and Anglican missions are situated. This quarter is called the Mart Mariam, from the church erected here in honor of the Virgin Mary. Tradition relates how it came to be built. It seems that a priest was sleeping in his house when a woman appeared to him. He asked, " Who are you ? " She answered, " I am Mary, the Mother of Jesus.

Build a church here in my name, and let all mothers who lack milk to nourish their children come to my shrine, and I will make their supply plentiful." So the women come with wax candles and incense to beseech her blessing. Even Mohammedan women frequent the shrine.

There are many pleasant rides about Urumia. One of these lies along the river-banks. Riding out of the Seir gate, we came opposite to the garden of Ikabal-i-Doulah, where the Kurds fortified themselves for the attack, and in which the palace was demolished by his own orders. Twenty minutes' ride along shaded avenues brought us to the college and hospital of the American Mission. A little beyond them is the river. It is a popular resort. Tying their horses to the trees, the Persians sit on the grassy banks and pass the idle hours with the samovar and kaleon, or, as is the case with some, with dice and cards. Some are dyeing and washing and drying native print goods; others are seine-fishing in the river. We came upon a gipsy village, where some of these nomads had been in winter quarters. They are a dark-skinned, rough, and uncouth people, who seem to have a cult of their own, though outwardly they are Mussulmans. In summer they roam about, living in black tents, the women telling fortunes as in Christian lands, using a book or a shoulder-blade, as the case may be. The men make seines and hair ropes, trade horses, and are considered loose-fingered. They pay tribute to the government.

We were here greatly attracted to the ash-hills of the fire-worshipers. Of considerable size, associated with an unknown past, they seem appropriate to the place where Zoroaster was born, and where the Emperor Heraclius (A.D. 625) destroyed a magnificent fire-temple, along with the city. I visited ash-hills at Degala, at Geogtapa, and at Sheikhtapa. They have been much excavated, and for centuries the ashes have been used as fertilizers. Coins, earrings, and bracelets of copper and gold, bowls, lamps, and other earthen utensils have been unearthed.   Pieces of broken pottery are dug up continually and are lying about.   Bones of men and animals are also excavated.   When building Geogtapa church, on the site of the ash-hill, large building-stones were dug up.   A Babylonian cylinder of unusual size was found.   It was purchased from the owner of the village, and is now in the Metropolitan Museum, New York.   At Degala niter is produced for the manufacture of gunpowder.   It is a strange fate that Ahriman should extract his weapons of destruction from the monuments of the worshipers of Ormuzd.   The ashes are dissolved in water and passed through a series of vats.   The niter settles at the bottom.   The sediment is boiled in a large caldron, strained, and spread in the sun to dry.   I secured several good specimens of ancient pottery from Degala hill—a flat red bowl, an earthen lamp of yellow tint, and a charred pot, probably used for boiling meat.   When they were seen by some people on the road to Tabriz, they inquired what they were.   The Persian who was with me, with the usual facility for prevarication, answered them: "They are skulls of Kurds."

One mound is a large pile of stones.   Tradition states that here Mar Guergis (St. George) was martyred by the fire-worshipers, and God punished them by a shower of stones, which overwhelmed the village and reared over it a monument of wrath.

On another day we rode twelve miles to the lakeside.   It was too cold for bathing.   Near the harbor Melek Kazim Mirza redeemed a plot of ground from the surrounding desert and built a house.   The house is dilapidated and the garden dried up, only a few fig and pomegranate trees and a tiny stream remaining.   The place was purchased for one hundred dollars by a lady in St. Louis as a resting-place for missionaries.   It has since become a lakeside Chautauqua.   For several weeks the preachers and teachers of the Protestant church gather here in an institute, where there are lectures and conferences.

It is this ruin which a captious critic of foreign missions has exaggerated into "one of the finest palaces in all Persia," and which, he says, "cost a large sum of money"!

Proceeding southward from Urumia, we entered Kurdistan. Our way lay through the low rice-fields of Baranduz to a village with the ill-omened name of Shatanabad ("Satanville"). Pent up in a little fort, on the top of a steep hill, are a few families of Armenians, surrounded by some Kurds. The streets are so narrow that horses can scarcely pass. The houses have no yards whatever. The Kurdish aga has a good establishment on the level ground near the village. We expected to find our load with bedding, etc., already there, but it did not come at all. Our Armenian hostess, moving around with her mouth tied up, did her best to make us comfortable. The family fowl occupied their accustomed place in the family room, and in the morning did not allow us to oversleep. On the next day we reached Sulduz, where finally our belated load arrived, having been delayed by robbers. They had come upon our servant Asdsadoor and the *charvadar*, thrown down the load, and examined it. Asdsadoor cast himself on the ground, kissed their feet, and begged them not to take the sahib's property or injure him. Finally they released him, only retaining some sugar and tea, a few *krans*, and some things that could not be identified.

Kurds frequently render the roads unsafe. When Miss N. J. Dean was on her way to America the *charvadar* was attacked, and her wardrobe and some curios were taken. Nothing was ever recovered. On another occasion Mr. and Mrs. Stocking were entering Salmas, when three Kurds attacked them. One drew his sword and began beating Mr. Stocking over the back, while the others helped themselves to the baggage, pistol, and field-glass. They then demanded money. Mr. Stocking having some time before given his purse to Mrs. Stocking, a Kurd leveled his cocked gun at him to enforce the demand. This was too much for the lady; she threw the purse to the robbers, glad to avert a worse calamity. One Kurd snatched off her bonnet, and was disappointed not to find any ornaments on her head.

Another American missionary was attacked just outside of the college gate at Urumia in 1893. He was stripped of his clothes and all the money he had with him. He was taken into a garden and left there, with injunctions not to raise an alarm for half an hour, under penalty of death. The government acted with commendable energy in endeavoring to capture the robbers. Finally the same gang, having attacked a house in Sulduz, were pursued by officers, driven to take refuge in a hovel, which was set on fire, and they perished in the flames.

The inhabitants of Sulduz and Ushmuk are Kurds and Turks, with about a thousand Armenians and Nestorians and the same number of Jews. The Turks are called the Karapapas ("Black-hats"). They came from the Transcaucasus at the time it was conquered by the Russians, preferring, like the Circassians, to forsake their native land rather than live under the rule of Christians. They were assigned this region by the shah as a buffer against the Kurds and Osmanlis, and the revenue and practical ownership of it were given them for their support. The khans live beside their peasants in strongly walled houses. The civil and military offices are in their hands. Colonels and generals are plentiful, and they are under obligation to furnish a contingent of soldiers to the shah in time of war. The khan of the village where we stopped sent us his salaams, saying, "The village is yours; won't you do us the honor of being our guests?"

Sulduz is in sharp contrast to Urumia, in that it is almost treeless. Material for building is very scarce. The sod is cut, dried, and used for bricks. The uncomely buffalo, wallowing in water, is a common sight. One of the amusements of the populace is to see these huge beasts fight. They will contend until their heads are covered with gore, and the victor will even try to drown his antagonist. Ushmuk is famous for a blue serpentine, from which are cut kaleon heads, pipes, vases, inkstands, and various ornaments. Upon the mountains, near the border of Turkey, is an interesting rock with a cuneiform inscription. Border disputes about land and flocks are very common. In 1892 one of these quarrels resulted in considerable bloodshed, and a joint commission from Turkey and Persia was sent to the spot to settle the dispute and fix the boundary.

Continuing our journey, as we passed through Laj we saw a crowd of people gathered on the banks of the river, and a horseman and two men on foot dashing across the river and fields. A fight, it seems, was on between the two villages. As the result, a man came to the surgeon's house in Daraluk with a deep, long sword-gash on his head. The surgeon being absent, his wife shaved the hair of the head with a common broad-bladed pocket-knife and dressed the wound.

A few hours' ride brought us to Soujbulak, a city of ten thousand inhabitants. It is an unhealthy place, the water of the river being defiled by the sewage of the city. During the cattle-plague in the valleys above, the carcasses of the animals were thrown into the river as the easiest way to get rid of them. Even the fish which abound in the river have a nasty taste, yet many people drink of it rather than bring water from the upper spring. No wonder that fever abounds !

Soujbulak is the capital of the district of Kurdistan. A garrison of Persian soldiers keeps watch over the Kurds. From here it is nine days by caravan to Mosul, through the Ravanduz Pass. Outgoing caravans were then carrying their feed, owing to the locusts having eaten up vegetation along the road. To the west are the forests of Leilajan, where there are large deposits of coal.

Soujbulak takes its name from the mineral springs close beside it, called soda-springs on Kiepert's map. There are more than a dozen of them, which are strongly impregnated with gas, and leave a thick deposit on the hillside. Near the city is the tomb of Pir Budak Sultan, some two hundred years old. The structure is about forty by twenty feet, with a central dome. The slabs are of alabaster, about ten feet long, and the inscriptions are in Persian. Budak Sultan was chief sheik of the Mukri Kurds when they came from Turkey. They are divided into two divisions; the chiefs of one are called begzadas, of the other agas. To the north of the city is a cliff-dwelling, reached with difficulty by means of ladders. Most of the inhabitants are Kurds. The remainder are a mixture of Persians, Turks, Jews, Armenians, Jacobites, and Nestorians. Boys grow up able to speak four or five languages without effort.

The Kurds of this district, including those on the Persian side northward to Mount Ararat, are variously estimated at from two hundred and fifty thousand to four hundred and fifty thousand in number. To the south, those of Senna and Ardelan are estimated at one hundred and twenty thousand, and those of Kermanshah at two hundred and thirty thousand, making a total of Kurds resident in Persia of from six hundred thousand to eight hundred thousand. A larger portion live in Turkey. They are undoubtedly the Carduchi of Xenophon, and have remained in a condition of semi-independence from the earliest times. Living on the borders of Turkey and Persia, they are in subjection to neither government, and can, as occasion requires, for the purpose either of plunder or of escape from punishment, move from one territory to the other. There are two divisions of them: some are permanent denizens of towns and villages; others live in villages during the winter, and roam on the mountains with their flocks and herds during the remainder of the year. Their language is akin to the Persian. It is rarely written, the Persian being the literary language for the Kurds of Persia; the Arabic, or Osmanli Turkish, the language for those of Turkey. Few of them can read or write. Their language has a number of dialects, corresponding to their separate districts.

Most of the Kurds are shepherds and farmers by occupation, though warriors by profession. Those of Soujbulak and other cities are, however, engaged in merchandise and the trades. They are fond of play, and are shiftless and improvident for the future. They borrow recklessly, at exorbitant interests, and become victims of the mortgagee. The aspect of their city is dilapidated and poverty-stricken. There is little beauty of garden or orchard. I called on a rich citizen who had a small orchard. Pointing to it and the bleak mountains beyond, he asked me if I thought there was any country in the world equal in beauty to Kurdistan. My reply was such as courtesy dictated. At the time of our visit the governor of Soujbulak was Saf-i-Din Khan, son of the Sirdar Aziz, formerly governor of Tabriz. He was an intelligent Kurd. He had bought an hydraulic machine for irrigation, and had ordered American reapers and threshers through an Armenian merchant.

Opportunely, while we were there, the *khallat* or robe of honor from the shah arrived for the governor, on the renewal of his appointment. The day of its reception was made a gala day. The bazaars were closed, and everybody turned out to meet the bearer. Companies of Persian soldiers attended him. Kurdish sheiks and beys were there with their mounted retainers, the latter splendid specimens of manhood, with sharp, fine-cut features, deep, dark, piercing eyes, and stately bearing. Courage and determination were strongly marked on their countenances. Their costume of gay colors, with full turban and wide-flowing pantaloons, is the most picturesque in all Persia. A band of them, mounted on their keen-tempered and fancifully caparisoned horses, each with many daggers and revolvers in the folds of his ample girdle, and a spear

twelve or fifteen feet long, or a Martini-Henry, thrown over his
shoulder, and a belt of cartridges buckled around his waist,
have a fierce, warlike appearance. The chief citizens were also
mounted, though every one else came out on foot. Bands of
music enlivened the scene. When the bearer of the *khallat*
approached, the governor dismounted and received the robe.
Returning, the procession marched through the streets to the
palace, the people crowding the roofs of the houses to see the
functionary pass. About an hour afterward I waited on the
governor to congratulate him. After some days he appointed
a day of rejoicing—a tournament on the plain about four
miles away. On such occasions all the people gather on the
meadows for a merrymaking. A clown is appointed king, and
rules the day, levying fines on the governor and others. The
Kurds have horse-races, the spear of each horseman being
poised in the air, and the fringe of his turban flying behind;
they present a picturesque appearance. With games, and a
freer mingling than usual of men and women, they grasp one
another's hands and dance the merry-go-round.

The Kurds in the villages have rude habitations, and are
filthy, unkempt persons. The village scene receives a pictu-
resqueness from the stork-nests on the roofs and in the trees,
and the flight of the birds everywhere about. Women and
children are seen returning with their bundles of herbs, gathered
from the hillside, with laughter and wild, shrill songs, as gay as
any picnic-party at home. Then milking-time comes round.
The flocks of cute little kids and lambs, which have been pastured separately, come skipping along with their "bah-bah,"
"mah-mah," each glossy black pet finding and being found by
its mother, and known to its owner by some natural mark. We
sat down to lunch in one of the villages. The women spread
a piece of the matting they were weaving for us to sit upon in
the low mud-hovel. With uncovered face and unconcealed
merriment they discussed us in lively Kurdish. We were as

good a show to them as a Dahomey village in the Midway Plaisance. We took some hard-boiled eggs from our saddle-bags to eat with our bread and milk. They told us in Turkish that milk and eggs eaten together would make us ill!

In one village I visited a sheik. Though a minor one, he had, so they told me, ten thousand followers, and was the owner of four or five villages. He was of noble mien, with long flowing robes, a turban and girdle of Kerman shawl, and a keen, intelligent eye. His house was plain, but much better than any in the village. He took us into the family apartment, where we saw the simplicity of Kurdish life. His wife sat by us, conversed freely, and smoked her pipe. The maid came and went without thought or fear of the strange men who were present. Dinner was served in an upper room. Boiled rice and chicken were brought in on a platter, placed on the floor before us, and the sheik and our party ate from the same dish. On the niche were a few books, chiefly religious, in Persian and Arabic, together with the Bible in three or four languages. Just before retiring for the night some young men came and honored us with music and singing, at once quaint and weird. The next morning the sheik held a reception for his followers. Each one came with a present in his hand. One wished to know where his asses had strayed, like Saul, the son of Kish. Another's property had been stolen, and he wished to discover the thief. Still another was sick and childless, and went away satisfied with a written prayer, or a pill, as the sheik might elect. Others look to him as a mediator, and through his merits expect to obtain forgiveness of sins. They even attribute to him power to help them when absent. It is his duty to minister to both body and soul, as well as to settle lawsuits and take the field as their leader in battle. Asceticism sometimes adds still more to the reputation of a sheik. One sheik was reported to have fasted forty days for nine successive years, subsisting each day on one fig only and

a little water.   The devotees eagerly take the water in which
their sheik has bathed or washed his clothes, and rub it on
their faces, or drink it, for its sanctifying qualities.

This part of Kurdistan was in 1891 a scene of much excitement.   The story reached us in Tabriz that a band of mounted
Kurds had come one night to a village where a Christian family from Tabriz was residing, and carried off a beautiful young
girl, compelling her to become a Mohammedan and to marry
a son of a Kurdish sheik.   The family were British subjects.
The acting British consul, R. M. Paton, Esq., demanded that
the girl be released and returned to her mother.   The Kurds
answered that the elopement and the conversion to Islam were
of the girl's own free will.   The consul demanded that the girl
should be brought before a proper tribunal to answer for herself.   This the Kurds refused, though it was repeatedly demanded by the Persian government.   Finally it was arranged
that Mr. Paton, the Osmanli consul, Beyjat Effendi (because
some of the Kurds were Turkish subjects), with some Persian
officials and a guard, should go to the scene.   Then what
strange and contradictory rumors reached us day by day!
Once we heard that fifteen thousand well-armed Kurds were
gathered, ready to die rather than surrender her; again that
the Osmanli consul was wounded and the British consul's life
attempted.   One day some Kurds, pointing a musket at his
head, compelled the Osmanli consul to sign a paper that it
was the girl's own choice.   Weeks passed without result, except the killing of several Persian soldiers and the submissive
payment of *mudakhil* to Persian officials.   At length the
affair became an international question, discussed in Parliament and telegraphed across three continents.   Several regiments of soldiers were sent to the front, and a Trojan war was
expected.   Finally the Kurds yielded, and brought the girl to
the Persian authorities.   At a formal examination before the
officials, the consuls, and her mother, the girl stated that she

had of her own will married the Kurd and become a Mussulman. The representatives of the nations and the army of the
shah returned, leaving the girl to her fate. During the excitement many Christians of Soujbulak and the surrounding country abandoned their homes, with much of their property, and
fled for their lives.

A day's ride from Soujbulak brought us to Mianduab ("Be-
tween-two-waters"), a fine plain lying between the Jagatai and
the Tatavu rivers. The road passes along the telegraph-line.
Soon after it was built, it is said, a party of Kurdish highway-
men attacked some Turks. One of the latter ran to a tele-
graph-pole and threatened to send word to Tabriz if they were
molested. The Kurds were alarmed and let them pass unharmed. East of the Tatavu the people are largely Afshar
Turks and Persians, transferred from Kerman by Aga Mohammed Shah. The lower part of this plain is a swamp-land,
covered with tall reeds and frequented by storks and wild
boars. A khan who had been indulging in the latter forbidden meat took carefully from his cupboard, and exhibited to
me as a rarity and precious medicine, a small bottle of lard.
Near this reed-forest is Dash-Tapa, a rock with a cuneiform
inscription. So little interest is taken in the inscription that
though I inquired of a number of persons in Mianduab, they
could tell me nothing of the whereabouts of the rock. Guided
by the map, after a two hours' gallop over the plain, I, however, came to the place, a small circular hill rising out of the
level plain. One side of the rock is smoothed off, and a space
about five feet by three is inscribed with the arrow-headed
characters. At the top of the hill are the ruins of a fort, and
the ground about gives back a hollow sound, as if there were
a cavity below.

On the upper part of this plain is the sepulcher of Hulaku
Khan, the Mongol conqueror. Thither several Armenian
friends accompanied us. On the plain we met the khan who

has charge of the telegraph, with horsemen and hounds on a hunt. He also went with us, but we found nothing remarkable at the grave. It was sunk in, and some broken stones were lying about. A villager told us that a man had a dream that there was a treasure in it, and that he dug it open, but found nothing save a skull and some broken dishes. Farther on we saw outlines of an old fort and traces of an aqueduct, which I imagine is the Top-Kala of Abbas Mirza, which he hoped would become the Woolwich of Persia.

Here a Kurdish kand-khuda met us on horseback. Dismounting, he came limping and fell at the feet of the khan, and besought him to telegraph his grievances to Tabriz. At the same time a woman came crying and begged to be avenged of her oppressor. Later a procession of thirty Kurds met us. Some gathered up dust by handfuls and threw it on their heads, and the whole company, with intense feeling, cried out, " Vy, vy!" One man was borne on the back of another and laid down before us. His bruised and beaten back was exposed to view, when a dozen cried with one voice, making known their complaint against the agent of the landlord who had maltreated them. They followed the khan to the city to telegraph their complaint to the government.

The life of the semi-nomads of this plain is peculiar. The family tent is about forty feet long, made of coarse black woolen cloth, and surrounded by smaller tents for provisions and cattle. A well is dug near each encampment, and the women come to draw water for their flocks as of old. The watering-trough was made of earth hardened in the sun. The villagers prepare their winter quarters in the same place. The building-material is a reed, fifteen to twenty feet high, which grows near the lake. A trench is dug six feet deep and somewhat less in width; a gable-roof is formed of these reeds compactly interwoven. In these underground houses they, with their cattle, spend the winter. From this reed they make racks for their two-wheeled carts, fences around their hay-stacks, matting or *hassir* for the floor, screens, walking-sticks, laths, tents, frail bridges, and other things. It is surprising how, in the absence of stones and timber, they utilize the material at hand. One thing that indicates their backward civilization is their manner of procuring light. They burn castor-oil. After paying rent for the ground, plowing, sowing, irrigating, gathering the beans, and threshing them out of the pods, comes the boiling and crushing of them. The latter is a peculiar sight in the towns. A large stone or brick plat-form is raised on a corner of the street, and men and women stand beside it crushing the beans with a heavy stone roller. After this they are again boiled, and, the sediment sinking, the oil is ready for the lamp, or to be administered by the glassful to village infants. I tried a dose of it once, and found the remedy worse than the disease it is designed to cure.

Since the Kurdish raid Mianduab has not recovered. Kurds do not venture into the town. For purposes of barter the Kurds and Persians have a country fair, called Kurd Bazaar, every Wednesday, on the plain west of the Tatavu. From a distance of two days' march, and from all directions, the Kurds, both men and women, gather with cattle, grain, butter, cheese, carpets, etc., for sale. The Persian and Jewish shop-keepers from Mianduab come with their imitation rifles, some even engraved "Providence Tool Co., U. S. A." Cattle and horse dealers come from the cities—to the number of two thousand on favorable days—a lively bazaar.

The Jagatai is a noble river. During a large part of the year ferry-boats must be used in crossing. Caravans are greatly delayed and often imposed upon by the ferrymen. We now turned our faces toward Tabriz and determined to hurry back, but our *charvadar* objected to haste. As he rattled the currycomb over the rough backs of the horses he muttered to himself about the injury done to his animals. He knocked his head against the wall until it seemed as if he would crack his pate.   His despair foreboded ill, and the next morning, when we arose, neither *charvadar*, horses, nor partial payment in advance were to be found.   Under cover of the darkness he had followed the road to Irak, while we had to fall back on donkeys.

The following night we spent at Binab, which means "founded on water." Water is reached at a depth of ten feet. Its principal mosque is illuminated every Friday by candles stuck in the recesses of the outer walls on the streets.

On the last day of our circuit of the lake we alighted at a caravansary at Ducargan.   In the darkness it seemed a quiet place, but in the morning it was full of the bustle of business. The porches and court of the caravansary were crowded with men buying, sifting, cleaning, and packing raisins.   What a gaping and staring ensued as a lady mounted her horse! They inferred from seeing but one side-stirrup that she had only one foot.   One man, seeing the slipper stirrup, came in to say that the lady had left her shoe in the saddle.   Her straw hat led to the remark that she had a basket on her head. "Why have you surrounded your eyes with those things ? " was the query called forth by the sight of my spectacles.

CHAPTER VI

THE KURDISH RAID

THE memorable Kurdish raid, under the leadership of Sheik Obeidullah, was causing great excitement in Azerbijan at the time of our arrival in Persia. Barricades had been erected hastily in the streets of Tabriz, in anticipation of an attack, while muskets and ammunition were called into requisition by many of the inhabitants. The foreign population was contemplating removal across the Russian frontier. The post had been interrupted for many weeks. The telegraph-lines connecting with Urumia and Soujbulak had not then been built.

A number of causes led to this raid of the Kurds. The latter felt that they had various grievances against the Persians. Sheik Obeidullah, in September and October, 1880, set forth their grievances in two communications to Dr. J. G. Cochran, the missionary physician at Urumia, with a request that the British consul be informed of them. The charges were that Shuja-id-Doulah had beheaded fifty Kurds without cause, and had done damage to the sheik's villages to the amount of one hundred thousand tomans; that Mo'en-id-Doulah had seized the chiefs of Ushnuk, fined them twenty thousand tomans, kept their women in custody, and inflicted other injuries.* Hamza Aga, another sheik, had a special

* The authorities consulted in writing this account are the reports of Mr. W. G. Abbott, H. B. M. consul-general at Tabriz, the diplomatic correspondence of Great Britain and the United States, the New York

grudge against the governor of Soujbulak. Hamza Aga and his followers had fled with their booty from Turkey into Persia. He had accepted an invitation to a conference to arrange with the governor, according to custom, what portion of the spoils should be given him. Being unable to come to terms the governor commanded the soldiers to seize the aga and put him in chains. Instantly the latter drew his sword, cut his way through the guards, slew four at the gate, and escaped to the mountains. He then got his clansmen ready for an anticipated attack, aroused other tribes, and sent word to Sheik Obeidullah that he was ready to join him.

Sheik Obeidullah now felt himself in a position to resent the treatment he had received. He was a remarkable man. Intrenched in his stronghold at Sheem-i-Din, in the district of Nochea, three hours' ride from the Persian border, he lived in state as a king-priest. Though simple in his dress and food, he had a considerable army of retainers about him. All who came were fed at his hospitable board, while orphans even were supported at his charge. His disciples came to consult him in matters of religion and conscience, revering him as an inspired guide. Next to the sultan and scherif of Mecca he was the holiest person among the Sunnis. Thousands were ready to follow him, not only as a chief, but as the vicar of God. He was descended from Mohammed, and claimed to be of the line of the caliphs of Bagdad. As a lawgiver and judge he was noted for his virtue, as well as for his impartial justice.

Sheik Obeidullah was ambitious. He had formed the project of an independent Kurdistan, after the manner of Bulgaria, uniting all the Kurds under his own rule. He showed himself friendly to the Christian populations, declaring that he would rule them with equity. He cultivated foreigners,

"Tribune," New York "Evening Post," and the letters of Rev. J. H. Shedd, D.D., Rev. Benjamin Labaree, D.D., and Rev. W. L. Whipple.

and sought to enlist the public opinion of the world on his side.

The power of Turkey had just been broken in the Russo-Turkish War. The Kurds were armed with modern rifles, received partly as gifts from the sultan and partly as the spoils of the battle-fields. They felt themselves strong enough to be aggressive. For several years the Turkish government had not collected taxes, and had kept them on good behavior by largesses. On the other hand, some say that the sheik was encouraged by the sultan to assert himself, as an offset to a plan of an autonomous Armenia, and to show that the Kurds were the predominant and superior race of the region.

Moved by such a variety of motives, the Kurds crossed the Persian border in October, 1880. One division, under Sheik Abdul Kadir, a man of passionate and cruel disposition, moved toward the south of Lake Urumia. Ushnuk and Sulduz furnished their contingent. They were joined by the Mangur Kurds, under Hamza Aga, and by other chiefs, who said they were sworn on the Koran to fight until death. Souj-bulak was taken possession of without a blow, the governor and garrison fleeing before their approach. The imam-juma of the Sunnis of Soujbulak issued a manifesto declaring the enterprise a *jahad* or holy war against the Shiahs.

The Kurds then crossed the Tatavu and attacked Mian-duab. Half of its inhabitants hastily concealed their goods and fled, meanwhile smearing their wives' and daughters' faces to hide their attractions. All that remained, to the number of three thousand men, women, and children, were ruthlessly put to the sword. Shiahs, Jews, and Armenians alike were massacred. The courts and house-yards were turned over and search made everywhere for concealed valuables. Household goods were seized and the houses burned; only the walls were left remaining. The villages as far as Binab and Maragha were plundered and burned. " Upwards of two thousand vil-

lages have been burned, and ten thousand persons are said
to be homeless," wrote Consul-General Abbott in his report.
The flocks and herds were driven off. The Kurdish women,
vulture-like, came with their pack-animals and carried off the
prey. Many of the warriors, too, scattered to take back their
spoils, so that, out of a horde reported from ten thousand to
thirty thousand strong, but a few thousand remained in the
district. This scattering proved that the Kurds were not
capable of regular warfare. The massacre was not only a
crime, it was an error; for it aroused the Persians to the resistance of despair, and destroyed whatever sympathy may have
been felt for the Kurds. It demonstrated anew the incapacity
of the latter for civilized rule.

The attack found the Persians unprepared. Anticipating
no trouble, the garrisons of Azerbijan had been sent to quell
disturbances in Khorassan. The government of Azerbijan was
in a confused state. The governor of Urumia, after suffering
violence, had fled. When warned of the approaching danger
from the Kurds, an official replied that he would send twenty
horsemen and capture Sheik Obeidullah. A telegram had
been sent by some friendly Kurds to the shah, informing him
that the sheik was coming, and that as their religious chief
they must obey his orders if he came, and hoping the Persians
would intercept him before he reached their district. This
telegram was never given to the shah,* otherwise he could
have made ready his forces.

* An Armenian wrote an account of these and other facts, giving the
names of the delinquent officials. This document was presented to the
shah, who called them to account. Shortly afterward the Armenian was
attacked at night in his own house in Teheran, and left for dead. Examination showed that the assailants had come, not to plunder, but to murder. The sequel illustrates several phases of Persian law. The shah
thought to execute the assailants, but the mujtehids gave decision that it
was not legal to put a Mussulman to death for attacking a Christian; that it
should be arranged by the payment of one hundred tomans blood-money.

An army of twenty thousand soldiers was hastened forward from Teheran, commanded by Hishmat-id-Doulah. He died *en route*, and was succeeded by the Sipah Silar, Mirza Husain Khan.* General Walter von Wagner and other Austrian officers accompanied the army. In the middle of October eighteen hundred infantry and two thousand cavalry reached Binab. A three days' skirmish with the Kurds resulted in the defeat of the latter, with a loss of two hundred killed and many wounded. The Persian loss was reported as twenty killed. The Persian command moved forward on November 4th and retook Soujbulak, the Kurds retiring to the mountains.

Meanwhile another division of the Kurdish horde appeared, on October 20th, at Mount Seir, near Urumia, under Sheik Obeidullah. The latter force consisted of eight thousand horsemen. In its leader's train were three hundred mountain Nestorians, under the Metropolitan Mar Yosef, of Nochea, who were forced to come at the command of the sheik. An Armenian, Simon Aga, of Diarbekir, also accompanied the sheik, ostensibly to protect the Christians. The Kurds were a very irregular body of troops, without tents or rations. They subsisted on their daily plunder. On October 23d Consul-General Abbott, with Dr. Cochran and Simon Aga, proceeded from the college to the city, at the request of the sheik, to make arrangements for non-combatants to leave the city. Mr. Abbott reports:† "I proceeded, on what I con-

---

The shah sentenced them to prison for fifteen years. Two years afterward the shah vowed to release a dozen prisoners if the aziz-i-sultan recovered from sickness, and these prisoners were among the released ones.

* He had been ambassador to Constantinople, had accompanied the shah to Europe, was for a time prime minister, or sadr-azam, and had been deposed, but not executed. He was at Kasvin, in semi-disgrace, when appointed to take command against the Kurds. He has since died in Khorassan.

† Consular Report No. 23. See also Dr. Shedd's letters of October 27th and December 16th, in the New York "Evangelist," 1880.

sidered to be an errand of mercy, toward the principal gate. On arriving within one hundred yards I sent on a guard to announce the object of my mission, but presently we saw that the Persians had opened fire upon him. In fact, within a few seconds we were all under fire, and in the midst of showers of bullets, which fell thickly on all sides. I and my companions beat a hasty retreat to the college, and I owed my life to the fleetness of my horse."

The citizens wished to surrender the city, and the mollas sent a deputation seeking to deliver the city to the Kurds; but the governor, Ikbal-id-Doulah, declared that "though all the others should surrender, he would be faithful to the king." Though he was disgraced and made a scapegoat at the end of the campaign, yet he endeavored, though unprepared, to drive back the Kurds. He had under his command two regiments of ill-fed and ill-clothed soldiers. These he led forth; but they were defeated, losing two cannon, and for a time were surrounded by the enemy. At this juncture the sheik might easily have taken the city. Then the governor sent to Dr. Cochran, asking him to request the sheik to grant twenty-four hours' delay and the city would be surrendered without bloodshed. The sheik was very friendly to Dr. Cochran, in consequence of courtesies received during a visit made to him at Nochea in the previous spring. At Dr. Cochran's request the sheik reluctantly granted the delay. This saved the city, for in the meantime the governor and his soldiers extricated themselves, reëntered the city, and prepared for its defense. They fought bravely, and for three days and nights there was almost incessant firing. At one time the Kurds captured the Charbash gate and the cannon within it, but could not hold their ground, though they cut off the water-supply. Negotiations for surrender were again begun.

All this time the Kurds were scouring the plain, plundering the villages, carrying off grain, cattle, and household goods, as well as money, and killing many of the defenseless inhabitants. The sheik desired to protect the Christian population, but in such barbarous warfare regulations were poorly obeyed. Twenty-seven Christian villages were pillaged, fifty Christians killed, and eight hundred families suffered partial or total loss of property. Nine of the Protestant congregations were broken up. One of those who suffered violence was Pastor Shimun, moderator of the Synod. He and Babilla, a theological student, were in the lodge of his vineyard near Degala. Mohammed Sadik, son of the sheik, and one thousand horsemen came suddenly upon the village. A party of them were welcomed to the lodge and told to take all or anything they wished. After sitting a short time, one of the Kurds said, "Why don't we kill these people ? " and stabbed Babilla, who cast himself from the roof and died of his injuries. Pastor Shimun was also stabbed and left for dead. After that they attacked the village. The number of Shiahs outraged and murdered was never estimated.

On November 3d Tamur Pasha, of Maku, arrived with five thousand soldiers and relieved the city. For some days the two forces skirmished. Then the Kurds attacked the Persian camp and were repulsed with loss. Being discouraged by this, and hearing of the defeat of Sheik Abdul Kadir at Soujbulak, they broke camp on November 11th and hastened back to their mountain fastnesses.

At their departure the Shiahs began to take vengeance on the Sunnis of the plain of Urumia, who had helped the Kurds to pillage Shiah villages. Many of the five thousand families of Sunnis in the district fled with the retreating Kurds. Those who remained and were discovered were killed and their villages plundered. Not content with this, the lawless soldiery of Tamur Pasha robbed and harassed and maltreated the Persian villagers who had escaped the Kurds, levying on them for whatever they wished. A writer in the Augsburg "All-

gemeine Zeitung" says: "They dispersed themselves about
the country, and committed such atrocities, even on their own
people, Shiahs and Nestorians, and also on women, as cannot
be described.   At first the aga beheaded every Kurd who fell
into his power, even amusing himself by cutting off their heads
with his own hand.   Later he beheaded about forty, until his
arm was tired, when he left the work to others.   Visitors to
his camp saw a row of prisoners who had just had their
tongues cut out."   Shortly afterward the Sipah Silar, with an
army under Austrian officers, arrived from Soujbulak and distributed his troops along the Turkish frontier for the winter.

The condition of the missionaries during this time was very
critical, shut off for six weeks from all communication with the
outer world, and surrounded by such dangers.   Dr. Cochran
and others, with the college students, girls' school, and five
hundred refugees, were in the college grounds.   "The school-
girls were allowed to leave the city.   Eighty-four little ones,
each carrying a quilt on her back and a book under her arm,
with Miss Dean and three men as an escort, marched to the
city gate, the Kurds outside and the Persians inside sending
stray shots among them all the time.   They reached the college without injury."   There, as a guest, was the British Consul-
General Abbott, who had come to investigate the condition of
the Nestorians, yet whose visit was connected in the public
mind in various ways with the coming of the Kurds.   The combined Union Jack and Stars and Stripes waved over the gate
of the college premises.   The college and *seir* were within the
Kurdish lines.   Though the sheik sent a message assuring
them of their safety, yet they were frequently in danger from
the accidents of war and the uncontrollable plundering instinct
of the horde.   Once a band of fifty Kurds attacked the college, trying to break down its gates; but they were ordered
away by an officer who came up.   Cannon-balls from the
Persian side flew past the college, and one was found within

its grounds. Many stray shots came near them. Rev. W. L. Whipple and the refugees in the city premises had hazardous experiences with rifle-balls, the bullets buzzing about them and falling into the yard. Several came through the windows of the room in which Mr. Whipple was sitting, and one passed . over his head while he was eating dinner.

Nor did the danger cease when the Kurds departed. The friendly attitude of the sheik and his protection aroused the suspicions of the Persians, and gave occasion to opponents to insinuate that the missionaries were in league with the Kurds and had invited them. In these excitements the fact that Dr. Cochran's intercession had saved the city was forgotten, and many were ready to believe the slanders. The slightest influence might have involved them in destruction. They ascribed their preservation to the "good hand of God upon them." One of the ladies wrote home during this time of danger: " Do not grieve for us; for if we die, where could we better fall than here at our post of duty?" In those trying times the friendship of General Wagner, a Magyar Protestant, was most valuable, and was highly appreciated.

Once a company of mollas went to the Sheik ul Islam, proposing to celebrate Muharram by a massacre of the Christians and missionaries.* He replied: " I have three things to say: (1) Remember that if the missionaries had not induced the sheik to wait a day he would have taken the city, and we all should have been massacred. (2) Remember how many of our people these men saved from starvation in the famine. (3) Think of the consequences! If you do this we shall be destroyed and Islam shall fall."

Mr. Abbott and Mr. Wright left Urumia October 8th, with a guard of horsemen from Sheik Obeidullah and a letter to Sheik Abdul Kadir. At Soujbulak they were entertained by the leaders of the Kurdish army, and under a guard of three

---

* Mrs. Shedd, in " Woman's Work for Woman."

hundred cavalry were conducted to the Persian lines. Hamza Aga was chief of their escort. They described him as a perfect Kurd, brave and chivalrous, but bloodthirsty and cruel when his passions were aroused.

It was thought that the Kurds would renew their raids in the spring, and military preparations were made in anticipation of that event. Negotiations were carried on between the Persian and the Turkish governments. An envoy extraordinary was sent from Constantinople, with an autograph letter from the sultan to the shah expressing regret for what his subjects had done. The sheik was summoned to appear at Constantinople to answer for his conduct.

A strong Persian force wintered at Urumia. In the way habitual to them they committed all sorts of ravages, cutting down the orchards for firewood, besides quartering themselves on the inhabitants. In the spring an army from the other provinces was mobilizing at Tabriz.

An energetic man, Mohammed Rahim Khan, Ala-id-Doulah, later the Amir-i-Nizam, was sent as governor of Azerbijan. His fame preceded him and filled the people with a wholesome fear. When he arrived at Zenjan he found a man creating a corner in grain. The fall of the man's head effected an instantaneous decline in the price of the commodity. The news of this worked like magic in Tabriz. The "bulls" of the grain market were henceforth afraid to hoard foodstuffs or make gain out of the life of the people.

He also meted out condign punishment to the traitors of the preceding campaign. Jalil Khan, himself a Kurd, had been commander of the Persian troops at Mianduab before the massacre. When the Kurds came against the place he led his troops out at one side of the city, while the Kurds entered at the other. Then he turned and helped to pillage and massacre the defenseless inhabitants. In the spring he surrendered to the Persians under promise of pardon. He was brought to Tabriz and shot from a cannon's mouth. His head was placed on a sword and borne through the bazaars, every shopkeeper giving a piece of money to the executioner. His sons were involved in the same destruction. Around the neck of one a long rope was looped loosely. Each end of it was seized by a soldier. Then twenty others, appointed for the purpose, beat and abused him until the gradually tightening rope relieved his misery. When we remember their treason, and their participation in the horrible massacre of those whom they were set to defend, we need not stop to condemn the manner in which death was meted out to them.

The Amir-i-Nizam led the army from Tabriz. His entrance to Urumia was celebrated by the sacrifice of thousands of sheep along the route of his approach. According to custom, he declared the sacrifice a gift to the poor. Then there arose a great uproar and disturbance, which soon assumed the proportions of a riot. This was occasioned by the people striving for the carcasses, and almost tearing one another to pieces to obtain them; and the soldiery had to interfere to quiet the outbreak.

The Persian troops were stationed in Mergawar, on the east side of the Kurdish mountains. The Osmanli troops advanced from the west. It was probably his serious position between two armies that led Sheik Obeidullah, who at first declined the invitation of the sultan, finally to conclude to visit his Majesty. A powerful escort conducted him to Constantinople, ostensibly as a guard of honor, but really as his custodians. A regiment of cavalry and two batteries of artillery gave an appearance of great pomp to his coming. The officials of the towns went out to meet and honor him; the people crowded the streets to receive him. They supposed he would be sent back as governor-general of Kurdistan. At Constantinople he was received in great state, loaded with presents, and treated as a noble guest. But soon it was apparent that the palace assigned him was his prison.

Among those whom nothing could deter from the open field was Hamza Aga. He had vowed to carry on the war until death, and, though opposed by greatly superior numbers, he initiated a campaign of destruction, with flying horsemen harassing the enemy at many points. He came into the region of Soujbulak with two hundred horsemen. The governor of Soujbulak, Hasan Ali Khan, Silar-il-Askar, a Kurd of Garu, had under his command a Persian force of four thousand, with which he could easily have conquered Hamza Aga. He preferred, however, his own way of dealing with the delinquent. He sent a deputation to Hamza Aga, desiring to treat with him, promising him, if he would swear allegiance, authority over southern Kurdistan, on condition of paying a small annual revenue. He invited the chief to a conference at a great feast, assuring him of safety by an oath and a kiss on the Koran, which he sent to him. Relying on this sacred and inviolable pledge, Hamza Aga, with fourteen of his men, became the guests of the governor. They were received with all possible respect. The whole camp united to show them honor. In the tent they feasted, smoked the pipe of peace, and made their terms. At a given signal the governor retired to an adjoining tent, where he concealed himself. The soldiers opened fire upon the tent in which Hamza Aga was seated, and riddled it with bullets. Immediately recognizing the treachery, he determined to sell his life as dearly as possible. Issuing from the tent, he hewed right and left with his sword, and slew a dozen before the treacherous bullets felled him. His head was cut off and sent to the commander-in-chief at Urumia, and the governor was counted worthy of double honor.

After this the army was turned against some minor tribes in Persia. One of these, the Shakoik Kurds of the mountains near Salmas, had been infesting the passes and making the roads unsafe. Their sheik was Ali Khan. In the previous year he was nominally on the side of the Persians, and gave a quota of soldiers to the shah; but it was believed that for one he gave in loyalty, he gave five to the enemy. The campaign against him opened in August. In the first action the Persians were worsted; five hundred were slain, the Kurds losing in captured about two hundred, and fifty heads were cut off and sent as trophies to Urumia. The final result was that these and other Kurds were brought into subjection, and since then they have made little disturbance in Persia.

Sheik Ali Khan was afterward brought to Tabriz. He occupied a small house under a guard, with permission to go about on foot, but not to mount a horse. In company with some ladies of the mission, and Dr. Samuel, his physician, I called on him and his khanum. The latter came into the room with uncovered face and sat down in the company. The sheik said he had been in a hundred battles, and that the scars on his face were the results of these contests. He said he had known fifteen men who did not deserve as honorable a death as decapitation; so he had thrown them down, put stones on their heads, and stamped them to death with his foot. One man he had strapped and put in water in the depth of winter until he froze to death. The sheik's eyes were by this time dim with age, and he faintly discerned in the cheek of one of the ladies a dimple. He inquired in what battle she got that scar!

The story of Sheik Obeidullah is so interesting that we must follow it to its close. In Constantinople he seemed to give himself up to religious meditation, his one desire being to visit the sacred shrines. He petitioned the sultan to be allowed to make a pilgrimage, and under this pretense made preparations for his escape. A correspondent of the New York " Evening Post " thus describes his escape: " During the fast of Ramadan, by giving out that he would pass the whole time in meditation and prayer, in imitation of the example set by the Prophet, he secured his chamber against the entry of any one who might have prematurely made known the fact of his flight. He thus gained a clear start of all pursuit of over twenty-seven days. A jug of water and a loaf were placed each night at the door of his chamber, and it only required that these should disappear regularly—as was easily managed through a devoted attendant—for those on guard to imagine that the sheik was always safe within. It was only on the sultan's noticing his absence from the service at the mosque and from the subsequent levee at the palace that messengers were sent to bring Obeidullah to the imperial presence, but found that the bird had flown."

The sheik hastened through the Caucasus and safely reached his castle. Here his sons collected a force of several thousand men and prepared to resist the Turkish troops. But the rising of the Hekri tribe of Kurds against him, on account of an old blood-feud, led him to despair of success, and he surrendered to the Turkish authorities. His sons again attempted to release him from the Turkish guards on the road to Mosul; but this proving futile, he was sent to Mecca, where he died in October, 1883.

One result of the Kurdish raid was the establishment of diplomatic relations between the United States and Persia. The danger to the missionaries in Urumia drew the attention of the government to Persia. Hon. R. R. Dawes, a member of Congress, and brother of Mrs. Shedd, of Urumia, took special interest in the matter. A despatch in the press from Teheran announced: "There is great excitement among the inhabitants of Urumia against the Christians—especially against the American missionaries—for their supposed complicity with the Kurds." On this version of the affair being received, Mr. William M. Evarts, Secretary of State, through Mr. Lowell, requested the Earl of Granville to extend her British Majesty's special protection to the American missionaries. Despatches from Teheran reached the commander-in-chief in Urumia just when the missionaries were having a formal interview with him to dispel the unjust suspicions. " His Highness proceeded to assure them of the confidence of the shah's government in the integrity and sincerity of all their actions, and its appreciation of their benevolent labors among the subjects of his Majesty the Shah." The prime minister of Persia replied to Mr. Abbott in these words: " I know these reports to be false. I know these men are our friends, and what good things they did for our people during the famine." Prince Malcolm Khan, Persian minister to England, wrote to Mr. Lowell: " I have always gladly availed myself of every opportunity to lend my feeble aid to those apostles of a civilization which I so earnestly desire to see introduced into my country." Consul-General Abbott, in his official report, says: " Such reports are mischievous slanders, completely devoid of truth. The United States have every reason to be proud of men who, at all times conspicuous for their practical piety, displayed at Urumia, amid famine, pestilence, and war, a coolness and pluck which will never be forgotten by those who were present during that season of trial." His Majesty the Shah showed his appreciation of Dr. Cochran's conduct by honoring him with the decoration of the Lion and the Sun.

After the danger was past the conviction remained that the United States owed its citizens in Persia efficient protection. Hon. Andrew G. Curtin, advocating eloquently the establishment of diplomatic relations, said on the floor of Congress: " We have more missionaries in Persia than has any other country. Surely those of our citizens who in self-sacrifice have penetrated the darkness which has covered that historic land, given them the Bible and its precepts, and established schools, deserve the active protection of this government."

In August, 1882, Congress passed a bill for the appointment

of a consul-general and *chargé d'affaires* at Teheran.   In the following year the office was changed to that of a minister resident.   Rev. Henry II. Jessup, D.D., a missionary at Beirut, declined the position, and Mr. S. G. W. Benjamin, son of a former missionary in Turkey, and an author of fine literary tastes, was appointed the first representative of the United States to the court of Persia, arriving June 9, 1883.

Up to the present time six gentlemen have occupied the position, with considerable intervals in which no minister was at the post.   This has gone far to neutralize the benefit expected from the appointment.   The mere statement of the fact is a severe criticism on the diplomatic service of the United States.   What continuity of policy, what development of commercial enterprise, what cementing of personal relations with the ministers of the shah, could there be when the terms of service of the American ministers averaged less than two years each?   Long terms are specially necessary in the American diplomatic service, since our representatives serve no apprenticeship.   Contrast it with the Russian service.   A young man enters that service, learns the languages and customs of the country, rises through the various grades, until finally he becomes consul-general or minister, thoroughly qualified for his position—a trained diplomatist.   Then, with his agents in every important city of the kingdom keeping him informed of every item of commercial or political importance, and with a government with a fixed policy standing behind him, he is master of the situation.   Other European and even Asiatic countries follow the same method.   There is in this matter urgent call for reform in the consular and diplomatic service of the United States.

CHAPTER VII

MOUNTAIN ARMENIANS AND NOMADS

LYING to the north of Tabriz and skirting the Aras River is a region called Karadagh. Its name signifies "black mountain," and indicates truly its character. Ten hours' ride from Tabriz brought us, at an altitude of eight thousand feet, to the summit of the range, which, continuing eastward, reaches an apex in the lordly Savalan, at an altitude of fifteen thousand seven hundred and sixty feet. Through these wild mountains our course led over high and precipitous spurs and through dark, narrow gorges—a terror to caravans, but a delight in themselves. Through the Joshin Narrows we waded the bed of a pure mountain stream, whose banks at some places were covered with shrubbery and flowers, while at other places high rocks excluded the sun. On the third day the hills bore a sparse growth of stunted pine, and on the lower ranges oaks formed shaded avenues. We lunched on moss-covered rocks, with faded leaves around us, and a rivulet rippling by our side. In contrast with the bleak, barren mountains of Persia in general, the scenery was quite a refreshment. The meadows and groves in the valleys and on the hillsides, with the elderberry and blackberry, currant and thorn bushes filling up the nooks, the new clearings with the hacked or charred oak-trees still standing in the midst of the golden wheat, the icy springs, the hollowed-tree watering-troughs, the banks of the Aras clothed in green—all presented a homelike view which was a surprise to us.   Yet the varieties of wild flowers—roses, snowballs, etc.—gave a luxuriance of color and perfume not often seen in Western lands.   Folk-lore, too, added its charm. A certain sweetly scented posy, we were informed, was created by Christ on the day of his ascension from a near hill, to be a perpetual and fragrant memorial of him.   A copious spring gushes forth from the foot of a hill, on which are a shrine and the altar of a saint.   It proceeds from his tomb, and renews the faith of all who quaff it.   Another tradition varies the story, and tells us that Jesus was buried on this hill, and Ali on the opposite one, on the summits of which they at times appear and converse with each other.   As a proof that Ali was in this region they show the prints of his horse's hoofs, perfectly formed in the solid rock.   The relic is covered with a stone hut for its protection.

When we were descending into the valley beyond, a fog, driven by the wind, blew up and enveloped us.   This called forth the story of a man from Ispahan who was traveling here and saw a fog for the first time.   It seemed to him the attack of some subtle and intangible foe, and he turned and ran from it to the main body of the caravan, crying out that an evil jinnee was assaulting them.

Karadagh has eighteen districts.   We passed through many of them, observing the character of the country and its people. It is rich in natural resources.   Its timber lands have supplied charcoal to the markets of Tabriz for centuries.   Walnut for veneering is exported to Europe.   Copper is mined at Asta-mol, Gushlak, and other places.   At Avon and Missan the villagers dig out iron, and the blacksmiths prepare plowshares, horseshoes, and other implements for their domestic use.   The mineral springs, famed for their medicinal qualities, are, according to the native expression, large enough to run a mill and hot enough to boil an egg.   The crop of cornel-berries was specially abundant.   Many women were thronging the groves picking and seeding them, and spreading them in the sun to dry.

The population is chiefly Mohammedan. The Armenian villages are scattered in groups among them. Karadagh was once a part of Pers-Armenia; now the roughest and poorest places are held by the Armenians. From the fair and fertile river-banks they have been driven. Every well-built and prosperous place is, without inquiry, known to be Mohammedan. As we approach an Armenian village, whether of ten or a hundred houses, we find the characteristics the same. The houses are arranged one above the other, so that the flat roof of one house is the front yard of the one above. For safety the houses are huddled together. A common spring, from which the women are seen coming with earthenware jugs on their shoulders, sends forth a stream which is bordered by a few truck patches. Beside the village each farmer has a threshing-floor, a surface of leveled ground, with a barn behind it. They form, like the houses, giant flights of steps ascending the hillside.

We usually lodged with the kand-khuda or village master; for entertaining is part of his prerogative, and his house is the best in each village. It consists of a single room, and that a half-cellar, for the back wall is in the hill. It is built of uncut stone and mud-plaster. Large unhewn oak rafters, covered with oak planks, support the mud-roof. The floor is simply mother earth packed down, and often not even leveled. A small low door and a diminutive skylight are the only apertures. There is no sign of a window, much less of glass for it. In the center of the floor is the *tandur;* at one end a fireplace, with imperfect flue. The smoke from the oven, fireplace, and black naphtha-lamp has coated the walls and rafters with soot. The furniture consists of an iron tripod for cooking, some tinned copper vessels, a tea-kettle, a primitive spinning-wheel, a carding-comb, a weaving frame, a pile of bedding, and a few cheap carpets. The naphtha-lamp is earthenware, and is in the shape of a shoe. The oil is poured in at the shoe-top, the handle is at the heel, and the wick at the turned-up toe. It has no chimney, and emits an odor and smoke which preclude any desire to burn the midnight oil. The room is cool in summer and warm in winter. By the side of it is a stable similarly constructed, only with the light more completely excluded. At one end is a raised platform, a favorite place for sleeping in winter, in consequence of the heat engendered by the neighboring animals. Along the house is a covered porch, partially inclosed with boards or intertwined branches. The yard, which is about twenty feet square, is inclosed by a similar fence. In this yard cows, buffaloes, sheep, goats, and donkeys gather for the night. The calves and cats, with the dogs, guests, family, and fleas, occupy the front porch in summer, and the hens are invited into the room to roost.

The family soon attracted our attention. The men are rugged and work-worn farmers. Some wear curious breeches of half-tanned sheepskin. The common shoe is the *charukh* or sandal, which each man manufactures for himself. A piece of leather is cut in oval shape, the edge is bent up all around, and holes are cut in the edges and loops inserted, through which the shoestring passes. The women are hardy and muscular, with the rosy flush of health. The men do the bulk of the hard work, yet the women do not shirk the spade or the heavy burden. Their dress, generally of red calico, ends above the ankle. The head-dress is sometimes a square of calico or silk, covering head and chin, and tied under the arms. At other times a tall wooden frame is placed on the crown of the head and covered with as many as twenty handkerchiefs similar to those in use by the Turkoman women. The head-dress is worn continually, but the face is not veiled, and social intercourse is unrestricted. Their love of ornaments is displayed in earrings of twenty or thirty silver coins, and in bangles and necklaces of coins also. The boys and girls are of a pure Caucasian type, fair and beautiful even in their homespun and untidiness.

There is a great lack of variety in their food. Wheat and barley bread, millet porridge, eggs, milk and its products, a few vegetables, and fewer fruits constitute their meager bill of fare. The drudgery of dish-washing is unknown. Meat is rarely eaten, except when an animal is diseased or injured and must be killed, or when a sacrifice is offered. In the course of a month we had meat only two or three times. A diet of bread and cheese or curd, bread and milk, etc., is interrupted only by frequent fasts, which exclude all animal products. A large part of the household occupation consists in attending to the milch cows, sheep, and goats. Milking the latter is quite a comical sight. The gate of the goat-pen is so low that the goat must bend its head to enter. It is held in the gateway by one woman, while another woman milks it. All milk is heated immediately, and most of it is made into *matsoon* and cheese. The *matsoon* or *yogurt* is a curd made by putting rennet in the heated milk and letting it sour for several days. From the soured milk butter is made. There are several kinds of churns. One is a large jar. When filled a piece of leather is bound over its mouth, and it is then rolled back and forward on the ground. The other kind is a hollowed trunk of a tree. It is suspended by ropes and moves as a swing. Cheese is made by allowing the whey to flow off without pressure. It is preserved by salting, and is sometimes mixed with herbs and buried.

Spinning and weaving dress-goods, carpets, and other fabrics are universal household industries. Though Manchester prints adorn the wife, yet she still " layeth her hands to the spindle, and her hands hold the distaff." Wool is carded by pulling it over a pair of long-toothed brass combs. Wool and silk are sometimes spun by a distaff whirled by hand. More frequently a spinning-wheel is used; the spinner sits on the floor and manages the thread partly with her feet. In many villages there are little shops where the silk is spun on a small machine. The cocoons are thrown into a caldron of boiling water mixed with sour milk. A man turns a wheel, about a yard in diameter, with a foot-treadle, and with one hand stirs the cocoons to loosen the fibers, while with the other hand he draws up the threads to be wound around the wheel. The refuse and loose fibers are spun by the women and made into head-dresses. In the mulberry orchards, where the leaves are gathered for feeding the worms, the trees are kept cut so that each one occupies but a square yard of ground. The seed-worms complete their work in three months, and are kept in the house during the winter. The weight of the annual silk-crop of Persia, which is derived chiefly from the Caspian provinces, is six hundred thousand pounds, of which thirty-two thousand pounds come from Azerbijan.

The farmers of Karadagh were wont to be cursed with land-lords. The villages were owned by the khans, who consulted only their own interests, not the good of the tenants. They went the round of the villages and levied on the people, eating their fatlings and depleting their hen-roosts. Not shahis, but revilings, were the reward of the peasants. Worse than the masters were the agents who collected the rents and taxes. The names of the householders were sometimes written on wooden tickets, and one of these was drawn out each day to indicate who should provide for the agent. These agents were cruel and dishonest. They extorted without mercy or chance of appeal. The regular dues were three parts out of ten of the crops and flocks, but more than a half was required to satisfy the owner and his men. The result of these exactions, with the insecure tenure, was that many people were driven away. They had no sense of security, such as would encourage them to build good houses or orchards. They fled

from one village to another. Some went to Tabriz and others
to Russia. Finally they made an appeal to the shah, through
the mediation of Bishop Stephanos. The shah was gracious,
and transferred the farming of the taxes to the bishop, who
appointed the priests to collect and forward the revenues.
Some villages were purchased by Armenian merchants. As a
result the Armenians were relieved from their oppressions.

The Armenians of Karadagh are not lacking in the exter-
nals, at least, of religion. They have churches, shrines, and
priests in abundance. Every village, however insignificant,
has its rough stone church, sometimes not more than ten feet
square. On some of the churches are bells, which have been
introduced of late years from Russia. There lives in the
region a Jerusalem pilgrim, who, with a great reputation for
sanctity, peregrinates among the people, dervish-like, tells their
fortunes, and eats their substance. He is blind and beggarly,
very ignorant, and apparently half-witted, which probably
adds to the reverence given him, as insanity is frequently con-
founded with inspiration. He came one day and interrupted
our meeting. After setting forth his own perfections, the
many languages he had mastered—each in a single night, with
a vast literature in each—the wide extent of his travels, and
an immense amount of gibberish, he ended with a vile and
violent attack on Protestantism.

At one place we saw a good sample of a village fight. We
had lain down to sleep in the common apartment, when suddenly there was a rushing to and fro of troops of infuriated
men and women, who made a bedlam of the village, and with
shoutings, curses, blackguarding, and general scurrility exhausted the Armenian vocabulary in doing to others as others
were doing to them. Mingled with the barking of dogs, the
quarrel made the night hideous; nor did they desist until they
had scarred one another's beauty.

A rite upon which great stress is laid by the Karadaghlis is the offering of sacrifices. Almost every village has its shrine and altar. These are usually on high ground, surrounded by groves of tall trees, and are regarded as most sacred. Various causes are assigned for the selection of these places. One acquired its sacred association because, when Christ mounted on an ox was traversing this country, the ox rested on the hill. Another is the place where the ox died. Yet another is the cave of a hermit of olden time. Another still is the tomb of two monks, John and James, who are declared by the inscription, in ancient Armenian, to have wrought miracles. The place of the tomb was disclosed to the Jerusalem pilgrim in a dream, and a church has since been built over it. Other sites acquired their sacredness from the descent of heavenly lights, supposed to be divine manifestations. Another cause is the beauty of the groves, and the size and age of some of the trees. There seems to be something natural in the veneration given to large trees. To these groves the axe is never laid. Some time ago the top of a tree, whose trunk at the base measured forty feet, fell to the ground. It has lain there and rotted, as no one dares to use the sacred wood. To warn off any Gideon, they tell of a Mussulman who, thinking there was honey in one of the trees, cut it down in spite of the protests of the Armenians. The tree broke in five pieces, one of which killed the axeman. Four of his sons died within a short time, and the fifth, fearing a similar fate, brought an offering for his preservation. The man should have known better, they said, for his uncle once ridiculed a grove, and when he looked around his neck became fixed in a crooked position. Thus does Baal plead for himself! I once ventured to speak against their superstitious belief in the sacred trees, and on the following night my horse fell into a well in the stable. Afterward this was cited as a punishment on me for daring to call in question the sacredness of the shrines. At one of the shrines food is placed on a rock, and the saints are supposed to come and consume it. A young evangelist, seeing that lizards came out of the crevices of the rocks, shot some of them in order to uproot the superstition of the people. The women meditated an attack upon him for destroying their saints. They confidently expected some definite and sudden calamity to come upon him, and were surprised to see him go about safe and sound the next morning. The priest chided him for spoiling his source of revenue.

Upon the altars at the high places sacrifices of sheep and goats are made, frequently in fulfilment of vows, on recovery from sickness or deliverance from some calamity, or with a petition for some desired blessing. After the sacrifice has been slain, with its face toward the east, and its blood has been poured upon the altar, the head, feet, and hide are given to the priest, and the remainder is taken home and eaten. After two weeks' abstinence we were glad to eat of it, without asking any questions. None of the sacrifice is burned, but candles are kept lighted during the ceremony. It seems to be regarded as a thank-offering, though some attribute expiatory efficacy to it. "They sacrifice upon the tops of the mountains, under oaks and poplars and elms, because the shadow thereof is good." (Hos. iv. 13.)

We had several interesting experiences with the Aylauts, or nomads of Karadagh. The greater part of its Mussulman population is settled in towns and villages, but some still retain their habits as wandering tribes. The plain of Moghan, part of which is Russian territory, is one of their pasture-grounds. The grass is said to grow so high as to cover a man on horseback. Moghan has been the camping-ground of many conquerors. Here, it is said, venomous serpents arrested the march of Pompey. Here, on Noruz, 1736, Nadir Shah placed the crown on his head, with a great pageant, at the same time demanding that his subjects should renounce the Shiah and adopt the Sunni faith.

Some of the nomads live in the villages during the winter. As soon as spring opens they leave the plains, carrying everything of value with them, and their houses become deserted and dismantled, not even a watchman remaining on the site. Some of their villages have cultivated fields around them, and a few men remain to garner the crops. A few plow arable land on the mountains, sow the seed, and return to reap in the following year. They are in a feudal state, the clans being subject to the khan or chief, who is their protector from injury and their leader in war. Their dependence on the shah is slight. They send an annual revenue to the government, and furnish their quota of soldiers in time of war. This semi-independence enables them to oppress all within their reach. Not infrequently we passed their encampments. Their black or brown tents, of homespun woolen cloth, were grouped on the hillsides. Sometimes they were surrounded with reed curtains. Their wealth consists of their flocks and herds, which, with their products, are exchanged in the towns for their necessaries. They are not particular how they add to their flocks. The villagers around Muzhumbar had been complaining of their cattle having been stolen. We saw the thieves driving away the cattle on the hilltops above us. Knowing the bad reputation of these nomads, we always passed their tents with some solicitude. One day, after escaping from the fierce dogs, we were breathing more freely, when three horsemen in a gully shouted at us to halt, as the khan wished to see us. We moved on slowly, with some trepidation, while one of them galloped forward, stopped our load-horse, and disappeared. After a few minutes of suspense, in which the muleteer threw down the lines in affright and refused to go on, the horsemen returned, followed by another and another, until twenty horsemen, headed by the khan, and each armed with two Martini-Henry rifles, surrounded us. We expected nothing else than to be robbed; but after convincing himself that I was neither a consular nor a government agent, but simply a "man of the Book," he let us go in peace, merely chiding us for not stopping to eat bread at his tent. We afterward learned that they had just been on the war-path against the village of Dinovar; but finding its inhabitants armed and headed by a colonel from Tabriz, from whose tent floated the royal ensign, they did not venture to attack them.

Another day we lost our way, and wandered over the rough mountains, along the sheep-paths, through jungle-like forests, amid an underbrush of low thorns. Finally we came upon an encampment of the Aylauts. Isaac went forward to reconnoiter. He was in a sorry plight, with hat banged in, coat in tatters, hands scratched by the thorns, and eyes red with pain. The women, with wild, disheveled hair, followed by troops of almost naked children and by savage dogs, surrounded him, crying, "Vy, vy!" and offered to patch him up, then threatened to pen him if he did not give a good account of himself. But they refrained from molesting him, and gave us a guide, who brought us quickly to our destination. On another occasion, one of the khan's relatives, Ali Beg, seized the bridle of Isaac's mule and demanded a present of sugar. We declined on account of the smallness of our supply. He answered our refusal with the full weight of his club on Isaac's shoulder, and brought his Martini-Henry into position for use. The American eagle was too far away, and he got the sugar!

Dr. Mary Bradford and Miss G. Y. Holliday, while on a tour in Karadagh, lodged at an encampment of Aylauts. They kept a sharp oversight of their goods, and fastened their horses' feet with chains and locks at night. The nomads refused to fix a price for anything, and seemed insulted that they should be asked to sell food; but they had the expectation of an *anam* or present of far more than the value. In the morning, after giving liberal presents, the ladies started. When out of camp a man suddenly appeared, holding a bunch of snakes in their faces, and demanded an extra *anam*. The prompt action of a fellow-traveler, bringing his gun to bear on the intruder, relieved them from their predicament.

A Turk, Alaskyar, told me a story of a Shahsevan girl from near Ardebil who had known him when a child, and who afterward married one of the chiefs. She became a robber in male attire, and, armed with sword, dirk, and gun, was in the habit of waylaying travelers. She attacked Alaskyar when he was on a journey, and demanded his money. Then she recognized him and asked if she were known, it being the custom to kill when recognized. He failed to recognize her. She then said, "You are Alaskyar. I am the girl who used to play with you!" Afterward she released him and exhibited her horsemanship. Tying a bag of stones around her waist, she galloped around, throwing them down and picking them up, shooting under her horse, and showing all the manœuvers of the Persian horsemen.

During the last days of our journey we had to pass through the camp of Rohim Khan, who, with several thousands of his clan, had pitched his tents on the bank of the Keleibar River. Probably every man, woman, and child among them is a thief. We passed unmolested through the encampment, but just as we had turned out of sight of the last tents a horseman galloped up unobserved from behind and cried, "Halt! The khan demands your presence." We remonstrated, and the fellow said, "You must either knock me down or come." To have attacked him would only have brought up his comrades, so we parleyed, trying to impress him with our rights and dignity as foreigners, but with small effect. He demanded that I alight from my horse, and, reinforced by some shepherds, he proceeded to put his demand into effect, and in a short time had me on the ground. I held on to the bridle until one of his aids drew his sword, when he assumed undisputed possession. Mounting, he galloped off; but the horse, stiff with a month on the mountains, did not go to suit his fancy, so he returned it soon, and we managed to strike a bargain with him, and, losers by some *krans*, were allowed to proceed on our way. We immediately went to the governor of Karadagh, at Ahar, an unpretentious place of five thousand inhabitants, and laid information before him as to these affairs. He offered to furnish me with a company of soldiers to return and chastise the nomads, but I declined. He then promised to send and have the parties arrested and imprisoned until orders should come from Tabriz for their punishment. The governor was a prince, but in dealing with these chiefs of the tribes he was comparatively powerless. His court was full of petitioners appealing from their oppressors. The executioner who served him, with his companions, had been waylaid a few days before, and after a musketry skirmish had been stripped of all his possessions. The roads had been so unsafe that the revenue of the province could not be forwarded to the treasury; some of it had been sent concealed in a charcoal caravan. One reason for the insecurity of the roads was that the governor of Azerbijan had compounded with the thieves and let them go free on their giving him part of the stolen goods. They immediately returned to plunder other victims. The governor of Karadagh was very friendly disposed. He had on his table a former edition of the Persian New Testament, which he had read with great interest. He was glad to receive the new edition. He honored us with a present of fowls and some sweets, and, owing to the dangerous state of the roads, gave us a guard to conduct us to Tabriz.

Shortly after this time the chiefs of the tribes drove out the governor, and the crown prince led an army against them and punished them and their chiefs, shooting some from the cannon's mouth, imprisoning and fining others. Since then Karadagh has been more quiet and safe.

CHAPTER VIII

A JOURNEY of four hundred miles by railway requires but the time of a fleeting dream. When, however, the same distance has to be traversed in the primitive method of Oriental travel, and amid Oriental scenes, it becomes important. Hours in one case become days in the other, and an ill-remembered sensation of swift motion is replaced by the experiences of two weeks' travel by caravan. It is true there is a speedier mode of travel even in Persia. Between some of the chief cities there are, in connection with the post, fresh relays of horses at frequent stations, and speeding at a gallop by night and day satisfies the foreigner's rushing impulse.

For our journey to Teheran we took the slower train. A large, burly Turk accompanied us, whose protruding bones and full muscular development made him well able to carry the name of the Imam Ali Askar. His black, furry, brimless hat concealed as large a surface of shaven head as any of his countrymen could boast of. His numerous waistcoats, of various bright-colored prints, each with a full frock, were bound with a leathern girdle. His coat of white felt, gathered in folds at the waist, extended out over the load as he was mounted upon it, and his slipper-like shoes, without heel-backs or fastenings, dangled in the air to the motion of the mule. A favorite amusement of the mule was " making Mussulman prayers," the stumbling and rapid rising of the animal suggesting the prostrations of the devotee of Islam. A favorite, and

138

at each successive time more ridiculous, position of the patient Ali Askar was sprawling on the ground.

The *charvadar* or muleteer had a coat of sheepskin, with the wool turned inside. His stockings were strips of coffee-sacking wound about the feet; the legs of the boots were open at the side, and bound tightly with strings of leather. He sometimes put on his boots before his night's rest, so as to be ready to start early. He slept in his clothes, except the mammoth hat of sheepskin, which served as a pillow. His place of rest was an elevated platform in the stables, without bedding. If the stables were full he tied the animals to a rope fastened to pegs in the yard, put the feed-bags over their heads, and slept beside them.

On leaving Tabriz the road to Teheran ascends quickly to a higher level, and as we passed the summer residences of the sadr-azam and the khallat-pashan, and the villa of the Russian consul, we could feel the air growing cooler. Morning revealed the earth covered with snow (September 14th), and gave us a cold ride over Shiblee Pass. Just beyond the pass we came upon a pretty sheet of water. It bears the paradoxical name of Kuri Gyol, or " Dry Lake," because of its smallness in summer. On the left side of it a road branches off to Ardebil and the Caspian coast.

The character of the day heightened the effect of the wretchedness by the roadside. The mud-hut where we lunched was certainly the humblest house of entertainment in which we ever ate. It was a low room ten feet square, with a manger in one corner, a refuse-heap in the other, a *tandur* or underground oven in the middle. A wild man appeared in the road, half naked, slinging a club in the air, and with singing and shouting running after it. He was powerful and well capable of handling his club. When we reached him he pleasantly demanded a *kran*. Every passer-by gives to him, as he is reputed to stone every one who refuses. He goes into the villages, and, throwing up large stones, lets them fall on his breast.   For this display of prowess he gets the shahis of the people.

But most wretched of all was the condition and appearance of the numerous lepers, who sat by the wayside begging, and crying out piteously, with scarcely intelligible voices, "Ya Yaradan Allah!" ("O Creator God!").   Repeated again and again, this refrain of the lepers is most touching.   Clad in rags and sitting upon the ground, their shelter a circle of stones piled up without a roof, or a dugout, or perchance a natural cave, they presented a revolting spectacle.   They were victims of the terrible elephantiasis—called *juzam*, from an Arabic root meaning amputation or mutilation—incurable, deadly, loathsome.   A picture of living death, they eke out a miserable existence.   Many frequent the roads in Persia, on the outskirts of cities or villages.   They are regulated by few laws, the one of separation from the rest of mankind not being rigidly enforced.   We passed a score and a half of these miserable creatures.   There is a village of them about six miles from Tabriz.   They cultivate their farms, and in some cases are well-to-do and prosperous, providing for themselves some, at least, of the comforts of life.   Their hamlet is called Payon, or the "Village of the Sick," and there are about five hundred of them, little, if at all, segregated.   To this village the roadside beggars belong, and there they take their alms and buy food; and whenever anything is needed from the city, some of those on whom marks of the leprosy are not evident pass the money to the unwitting shopkeepers.

The origin of the community is interesting.   About forty years ago Aziz Khan Sardar was governor of Tabriz.   Some of the leading men called his attention to the promiscuous way in which lepers were allowed to mingle with the people. To check this he ordered them to be collected from all Azerbijan, assigned them a section of land, furnished them with

oxen and farming implements, and established them as a separate community.   At first they were given charity, month by
month, from the public treasury.   If it was delayed beyond
the regular time they came trooping down to the city.   Now,
on the contrary, it is said that they pay taxes to the government.   During the famine they invaded the city at night with
demands for bread.   Some of the missionaries have visited
them.

As the days passed on we observed who with us made up the
caravan.   We were scarcely one caravan, as those who traveled
with us started, according to custom, on their day's journey
about midnight, or during the third watch, reaching their destination shortly after we of Occidental habits had started.   We
found our companions to be chiefly pilgrims for Meshed.   One
section were taking the bodies of their dead, perhaps exhumed
after months of repose, to deposit them in the ground consecrated by the dust of the Imam Reza.   What a long and dreary
funeral-march!   Many of the pilgrims were women, with children of all ages, starting out with alacrity on their thousand-
mile pilgrimage.   Some were mounted on horseback after the
manner of men.   Others were packed away in *cajavahs*—
wicker baskets or boxes, fastened together and slung over the
horse, and then filled with women, babies, baggage, or stones
to balance.   More, however, preferred the *takhtarevan*, which
may be briefly described as a large box, with windows or slid-
ing doors in the sides, placed on two long poles serving as
shafts, in which the mules are hitched, one before and the
other behind the *takhtarevan*.   We did not envy them their
stylish mode of travel, for we had tried it.   It is very slow,
tedious, and expensive.   A man trudges alongside to steady
and guard the vehicle.   Once, in crossing a stream, the fellow
abandoned his post to go over a foot-bridge.   The hind horse
stopped to drink, the *takht* turned, and the lady was in a
perilous position.   Ali Askar waded to the rescue, and carried

her to dry ground. Then his wrath vented itself on the delinquent *charvadar* with harmless blows with the broadside of his sword. He quickly stirred him up to extricate the *takht* from the water.

The fourth day brought us to Turkomanchai, a village picturesquely situated between high hills. It looked neat at a distance, but on near approach was as filthy as other villages. It is known only as the place where the treaty was signed between Persia and Russia after the invasion of 1828–30. The treaty gave the Russians the provinces of Erivan and Nakhejevan to the Aras River. Its bed is broad and deep, though in summer almost dry. It had been swollen by the recent rains, yet we preferred to go mainly by the river-bed. We crossed the stream nine times in its winding course, and reached the city of Miana, welcoming Sunday. There is little difficulty in getting a caravan to stop over Sunday. The principle in the law of rest is so clearly recognized by the *charvadars* as a necessity for their animals that it is their habit to rest one or two days in a week.

Miana is a district capital of ten thousand inhabitants, situated near the junction of three considerable streams, which, with their numerous tributaries, are lined thickly with villages. Miana, Zenjan, and Kasvin are the relay stations of the Indo-European telegraph-line between Tabriz and Teheran, in charge of German operators. They are also the post-offices and main caravan stations on the king's highway. Miana fairly represents one of the old towns of Persia, with small yards, separated from one another and from the crooked streets by high walls; houses mostly one story high, built of adobe, having pretentious windows covered with oil-paper, the roofs piled up with manure fuel; and with the threshing-floors at the entrance of the main streets—overgrown villages.

The Miana mosque, in the midst of hovels, speaks of the strength of Islam. It has a large green glazed-tile dome and

a tall minaret, and is a shrine hallowed by the dust of an imam-
zada. When a caravan comes within sight of the sacred dome
it stops, and each one places a stone of witness, so that a pile
has accumulated. This mosque is famed for giving sight to
the blind. Its efficacy is probably the same as that of a
mosque in Tabriz, where a miraculous cure was said to have
taken place. The news of the event was heralded through the
city, and for three nights the roofs were aglow with bonfires,
and for three days there was rejoicing, because God had visited
his people. It turned out that the man had merely fixed his
eyes blind, and had them conveniently relieved within the precincts of the mosque.

To this place also the prediction of the approaching end of
the world had reached, then so much talked about by newspapers. The molla announced that Miana would be destroyed
by an earthquake at the end of Ramadan. The people of
the Shahi peninsula thought it would be by a flood, because
the rising of Lake Urumia sometimes leaves them on an island
for six months; while the molla had in remembrance the earthquake which a few years before had shaken the whole neighborhood and totally engulfed some villages.

But more than for mosque or for earthquakes Miana is
famed for its bug, called *gana*. Little is known of the nature
of this bug, and some travelers have not hesitated to call it
a humbug. There is no doubt, however, of its reality, for it
abounds in the district. Its bite is poisonous, producing large
hives, and bringing on a fever which is sometimes fatal. The
gana does not bite the inhabitants, but only strangers. Fortunately we had comfortable quarters in the station of the Indo-
European Telegraph Company.

Soon after leaving Miana we ascended the Pass of Koflan
Kuh. It is the highest point between Tabriz and Teheran,
marking the boundary between Irak and Azerbijan. The
pass is not a difficult one, only a long winding stretch of steep

hill. The road is good, one side being paved for military
purposes. This was done first by the Turks, and was repaired
by the Russians in 1830, and since by the shah from time to
time. Descending, we crossed the Guzul Uzun or Sefid Rud
River, one of the longest rivers in Persia. It is four hundred
and ninety miles from its rise in Mount Zagros to its emptying into the Caspian Sea. The bridge over it at this point is
said to be eight hundred years old, and is well preserved. An
interesting romance is connected with it. A maid of Shiraz,
left an heiress by the death of her father, refused all offers of
marriage and devoted herself to ministering to the needs of
mankind. Finally she came to these solitary mountains and
built a castle, the ruins of which still frown down upon us, and
there lived while she superintended and built from her own
means this bridge. It is considered religiously meritorious to
do such benefactions. Another woman built one near Teheran, and as she deemed it criminal neglect in the king not to
have erected one before, she invoked a curse upon him, and
wrote this inscription on the bridge: " Let no king pass over
here forever!" It is said· the shah, coming to the bridge,
turned aside and went through the stream. That shahs have
not neglected their duty since then appears from several fine
bridges now spanning the stream on this road.

The region of country we were traversing is a high plateau.
The character of the landscape is very monotonous—undulating hills succeeding one another as far as the eye can reach,
without a sign of a forest, or even a tree of natural growth.
Lifelessness is the chief characteristic. The bleak, barren
hills are dead beyond imagination. No tree, no shrub is there
—only the stunted thorn-bush struggling for existence. One
species of bush is seen, here and there, which remains green
in the desert; and since there is no water visible, the natives
think it must have a spirit or life in itself. These bushes are
often covered with rags, offerings to this spirit. Lizards, both

numerous and active, continually dart before the eye. There
are literally millions of them. They are divided into believers
and infidels. The latter it is lawful to kill. In some desolate
regions the telegraph-poles appear as the only signs of the
great world's civilization. They afford a strange but real com-
panionship in the long weary hours of travel. The columns
of dust interest us. Beginning afar off, the column gradually
takes shape and rises, moving along regularly before the wind,
until it stands as high as the eye can reach, and apparently
not more than two feet in diameter. The entire absence of
farm-houses from the open country—all being collected into
villages—gives additional weariness to the long distances, without the sight or sign of a habitation. When a village does appear it looks so much like the dry hills around it as to be scarcely
distinguishable.

On the third day from Miana the landscape along the Zenjan River presented a pleasing contrast. It is well watered,
with many groves and grassy plots. On the flats were the
tents of the farmers, camped near their work, and around
them their fields of rice, castor-beans, cotton, and grain. After
such a day we arrived at Zenjan, the capital of Khamseh, a
small province. The caravansary at which we stopped was a
good sample of such in Persia. Though having accommodation for a thousand horse, there was nothing for travelers but
a few bare rooms. We remained a day, and found the city
an active, busy place. Its bazaars were full of goods, and full
of life as well. Zenjan is noted for its manufactures in brass.
The sound of the furnace did not cease at night, and in the
morning we awakened amid the din of a hundred anvils. The
display of fancy leather-work was attractive, but that which
gives Zenjan its European reputation is its beautiful filigree-
silver work. There is here a fine-looking mosque with blue
glazed-tile dome, and several graves of imam-zadas.

Of its twenty thousand inhabitants all except a dozen families of Jews and Armenians are Mohammedans of various sects. Many of the Babis, the sect which has proved so troublesome to the present shah, are domiciled here, the scene of their strong resistance to the government. The chief molla and thousands of the inhabitants had become adherents. When the government undertook their suppression they made a determined resistance. The fervor of the leader inspired the followers; they resisted with fury and enthusiasm the forces of the shah for eight months, giving no quarter and asking none. The women, with an energy equal to the men, joined in the defense of the barracks. When, reduced by hunger, they were given opportunity to renounce their prophet, the Bab, they resolutely refused, and died with the courage of martyrs.

A day's ride from Zenjan brought us to Sultanieh. Just before entering it we passed a summer palace and fort of the shah. When Sir John Malcolm came to Persia as ambassador from England he found Fath Ali Shah encamped here, with a retinue of forty thousand soldiers and attendants. Then he exhibited for the first time in Persia an electric battery and a magic lantern, and also introduced carriages. At that time the shah conferred on him the Order of the Sun, but he refused to receive it on the ground that it had just been created for Napoleon's ambassador, General Gardane. For this reason the shah created the Order of the Lion and the Sun, and conferred it first on the English ambassador. These orders are an imitation of European custom.

The camp of Fath Ali Shah formed a regular city of tents, with bazaars, etc. Soon the soldiers would grow discontented with inactivity and wish to fight; and Russia being the nearest enemy, it was almost certain the quarrel would be with her. So by treaty Fath Ali Shah was prohibited from assembling such a large body of troops here. The present shah repaired the palace, but rarely occupies it.

Little remains to attest the former greatness of Sultanieh.

Who would think that the miserable village of one hundred and fifty houses had once been the capital of Persia, and gloried in the riches and retinues, and had been adorned by the munificence, of several lines of shahs? Many earthmounds and the yet discernible traces of walls might lead us to suspect it had a history. But, fortunately, it is not left without a witness. Several monuments still attest its former greatness. One of these is the ruin of a mosque, beautiful even in its dismantled condition. It is a large structure, the dome itself being one hundred feet in diameter and one hundred and twelve feet high. The walls are nine feet thick. The interior and exterior are covered with glazed tiles, the dome being one continuous surface of blue tiles, resplendent from afar. The pillars are of variegated colors, worked in patterns. The interior workmanship is to a considerable extent a mosaic of gilded tiles. A frieze of alabaster, which formerly completely surrounded the interior, and on which was engraven the whole of the Koran, together with much other fine workmanship, has been removed to Teheran. We secured several tiles which had fallen. The mosque was built by Mohammed Khuda Banda, the first Shiah of the Mongol shahs of Irak, whose dust it contains and whose fame it perpetuates.

The next station, Horam Dara, is a beautiful shaded spot. Some stone formations in the mountain near by have an interesting legend connected with them. They appear as if a shepherd, leaning on his staff and surrounded by his flock, had become petrified in living position. This has given rise to the story that Ali, in his wanderings, had arrived here weary, and being rebuffed on requesting a cup of milk from the shepherd, pronounced a curse upon him, and instantly he and his flock were turned into stone.

Two days more of travel brought us to Kasvin. With Tabriz it has the honor of being singled out for mention in

" Paradise Lost," as indicating the distant Orient in the days of Milton. It is the center of a transit trade, having the most accessible road to the Caspian Sea. It has also a place in history as the capital of the Safavi shahs, the birthplace of Lokmân, the fabulist, the scene of memorable battles, and the terminus of Heraclius's Third Expedition. One of the relics of former days is a system of reservoirs, in which a supply of water is reserved for the dry season. The water is stagnant for months, and yet is the constant drink of the people, and in consequence readily breeds disease. Here ague attacked us, and, as it continued for three months, the pleasure and profit of the journey were greatly lost.

An agreeable surprise at Kasvin was to find a hotel, far better than any we had previously met with in Persia. Instead of empty rooms, with scarcely a strip of carpet, it was well furnished, and meals were served in European style. It even excelled in providing not only combs, but also toothbrushes and nightcaps for public use! The building, substantially built of brick, and standing at the head of a broad avenue, is an ornament to the city. It is also the depot for the carriage post-road, which has lately been completed from Teheran. Our admiration for the roadway was great. It is straight and solid, full thirty feet wide, and extends along a level plain. At every four miles are post-houses, some of them for guards, others for the accommodation of travelers. At every fourth house the horses are exchanged for fresh relays. Even with break-downs and smash-ups the rate of travel is rapid. During our last day's journey our course lay along a canal. It is a stream of pure mountain water, turned from its course toward the capital. A porous soil and evaporation cause the loss of six sevenths of it, and exposure in the course of twenty-four miles corrupts its purity. Still the accomplishment of such a work, and the construction of the post-road, are to the credit of modern Persia.

After gazing for hours upon the outstretched habitations and the lofty mountains in the background, we were right glad, as we neared the gates, when the Rev. Mr. Potter met and welcomed us to Teheran.

Teheran, the capital of Persia, is called the "city of the shadow of God," the "footstool of the King of kings." It can boast of no glorious past. Though the neighboring plains contain the mounds and ruins of great cities, it was only in the latter part of the last century that Teheran emerged from obscurity. The first records tell of it as a village of underground huts, affording a retreat from the heat of summer or from the ravages of plundering hordes. It was chosen as the capital of Aga Mohammed Khan, the founder of the Kajar or reigning dynasty. His preference for it was doubtless owing to its proximity to his own tribe in Mezanderan. Now Teheran has assumed the position of the political center of Central Asia. Here the legations of England, France, Russia, Germany, Austria, Holland, Turkey, and the United States represent their respective countries and carry on their political intrigues. In a century its population has increased from fifteen thousand to two hundred thousand. Because of its modern growth it has partaken more largely than any other Persian city of a European element, and been influenced by Western ideas. The old style is seen in the high walls and deep moat which surround the city. On each side of the town are two large, well-built, and handsome gates. The pillared fronts are of various-colored bricks, worked in mosaic, with picture representations. The old part of the city, too, is as truly Persian as possible, filthy and miserably built. On the other hand, broad avenues, well paved and bordered with shade-trees, new styles of houses, embassy grounds laid out like an English park, phaëtons and carriages, telegraph-poles and tramways, street gas-lamps and the electric light, restaurants, drug-stores, photograph galleries, and Framghi stores strongly attest that

Western life has invigorated the stereotyped East. The bazaars, too, while presenting the same general characteristics as in other cities, have wider avenues, and enjoy more of the much-needed sunlight. They are well stocked with imports, and those which deal in European goods attract the briskest trade.

The life-center of the city is in the vicinity of the public square or *medan*. This covers about the space of four city squares, is stone-paved, and is adorned with water-fountains. Here the electric light is exhibited. The city's main illumination is, however, by gas, which was formally lighted for the first time, with public ceremonies, the night after we arrived. The *medan* is used for royal exhibitions, and as a drill-place for the soldiery. Partially surrounding it is the *top-khana* or armory, from the windows of which the field-pieces stare out. Back of the *medan* is the ark or citadel, the most important building in the city. It is surrounded by a strong wall, with towers at intervals, and contains, besides the city palace, the hall of judgment, the treasury, the arsenal, the royal college, and the theater. These buildings are good, substantial brick structures, rarely attaining a second story, yet fantastically ornamented in Oriental style. We made repeated efforts to obtain admission to the "Palace of the Sun," to see the crown paraphernalia and jewels, of which the diamond called the "Sea of Light" is among the most precious in the world. Though disappointed in this, we had free access to the throne-room. On its walls are paintings of the shahs of the Kajar dynasty, while the ceiling and the walls are ornamented with arabesques, profusely inlaid with looking-glass, which reflects the gorgeousness of him who "sits high on the throne in royal state." Two doors are objects of great interest. They are of large size, covered completely with Shiras mosaic —an inlaid work of minute particles of wood, brass, and bone, of different colors, which is highly artistic. The throne itself is generally considered to be one of the trophies of Nadir Shah from the conquest of Delhi. It is a platform of white marble, about ten by fifteen feet in area, raised on carved figures of lions, and ascended by marble steps. It is inlaid and ornamented with gold. On it rugs are spread, and the shah sits after the manner of the Persians. Here, on his birthday, he holds salaam and receives the congratulations of the people.

We were greatly interested in the royal college, where we were received by the president and by some of the professors in the reception-room, and there the preliminaries of coffee-drinking took place and other hospitalities were dispensed. We were conducted through the institution by Mr. John Tyler, professor of English, now the efficient interpreter of the United States legation. The plan of the building is a hollow square, the rooms, one story high, all facing the inner court, and opening on a veranda which surrounds the court. The court itself was laid out with shrubbery and flowers. The first room we entered was the French class-room, where, under a Persian teacher, a large class was reciting and taking good hold of the language. The walls of the room were covered with very fair pencil-sketches and oil-paintings, the work of the pupils. In the English room Professor Tyler showed us a class of bright boys translating our mother-tongue, which is making much advance in Persia. These, with Russian, Arabic, and Turkish, are the foreign languages taught. Had we come in the morning the sciences would have been on the programme. There was some scientific apparatus and a small library representing many languages. Thence we crossed into the music-hall. We found pianos and organs, and, more than all, were entertained by a full cornet band, composed of the pupils. The music-hall was built by the shah for the royal theater, with stage and scenery; but the mollas objected to plays being introduced, so the shah refrained from executing his purpose. We were

then led into the gymnasium, where the attempt of the youthful Persians to go through the antics of the trapeze-performer
afforded us no little amusement.   It was certainly time to
refresh ourselves, according to Persian custom ; so we repaired
again to the reception-room, and were served with ice-cream
and tea, after which we looked in at the photograph gallery,
where every scholar has a chance to learn photography in
regular curriculum.

The extent of the curriculum, the drill, and the evident success of the instruction in the shah's college were a great surprise
to us.   The number in attendance was two hundred and fifty,
composed of Persians and Armenians, with a few Hindus.
All the native races and religions are admitted.   Christians
are allowed to stay away on Sunday if they desire to.   Tuition
is free.   Not only so, but all are in some degree supported.
Some are given only a few tomans, while others have full support, the morning and evening meals being provided at the
college.   The shah furnishes the funds, and the running-
expenses are said to be sixty thousand dollars a year.   His
Majesty's object in maintaining the college is to prepare educated officers for the army and the civil service.

Leading out from the *medan* radiate the broad avenues of
the city.   One of these, lined with poplars, extends far beyond
the city limits.   It is the popular riding-course.   It leads to
the summer palaces, to the mint, and to the mountain villas,
where the hot season is spent.   We took a ride along this
shaded avenue.   Within the city there were activity and bustle
everywhere, in preparation for the shah's return after some
months' absence.   The houses and walls were being festooned
and decorated with flags and bunting, arches were being
erected, the gates—especially that through which the shah was
to enter—were being adorned.   The work was under the
superintendence of the Austrian prefect of police.   The shah
was then at the palace called Negaristan, awaiting the com-

pletion of the preparations to receive him.   Passing by this
palace, we found admittance to the Takht-i-Kajar, a palace
built by Mohammed Shah on a hillside.   The building is
inferior, but the garden is dense with foliage and sparkling
with large fountains.   From its terrace a fine view is obtained
of the city and of the country beyond, as far as the royal
menagerie, the cemetery of the fire-worshipers, and the golden
domes of Shah Abdul Azim.

As we returned to the road an unusual sight greeted our
eyes, namely, the puff, puff of smoke from tall chimneys.   May
this forerunner of steam woolen factories in Persia have numerous successors !   The mint, too, puffed forth as honest smoke
as if the coin were not being badly debased in its fires.   We
were permitted to examine minutely the processes of the mint.
The metal was handled in the loosest fashion, the coin falling
down and rattling on the floor at our feet.   The work is now
in Persian hands, after having been started by Europeans.   It
is on so limited a scale that the whole process was easily
followed, until many a "sun-rising-behind-a-lion" appeared
bright and new before us.   The debasing of the coin has de-
preciated all manufactures of silver in Persia.   The transfer
from the Caspian to Teheran of the first steam-engine for the
mint was a matter of great difficulty.   It stuck in the mud
coming over the mountains, and there remained for a considerable time.   The first one brought into Azerbijan was drawn
on wheels with much trouble.   Lack of fuel, however, prevented its being utilized for purposes of irrigation in Kurdistan,
as was intended.

On another occasion a party of us went to Rhé, the site of
the ancient Rhages.   In its day it flourished contemporary
with Nineveh and Ecbatana, and was a prominent city under
Grecian, Parthian, and Arab supremacies.   It receives mention in the Zend-Avesta, and in Tobit and Judith, and was an
encampment of Alexander in his pursuit of Darius, and the

birthplace of Haroun-al-Raschid. It reached, in Mohammedan times, a population of a million and a half. Now it has
almost disappeared. Its site, about six miles from Teheran,
is for the most part cultivated fields. There still remains, however, a village named Shah Abdul Azim, in memory of the
saint who gave it its chief attraction. This is the mosque built
by him and containing his tomb. It is enriched by many and
costly gifts, and burial within its precincts is considered a privilege. The shrine is a great resort for the devout. Every
Friday, especially, crowds go there to worship. A railroad
has since been built to it—the first one erected in Persia. We
had merely time to gaze at its gold-covered dome, while we
busied ourselves in viewing the ruins of the ancient city. In
the midst of mounds of debris several strongly built towers
yet remain in different places, one with Cufic inscriptions of
comparatively late date. Over a ledge runs the line of the
old wall. Pieces of pottery, old coins, and ornaments are
occasionally found.

In the neighborhood were other objects of interest. Just
on the rock above a large fountain where we lunched there is
a carving in relief, after the manner of those made in ancient
times. This was made by Fath Ali Shah, and is a representation of himself and his counselors. Another represents him
on horseback in the chase, in the act of spearing a lion. The
present shah also has had such a monument made for himself,
in the Elburz Mountains, on the road to Resht—a sculpture in
relief of himself and his viziers.

The last sight of the afternoon was the cemetery of the
Guebers or fire-worshipers. It is a well-known fact that the
fire-worshipers do not burn or bury their dead, but expose
them in the open air to the ravages of birds and the influence
of the atmosphere. The few remaining adherents of this ancient religion continue the primitive custom. This cemetery,
far up on the hillside, can be seen from a great distance, be-

cause it is whitewashed.   Within the cemetery is a tower not more than fifty feet in diameter, with a circular wall about thirty feet high.   No door appears, nor is there any way of ascent.   A ladder is used at the time of the deposit and exposure of a body, and then removed.   By going farther up the hill we were able to see the grates upon which the bodies are laid, and through which the crumbling bones fall.   We saw no sign of the dead, though, and it is probable that the little community of three hundred do not often have occasion to form processions for the long march from the city to this "tower of silence."

CHAPTER IX

I VISITED Hamadan and Takht-i-Suleiman, the Median Ecbatanas, in 1892. I traversed the same road as in going to Teheran, as far as Zenjan. Thence to Hamadan the way is remarkable for little else than the number of shrines on it. It is one of the routes from Transcaucasia to Kerbela, and the shrines have been multiplied for the gratification of the pilgrims.

What an interesting sight it was when, on the thirteenth day's march, the snow-capped Alwand (ten thousand feet high) appeared with the city at its base, and the fertile plain stretching in front! Hamadan, the southern Ecbatana, the Achmetha of Ezra vi. 2, the capital of the Medes and Persians, renowned for its palace of Darius and Xerxes, and the tomb of Esther and Mordecai—how much history centers in it !

Hamadan has now about forty thousand inhabitants, a few of them Armenians, four thousand Jews, and the remainder Mohammedans. It lies sixty-one hundred and fifty-six feet above sea-level, and has a healthful climate, notwithstanding its filthy streets and malodorous surroundings. It is on the highway to Turkey, about forty-five miles from its border. It is the fourth city in the kingdom in commerce, and is especially noted for its leather. What antiquities has it? Excavations have not been made. What lies buried of the city captured by Cyrus, Alexander, and Antiochus the Great is unknown. It is even uncertain what descriptions in the classics or in the Book of Judith apply to this city. Our eyes, wandering in search of antiquities, discovered here and there a pillar or a carved slab; but it was hard to imagine, as we passed through the narrow, crooked, muddy streets, that this was the glorious capital of Media. The obliteration of the ancient grandeur has been very complete. During our stay our friends piloted us about and showed us the lions. One of these is such in no figurative sense. Just outside the city is a mammoth stone lion, said to be of the Median period. No wonder its eyes are dimmed and its outlines somewhat rubbed away by twenty-five hundred winters. The people regard the lion as a talisman against evil. On the same side of the city is the Hill of Ahasuerus, called Musallah, where the great palace, fourteen hundred and twenty yards in circumference, described by the Greeks, and the treasure-house of Ezra vi., are supposed to have stood. All the ruins that appear on it are modern, for it was leveled by Mohammed Shah.

Jewish peddlers brought us old coins, seals, arrow-heads, and teraphim, which had been found in the plain above the city. The ground is overspread with numbers of these small relics. The search for them is a systematic industry, farmed out by the government for revenue. The contractor buys the privilege by taking off the earth to the depth of a yard or more. Trenches are then dug. The soil is dissolved in water and flows into dams, where the heavy matter sinks. The gravel with the jewels, coins, and other relics is picked over, and the valuables separated. Many acres have thus been worked over. Sometimes valuable antiques are discovered.

One day we went a two hours' ride on horseback up the side of the Alwand (Orontes), to see the cuneiform inscriptions of Darius and Xerxes. They occur in a defile of the mountain, called the Ganj-Nama or "Treasure-writing," through which the ancient road to Babylon passed. The tradition

is that they tell where a great treasure is concealed, and whoever shall stand and read in audible voice the inscription shall
have opened before him the treasure deposit.   How true this
was!   For the Ganj-Nama with its trilingual inscription furnished the clue to the cuneiform alphabet, and so opened the
treasures of the libraries of Nineveh and other cuneiform literature.   Sir Henry Rawlinson, in his investigations, first examined the Hamadan inscriptions, and added to the letters of the
alphabet discovered by Grotefend and Lassen.   He was thus
enabled to begin the study of the language and to translate
the cuneiform inscriptions everywhere.

Preparatory to writing the Ganj-Nama, the red granite rock
was cut into and smoothed off.   The inscriptions are in two
tablets, each about five feet by six, with three columns of
writing, of twenty lines each.   They are written in Persian,
Median, and Babylonian.   The inscription on the left is
by Darius, and the other one by Xerxes.   The former is as
follows: "The great God Ormuzd, he it is who gave this
earth, who gave that heaven, who gave mankind, who gave
life to mankind, who made Darius king, as well as king of the
people, and the lawgiver of the people.   I am Darius, the
king, the great king, the king of kings, the king of nations,
the son of Hystaspes, the Achæmenian!"   The inscription of
Xerxes is almost word for word the same.

Similar and important inscriptions and figures commemorating Cyrus, Darius, and Xerxes are at Murghab or Pasargada,
Behistun, Persepolis, Naksh-i-Rustam, and Van.

Other sights of Hamadan are the tombs of Avicenna (Ibn-
Sînâ), the celebrated physician, and of Esther and Mordecai.   The latter stands in what was once a Jewish cemetery,
in the midst of the city.   A Mohammedan mob tore up the
other gravestones and leveled the surrounding ground, making
of it a public square.   The tomb which remained is an unpretentious structure, with a dome about thirty feet high.   It is

entered by a low door, made of a single stone moving in
sockets, in which the ends of the stone fit. The rabbi in
charge unlocked the door for us. The two tombs are covered
by wooden sarcophagi, carved with Hebrew sentences, and
black with age. Engraved stones, rescued from the old tomb
destroyed by Tamerlane, are placed in the walls. They are
eulogies of Mordecai and Esther. Under the framework
lamps burn continually. At one side is a place where pieces
of the Old Testament are thrown, too old for use, and too
sacred to destroy. This shrine is held in great veneration by
the Jews, who make pilgrimages to it, especially during the
feast of Purim. The tomb of Avicenna is ornamented with
stucco-work, which is said to be the most artistic in Persia.

On leaving Hamadan we had for a week almost continuous
rain and mud, and in the short November days it was not easy
to make our thirty or thirty-five miles a day. One must get
accustomed to many things in such a land as this. We became somewhat used to cholera, which prevailed more or less
through the region we passed. At Bejar the cemetery was
inside the town, so they had interred those smitten down
by the cholera near a village. The villagers, enraged and
alarmed, had disinterred the bodies, and the case had developed into a quarrel requiring government interference. In
one lodging there were two cases of measles in the next room;
in another three children had the smallpox, and before they
had recovered the parents celebrated the wedding of their
daughter with a feast for a hundred guests. At several places
we encountered the poison-bug, and had pustules on our skin
for some weeks.

A mishap to a fellow-traveler illustrated several points of
Mohammedan devotion. He was saying his morning prayers
by the roadside, having given his horse to another to hold,
and was facing Mecca. In the midst of his prayer he heard
sounds of horse's hoofs behind, but turning his head would

have invalidated his prayer. When he finished he looked around to find the man galloping over the field with his horse and three hundred dollars in money, which sum was in his saddle-bags.

Toward the end of a week we came to the district of Afshar, a name given from one of the seven Guzul Bashi tribes. Afshar is an interesting region historically and scientifically. Here Antony was defeated by the Parthians, and made good his retreat over the Sahend Mountains. Long before that time the Medes had their capital, the northern Ecbatana, at Takht-i-Suleiman. Our visit to this place was one of the pleasantest excursions of my Persian sojourn. Striking off the caravan road, we went higher and higher up the hills. From certain peaks there were visible wide regions of Kurdistan, very picturesque and grand. By noon we were nine thousand feet above sea-level. We lunched by the ruins of Takht-i-Suleiman. This means the "Throne of Solomon," and the popular idea is that Solomon, king of Israel, here held court, with the divs and jinns to do his service, and the birds as his messengers. On the neighboring peak, ten thousand feet high, called Takht-i-Balkis, they placed the palace of the queen of Sheba. There two hundred divs built her palace in a night, at the bidding of Solomon. She demanded a house made of the bones of birds, and thereby hangs the tale of how the owl outwitted Solomon. The wonderful rock formation on the hillside is supposed to be a great dragon, which came to attack the palace and was turned into stone, as it is at this day. At a short distance from the place is a "bottomless pit," where the divs were confined. Natives say that it goes through to the New World. Such is Takht-i-Suleiman in legend!

Historically it probably derived its present name from Suleiman Shah Abuh, of Kurdistan, who lived in the thirteenth century. Anciently it was the capital of the Medes, where

Cyrus deposited the wealth of Crœsus. Later it was called Ganzaca by the Greeks, Kandzag by the Armenians, and Shir by the Arabs. Pompey and Antony marched against it. Here Heraclius destroyed the celebrated fire-temple in which the image of Khosru was enthroned, and surrounded by emblems of the sun, moon, and stars. Here Bahrâm was attacked by Narses and Khosru Parviz. When the Arabs took it the jeweled throne of Kai Khosru was thrown into the lake. Rawlinson argues that it was Takht-i-Suleiman that Tobias of the Book of Tobit visited.*

This hill, where the palace of Deioces stood, is of peculiar formation. An active lime-sinter has been flowing copiously for ages, and has deposited the limestone on its side until it has formed a hill two hundred feet high and of large circumference. On the summit of this hill is a fountain or lake three hundred paces in circumference, of pleasant taste, clear and beautiful, and flowing strong enough to form a small creek. The stream has flowed to one side and made its deposit in a winding, serpent-like shape, from ten to twenty feet high and several yards wide. This formation, possibly an incrusted wall of the old defenses, is what the native imagination has called the petrified dragon. The fountain or lake was supposed to be bottomless; but an Afshar girl having thrown herself in because of disappointment in love, a chief ordered it to be sounded, and it was found to be about one hundred and sixty feet deep. Around the fountain the palaces were built, the walls of the fortifications encircling one another on the hillsides. The wall is three quarters of a mile in circuit and twelve feet thick. The solid masonry arches of a cellar are in a good state of preservation, with walls fifteen feet thick. Rawlinson thinks they are a part of the great fire-temple. A magnificent arch, tall as a four-story building, and covered

* " Journal Royal Geographical Society," vol. x.

with tiles and stucco-work, is the ruin of a palace or mosque built by Abaka Khan Mongol (A.D. 1281).

Some distance from these is another hill covered with curiously shaped limestone formations. We climbed its steep, rocky sides and looked down into the crater—an immense pit left by an extinct fountain of a lime-sinter. Its size is seventy feet by one hundred and twenty, and three hundred and fifty feet deep. Pigeons and other birds have built their nests in the recesses of the cone. Its bottom is dry, and a strong sulphurous smell exhales from it, appropriate indeed as coming from the prison of the divs. Another of these lime-sinters has formed quite a lake, on which is a floating island covered with grass.

In the process of these formations, and by volcanic action, there have been brought to the surface of this region mercury, arsenic, sulphur, and other minerals. During our visit Mr. David Ferguson, civil engineer, of Glasgow, with eight Englishmen, was there prospecting for the Mining Corporation. The accountant of the company was Mr. Galosd Vartan, an Armenian British subject, who is now secretary to the British consul-general at Tabriz. We were their guests over Sunday, and I preached to them. It was the first time a sermon had been heard in that region since old Nestorian times. Mr. Ferguson had been specially prospecting for cinnabar and mercury. They had sunk some shafts and got some samples. They found traces of the mines having been worked in bygone ages. By whom ? Mr. Ferguson named the horse he rode while investigating the region Cinnabar, and soon the Persians invented the story that the horse was very intelligent, and by smell or some other faculty knew where the mines should be opened, and led his master to the spot. An English mining-camp in Afshar gave us hope that soon the steam-engine might do greater work there than the divs of Solomon. But unfortunately the mercury failed to materialize in sufficient quantities, and the corps of workmen, after two years of mining, went back to England. The expenses for machinery and travel were heavy, and the engineer received five thousand and each artisan one thousand dollars a year. It is a matter of great regret that this effort to develop the resources of Persia did not succeed.

From Afshar we crossed the Pass of Mahi-Bulak to Sain-Kala. On the right of the road are the grottoes of Kereftu. They are a score of excavated rooms, with many winding passages. Over the entrance is a Greek inscription. Ker Porter, who described these grottoes in detail, supposed they were used for the initiation of neophytes into the religion of Zoroaster. Thence we came along the Jagatai River to Mianduab and back to Tabriz.

CHAPTER X

THE CONDITION AND NEEDS OF PERSIA

PERSIA in the past has been the scene of great historic events. As a "land of Oriental splendor" it has appealed to the imagination of the Western world. Persia to-day suffers by the contrast. Though much reduced in territory, it is still an extensive domain, extending seven hundred miles from east to west and nine hundred miles from north to south, and comprising six hundred and twenty-eight thousand square miles—a territory equal to France, Germany, Great Britain, and Ireland, with several of the smaller states of Europe, or to that part of the United States lying east of the Mississippi and north of Tennessee. But its uncultivated area is said to be three fourths of the whole, while one salt desert is as large as Great Britain, or as the States of New York and Pennsylvania. The central part of the country is an immense plateau, three hundred and forty thousand square miles in area, with an average altitude of thirty-seven hundred feet above the sea. The Elburz range bounds this central plateau on the north, and the Zagros on the west and center. These mountain-ranges are seven or eight thousand feet in altitude, and rise to such noble peaks as Ararat, Sahend near Tabriz, Savalan near Ardebil, Alwand near Hamadan, and Damavand near Teheran, all ranging from twelve thousand to eighteen thousand four hundred and sixty-five feet, and several of them covered with perpetual snow. On the other hand, the southern coast is a region of intense heat, the northern provinces

164

which border on the Caspian lying below ocean level and producing semi-tropical vegetation. The words of Cyrus to Xenophon are true of modern Persia: "People perish with cold at one point, while they are suffocated with heat at another."

The central plateau has a delightful climate. Its atmosphere has been pronounced "remarkable above that of all other countries for dryness and purity." The seasons come with healthful regularity. Tabriz has a climate of special excellence. The summer heat is moderated by a mountain breeze, which penetrates every nook and corner, purifies the air, and makes the nights delightfully cool; yet the atmosphere is so dry that sleeping in a draught is not injurious. Sunstroke is exceedingly rare.

A false impression concerning the heat of Persia prevails in Western lands, notwithstanding the fact that travelers have reported definitely concerning its winters. Rawlinson * speaks of snow to the depth of several feet, and of a keen wind, "the assassin of life." Ker Porter † says that "scarcely a day passes in winter without one or two persons being frozen to death in the neighborhood of Tabriz." In 1881 snow fell near Tabriz on September 13th. In Urumia sleighing has continued for as long as four months, the temperature at times reaching 7° F. below zero, and insuring a good crop of ice for the following summer's use.

Notwithstanding the wide extent of territory and the variety of climate possessed by Persia, it has been for some centuries in a state of weakness. It is but a shadow of the Persia of the past. Its population is small and sparse. Even its most fertile plains have no such diversity of population as is found in India or China. The total population is estimated at nine millions, of whom two millions are nomads. The races represented are Persians, Tartars or Turks, Kurds, and Lurs, with

* "History," vol. ii., p. 285. † "Travels," vol. i., p. 257.

about one hundred and fifty thousand Armenians, Nestorians, Jews, and Parsees.

It might be profitable to discuss the question whether this low condition of Persia is hopeless and irremediable. That can best be determined by considering whether the causes of its decline are in the land and the people, or in conditions and circumstances capable of change and amelioration. I believe the latter can be shown.

In the first place, the decline of Persia is not due to sterility of the soil. The cultivated parts of Persia are rich and productive. When irrigated it is only necessary "to tickle the soil with a hoe and it will laugh into harvests." Its wheat has been pronounced the best in the world. It produces also rice, barley, millet, and maize. Its gardens are famous. Its grapes and peaches (*Pomum Persicum*) are most luscious, and are, on the average, better than any I have known. Grapes in the bunch are hung in a dry place and kept until March. The other fruits largely cultivated are the apricot, nectarine, almond, pear, pomegranate, orange, lemon, mulberry, melon, *eda* or singian-date,* and the fig, all of which are of good quality, while the cherry, apple, plum, and some of the other fruits are of inferior flavor. The sunflower-seeds are used for food on the Caspian coast. Nuts and berries grow wild in the forests. Excellent honey is abundant. Most of the common garden vegetables are now cultivated, and a great variety of herbs are used. Sugar-cane is at home in southern Persia. Silk, tobacco, and opium are extensively grown. Cotton is a good crop,† and it is stated that enough cotton could be raised

---

* The *eda* is the size of a peanut. It is very abundant, and is the food of the poor. Though worth a cent per pound, one date was sold by an enterprising Persian at the Chicago Exposition for a dollar. Its leaf and blossom are very beautiful, and have a delightful perfume.

† Ten million pounds of cotton, eight million pounds of wool, and one million two hundred thousand dollars' worth of opium are yearly exported.

in Persia to supply the markets of western Europe. Flowers, both wild and cultivated, flourish in great beauty and variety. The domestic and wild animals of the temperate zone are also found in Persia. Trout are abundant in the mountain streams, and salmon and other fish provide a profitable industry in the tributaries of the Caspian. A country with such a climate and soil, and perfecting such products, certainly has capability.

Not a little of the uncultivated portion of Persia is desert, much in the same way as Colorado and California once were. Only irrigation is necessary to produce abundant fertility.

Nor is Persia lacking in mineral resources. These are as yet largely undeveloped; but coal, iron, lead, copper, arsenic, mercury, sulphur, asbestos, mica, marble, and manganese are found, and some of them are at present being mined. Gold-dust is found in the Jagatai River, and in the naphtha-springs near Bushire. The pearl-fisheries of the Persian Gulf are very productive, while the turquoise-mines of Khorassan are pronounced the richest in the world.

Nor is there any inherent lack of vitality in the people. The races show no exhaustion of energy; the men are strong and the women prolific, and freer from disease than their more civilized contemporaries. The Kurds, Lurs, and Tartar Turks have the usual vigor of mountain tribes accustomed to nomadic life. The peasants are sturdy, healthy, and inured to hardship. The men of the cities have fine physiques and good constitutions. The rate of mortality among infants is high. Perhaps not one in six survives; indeed, it is said that not one in ten reaches maturity. This mortality is due to no racial decline, and could be largely remedied. Nature carries on the struggle for existence against the neglect, ignorance, and indifference of parents. Exposure, improper clothing, injudicious diet, and other breaches of sanitary laws, carry off the children to early graves.

The present inhabitants of Persia, like those of Europe, have had the advantage of a mixture of blood.   Over the lands of the Medes and Persians and Parthians have swept Arabs, Seljuks, Turkomans, Mongols, and Turks in their successive incursions and conquests.   Iran and Turan have been commingled.   The last hordes from the steppes of Central Asia have left the most distinct mark and retain the ascendancy, the ruling Kajar dynasty being of Tartar-Turkish extraction. The present people is the resultant of the fusion of these many elements through a long series of years.   Their physiognomy is a mixed one.   Just as the Osmanlis have been improved in beauty by the mixture of Georgians and Circassians, so the Tartar Turks of northern Persia have been refined by admixture with the Persians.   In color they are slightly darker than Anglo-Saxons, of medium height, with prominent but, on the whole, agreeable features.

Famine and earthquake have had some effect in keeping down the population of Persia.   But the former is due to unscientific agriculture and to a lack of proper and extended irrigation, together with a want of good facilities for transportation.   The famine of 1879 was partly caused by the substitution of the culture of opium for grain.   The ravages of locusts caused a scarcity of food in Karadagh in 1890.   The central plateau of Persia is volcanic, and scarcely a year passes without some shocks of earthquake.   Frequently these seismic shocks are severe enough to cause walls and houses to crack and crumble, burying numbers beneath them.*   Sometimes they are overwhelming disasters.   On November 17, 1893, an earthquake destroyed every house in Kuchan, Khorassan.   On that occasion twelve thousand persons were killed, out of a population of twenty or twenty-five thousand, and fifty thousand head of cattle perished.   Within a week one hundred and sixty distinct shocks were felt.   The town had been partially rebuilt when it was again destroyed in January, 1895.

* This was the case in Tabriz, August 2, 1874, and again in May, 1883.

One hundred women in a bath-house were crushed to death. Survivors suffered severely from the intense cold. Notwithstanding these calamities, earthquakes are neither severe nor frequent enough to count as an important factor in the problem of population.

Nor is the backward state of Persia due to any intellectual feebleness. The Persians have alert, active minds. They are untrained and unscientific, but naturally intelligent, subtle in argument, sharp in business, skilful in imitation, artistic in execution, socially entertaining, fond of humor, delighting in poetry and music, and remarkably well informed for their limited opportunities. Persian art and civilization gave birth to Arab culture in Bagdad and Spain, with its philosophy, mathematics, amd architecture. Persian poets have sung in immortal verse. Henry Martyn's estimate of them was: "They are a people clever and intelligent, and more calculated to become great and powerful than any of the other nations of the East." Minister Benjamin remarks: "Persia, if the powers would let her alone, has vitality enough to carry her to another epoch of national greatness."

Nor is there lack of ability in the rulers of Persia. Nazir-i-Din, the present shah, is a man of marked talent, great energy, strong grasp of the details of administration, fine discernment in politics, alert to the demands of the times, and with an earnest desire for the progress of the realm. Coming to the throne in 1848, at the age of nineteen, he has had a lengthened reign, characterized by peace, progress, and prosperity, which has few equals in the annals of Persia.

I saw the shah when he passed through Tabriz *en route* for Europe on the occasion of his last visit. His Majesty traveled with an immense caravan, miles in extent. He is said to have had eighteen hundred horses and mules and four thousand soldiers in his retinue, with all the necessary instruments, even to the bastinado, for administering punishment. Two sets of tents and appurtenances were used, one set being forwarded and made ready for his Majesty's arrival, while he leisurely remained at ease in the other. He rode in a carriage over the stretches of good road, and took to horseback over the rough or mountainous regions. Three weeks were occupied in his progress from the capital to the border. Great preparations were made at Tabriz for his arrival: "The way was prepared, the crooked made straight, and the rough places smooth." Bridges were repaired, streets cleaned and paved, many walls rebuilt and whitened, shops adorned, and thousands of street lamps put up before the houses, so that the city was for the first time brilliantly lighted. A triumphal arch was erected at the head of the avenue (Kheaban) entering from Teheran. It was covered with flags and bunting, together with the national emblems—the Lion and the Sun. The base was covered with sod, in which pots of gay flowers were placed. The crown prince, the governor-general, and many of the officials, with their retinues, went four days' journey to meet the shah. He entered the city, in the gaze of thousands of his subjects, adorned with jewels and decorations, and accompanied by a retinue brilliant with colors and gold. Foreign residents who went out to meet him were saluted most graciously. A group of Christians, chiefly Armenians, presented an address to his Majesty, and sang songs of welcome. At night there were illuminations and fireworks all over the city. On the next day there was a military review in the Medan-i-Mashk, or drill-ground. The shah alighted from his carriage, walked into the *medan*, answered the salute of the soldiers, and then took his position on the stand to witness the evolutions. He was dressed in a plain black suit, and the Vali Ahd in one of grayish blue. The uniformed officers were splendidly mounted. General von Wagner, the Austrian drill-master, rode along the lines with sword drawn, and giving his orders in a stentorian voice. The results of his painstaking efforts to improve the royal army were evident.

After the review a company of acrobats, dressed in red and yellow, gave a gymnastic exhibition. While the review was in progress we had a good view of the shah. He had a truly royal mien, filling the popular ideal. His appearance was more youthful, and his strength greater, than one expected to find in a man past sixty, who had borne the cares of empire for over twoscore years.

On the following night the city was again illuminated, and the sky bright with pyrotechnics. Around the edges of the flat roofs of the houses little earthen bowls were placed and filled with flaxseed or castor oil, and with wicks of twisted cotton. Their light made the city brilliant. On the morrow a great crowd poured out on the road to get a glimpse of the royal party.

The Vali Ahd or crown prince of Persia is Muzaffir-i-Din, the eldest son of the shah by a royal mother. He has never been tried by the great responsibilities of government, so that his capacity is largely unknown. One marked characteristic of the prince is his religious disposition. He is a man of faith, free from the rationalistic tendencies of some of the ruling class. He is devout in his fulfilment of religious rites, and a total abstainer from intoxicants. He has a humane and sympathetic nature. The mother of a condemned man can appeal to him with large assurance of mercy. He is a friend of education, taking a great interest in the government school at Tabriz, having European tutors for the education of his sons, and encouraging his interpreters to translate standard works into Persian. He is much interested in telegraphy, photography, and like practical arts. He has a fondness for flowers and for new and rare plants, and enjoys tent life and the pleasures of the chase, often camping with his retinue on the mountains.

For some years the Zil-i-Sultan, the eldest son of the shah and the governor of Ispahan, was regarded as a rival of the Vali Ahd for the succession. But the disfavor of the shah, and later an affliction of blindness, have removed this possibility. When word of the critical condition of the Zil-i-Sultan's eyes reached Tabriz the Vali Ahd sent word to the mosques announcing the fact, and requesting that prayers be offered for his brother. The Vali Ahd has lately strengthened himself by the marriage of his children with some of the most powerful nobles of the realm.

One of these royal weddings attracted special attention, and furnished an interesting exhibition of how such events are conducted in Persia. This was the wedding of Izat-i-Sultanah (the "Glory of the Kingdom"), the eldest son of the Vali Ahd, with Malaka-i-Jehan (the "Queen of the World"), a daughter of the Naib-i-Sultanah, minister of war and son of the shah. The marriage contract was executed by proxy at Teheran, in the presence of the shah. The princess was brought to her royal husband in a *takhtarevan* (moving throne), covered with a rich Persian shawl, and was accompanied by a military guard and a caravan of one hundred and forty pack-animals, loaded with a dowry of the finest articles of the land. On her approach to Tabriz a letter was sent to the prince announcing her arrival, and he went out to meet her. There was a great *peeshvaz* and popular reception. The bazaars were closed by order of the government. The consuls, officials, and the whole city went out to meet the cavalcade. In the midst of the gaiety an untoward incident occurred. The prince—master of ceremonies—accused another prince of pressing too near the carriage of the princess, and ordered him to be beaten on the spot.

The princess was conducted to the palace in the Bagh-i-Shamal or "Prince's Garden." A week of festivities followed. These had two centers: one at the Bagh-i-Shamal, in charge of Prince Ayn-i-Doulah, the other in the city palace, in charge of General Nazm-i-Sultanah. These officers spared no expense in making the occasion one of unusual magnificence. Feasts were held for different classes on successive days. First the princes and highest officials, then the mollas, followed by the consuls and foreign officials and the wealthy classes in general, were fêted. Music and acrobatic entertainments were part of the festivities, except on the day when the mollas were invited. Free dinners and tea were served to the public. Magnificent presents were made by the nobles. It was reported that the Zil-i-Sultan sent a gift of ten thousand tomans, and other officials one or two thousand gold pieces. Seven or eight arches were erected by prominent noblemen, spanning the road through which the wedding procession must pass in going from the Bagh-i-Shamal to the residence of the Izat-i-Sultanah. The arches were covered with bunting, flags, and transparencies inscribed with mottoes from the poets. They were ornamented with glassware, lamps, and lanterns. The nobles vied with one another in making this display, expending on it, it was said, forty thousand tomans. Tea was freely served under these arches, while the " Prince's Garden " was gaily decorated and thrown open to the public.

On the wedding night the élite gathered on the line of the procession. The princess, completely veiled, after the custom of the country, and with a French bridal veil over all, was seated in a closed carriage, and escorted by the crown prince and a company of soldiers, amid a display of fireworks and an immense concourse of people, who thronged the streets and looked down from the roofs. When they reached their destination the crown prince presented the bride to the young prince. On the following days festivals were continued in the palace and among the ladies of the harems.

From this digression regarding royal persons and customs I return to the consideration of the ability of the shah as a ruler, and will now present some facts concerning Persia during his reign.

The shah has steered the ship of state in comparatively peaceful waters. While neighboring countries have been convulsed with great wars, Persia has been slightly disturbed. The expedition of the English (1853) on the Persian Gulf did not assume large proportions. The Afghan War and the siege of Herat brought little trouble to Persia. The insurrection of the Babis, and a few raids of the Kurds and Turkomans, complete the list of the country's troubles. Persian territory practically remains the same, while Turkey has meanwhile been bereft of many and populous provinces. The island of Ashorabad and a part of northern Khorassan have passed to Russia, while the district of Kutur was recovered by Persia by the treaty of Berlin. The definite settlement of the boundaries has tended greatly to preserve peace. The present situation is in striking contrast with the state of things that prevailed in the eighteenth century, when Persia was in perpetual anarchy, and when for a period of fifty years the throne was occupied by eight shahs, while large provinces were temporarily torn from the kingdom by rebellious khans.

The enlargement of the diplomatic intercourse of Persia has been marked. In addition to the envoys from England, France, Russia, and Turkey, there have been added the Austro-Hungarian, German, Dutch, and American, while the representatives of the shah are now stationed at the important European capitals. The shah has formed treaties of commerce with the great nations of the world, and the rights and privileges of foreigners have been guaranteed. The importation of African or Arabian slaves has been discountenanced, and treaty engagements have been entered into with England for the abolition of such trade on the Persian Gulf. Commerce has advanced with huge strides. Notwithstanding many drawbacks, the reign has been one of greater commercial enterprise than Persia has seen for centuries. The volume and variety of both imports and exports have increased. Regular

اداره تلکرافی دولت علیّهٔ ایران

...

۱۳۲
سنه

این از روی صه تبریر

اطلاعات	تاریخ اصل طلب		عدد کلمات	نمره
	دقیقه	ساعت	روز	۹	۱۰

وسون صاحب تکراف بیت دیشم، اوکوست نرسید هرکرو

بواسطهٔ تلکرافخانه	کرفته شد		کبرلهٔ مطلب
تاریخ ۲۴	شهر دی لکراف ساعت دقیقه		میرزا مهدی خان

PERSIAN TELEGRAM.

steam communication from the Caspian Sea and Persian Gulf ports has facilitated traffic. A system of custom-houses, no more annoying than those of other lands, has been established. A royal mint, run by steam, has given a more uniform system of coinage. The letter-post has been much perfected. In the time of Cyrus, and also in the time of the Mongol Gazan Khan, letter-carriers went with frequent changes of horses over the royal highways; but this, I imagine, was largely on official business. The first American missionaries received their letters in Urumia by sending a messenger to Tabriz once a month, to bring the mail which had been forwarded from Constantinople by English courier. Since then connection has been made with the International Postal Union. The issuing of stamps was begun in 1877, and post-offices have been established in all the chief cities and towns of the kingdom. They now number ninety-five. A fairly good system is in operation. It sometimes lags, as in the winter of 1893, when it took five days to carry the mail between Urumia and Tabriz, a distance of one hundred and twenty-five miles. The mail from the United States reaches Tabriz in four weeks. Eight mails arrive weekly from different directions.

The telegraph system was introduced in Persia by the Indo-European Telegraph Company. After extending it from London through Germany and Russia, it enters Persia at Julfa, and goes through Tabriz to Teheran, where it meets the Indian government line. The Persian government has the privilege of putting wires on the company's iron posts. The telegraph has since been extended to every important place in the kingdom, and two lines connect with Turkey, making in all a telegraph service of forty-one hundred and fifty miles. It has become one of the great institutions of government. Its officers are given rank as colonels and generals. They are the shah's special and trusted agents. They must make daily reports to him, giving an account of all the events of their

district or city.   The slightest disturbance is immediately reported to the capital.   A restraint is thus put upon oppression,
for a governor never knows how much may pass over the
wires.   Much government business is carried on by telegraph.
A governor is even called to the telegraph-office, and the shah
from the other end of the line consults with and directs him
in detail.   Moreover, the telegraph-office is a quasi place of
refuge.   Any one having an appeal from a governor or other
official to present to the shah can take refuge at the telegraph-
office, send a direct petition, and remain in security until his
answer is received.   This is exemplified by a circumstance
that happened when the export duty on raisins was increased
arbitrarily at Tabriz.   The leading Armenian merchants, representing an annual trade of hundreds of thousands of tomans,
proceeded to the telegraph-office and remained until their
grievance was redressed.   When Fath Ali Shah died in Ispahan
in 1834, the news by swift royal courier was two weeks in
reaching the heir-apparent in Tabriz, and rival claimants had
time to prepare for revolt.   Now the death of the shah could
be communicated instantly to the Vali Ahd by telegraph connecting with his own palace.

The telegraph is not kept in the best repair, and sometimes
days are required for an answer.   On the road through Ghilan
the wires are attached to trees, whose movement, dampness,
etc., often interfere with communication.   The London "Times"
says that a telegram was sent from London announcing that a
high official from Europe would reach Resht in a fortnight.
The telegram was received the same day in Teheran by the
European line, and delivered to the Persian line to be forwarded.   The official arrived in Resht, and the telegram was
received in his presence eighteen days after its despatch!

Very little has been accomplished in the way of providing
railways for Persia.   A line six miles long, from the capital to
the shrine of Shah Abdul Azim, was opened in July, 1888.

One was started from Mahmoudabad, on the Caspian, to Amol, twenty-five miles distant. I believe only twelve miles of it were finished. It was a calamity for Persia that the Reuter concession could not be carried out, for by this time Persia would have had its territory bisected with railways, and its resources developed. On the Shah Abdul Azim road an accident occurred in 1888, shortly after the railway was opened. A Mohammedan got on the train without a ticket. Instead of paying his fare he jumped off and was killed. A crowd, headed by a molla, and incensed that this foreign machine should kill a Mohammedan, attacked the engineer and fatally wounded him. In his dying struggles he drew his revolver and shot the molla. The mob destroyed the engine and part of the track. The foreign ministers laid claim for damages. The road had been built by a Belgium company, and the engineer was a Russian. Damages were fixed at one hundred and twenty thousand dollars, with an allowance for the expenses of the road during the time it remained idle; and a pension of twelve hundred dollars a year was granted to the widow of the engineer.

There is a tramway in the city of Teheran, and a hundred and fifty miles of carriage-road branch out from the capital, while a few hundred carriages have been imported by the nobility. The mining of coal at Teheran, the use of Russian petroleum throughout the country, and gas and electric light in the public squares of the capital, are all signs of progress. Knowledge also has advanced—knowledge of medicine, of geography, and of the world at large—while photography and dentistry are prosecuted as successful arts in the large cities. Mechanical arts, including working in wood and iron, have also developed. The standard of education has been raised by the founding of the royal college at Teheran, and other advanced schools in Tabriz and Ispahan. A ministry of the press has been established since the shah's last visit to Europe.

Several newspapers are published in the capital. The "Iran" is the official organ of the government; the "Scherif" is illustrated with pictures of prominent officials in Persia and in Europe. Other papers are the "Itila," "Tarhenk," and "Teheran," devoted to politics and literature. In Tabriz several attempts have been made to found a Persian paper. In 1878 the "Ruznama-i-Tabriz" was started, and subscriptions paid up. Only four numbers, however, were issued, for the Vali Ahd suppressed it, saying that he did not want all the bad things that were happening published. Another paper in 1881 had a brief existence. Still another, called the "Naziri," was founded in 1894. For fifty years the "Rays of Light" has been published by the American Mission at Urumia in modern Syriac. The "Shavig," in Armenian, was established in 1894 in Teheran.

Another encouraging fact is the growth of population in Persia in the last fifty years. In nearly every community careful inquiry establishes the fact of an extension of the population. Teheran in 1800 had fifteen thousand inhabitants; now it is reported to have two hundred and ten thousand. Tabriz has also increased in population. Drs. Smith and Dwight reported it in 1832 as containing sixty thousand inhabitants, with sixty or seventy families of Armenians. Sir Ker Porter, in tracing the limits of the inhabited city, says that the ruins extended three miles to the northeast and two miles to the southwest of the Kala. The places described as ruins are now occupied by dwellings. The city is estimated to have a present population of from one hundred and fifty thousand to one hundred and eighty thousand.

Having shown that Persia has made some progress of late years, and that its backward condition is not due to an adverse climate, to sterility of soil, lack of natural resources, exhaustion of race-vitality, intellectual feebleness in its people, nor to incapacity in its rulers, let me point out some things which

Persia needs to make its progress more rapid and to ameliorate its condition.

One urgent need is the development of internal improvements. The country must be thoroughly irrigated. Occasionally a summer cloud-burst will cause a flood to pour through the village streets and into the yards, carrying off the sheep and throwing down the walls. Elsewhere, save in the Caspian Sea basin, the rainfall is not sufficient in most districts between the middle of June and the end of September. Reservoirs must be built to retain the spring freshets for summer use. Artesian wells should be bored. What has been done in California and in Colorado, by the French in Algeria, by the English in Egypt, and by the Russians in the Transcaspian province, the Persian government must do in its own territory. Thousands of square miles could thus be redeemed for cultivation. Nor would the expense be beyond the power of the government, and would soon be covered by the sale of the redeemed lands. A change of land-tenure would also be beneficial, by which the *ryots* or peasants would be enabled to buy the village lands from the landlords, subdivide them, and pay the taxes directly to the government. Improvement in agricultural implements is greatly needed. The plow of the days of Xerxes no longer suffices. Wagon-roads and railroads must be encouraged, even by the granting of subsidies, if necessary. A great mistake is made in compelling capital, whether foreign or native, to fee numerous officials for the privilege of initiating new enterprises. Concessions should be given, with a subsidy and land grant, as in our great West, in the northwest of Canada, and in other countries, rather than that decades should pass with the country undeveloped.

Again, the development of Persia depends upon certain political reforms being accomplished. Official corruption is universally prevalent. Governors, judges, and minor officials now must give presents to obtain their appointments and to retain their posts year by year.   They have no fixed salaries, and consequently live by fees from litigants and even criminals, and otherwise reimburse themselves.   The expenses of governors are greatly increased by custom.   Their establishments must be on a grand scale and at their own expense.   A great retinue and large stables are needed to maintain the customary pomp.   They must provide lavish entertainment daily for many persons.   The Amir-il-Askar, a governor of Tabriz, once said to a petitioner, " If your business is about the army, go to such a one; if about the taxes, go to such another one," etc., naming all the departments; "but if you want a breakfast I am at your service.   Entertaining is my business."   Legitimate fees are not enough to enable such a host of officers to keep up large establishments.   The result is great corruption and bribery, and the sale of justice to the highest bidder.   There should be fewer officials, and they should be paid such salaries as to make them independent of bribery and peculation.   The Amir-i-Nizam, Hussein Ali Khan, by concentrating much power in his own hands, was enabled to maintain the customary dignity, and at the same time befriend the poor.   At a time when the bakers combined to increase the price of bread he summoned them and imposed fines upon them.   When their supply of wheat was scanty he opened his own granaries and sold at a low price, that all the people might have cheap bread.   He also summoned the grain merchants and landlords, and asked, " Why have you made a corner in the people's bread ? " They replied, "We have no grain."   He said, " Will you put your seal to a paper certifying that you have none ? "   They were afraid to do so, lest when their grain was found it would be confiscated, so they concluded to sell to the people at a lower price.

The number of nobles, with the title of khan, holding an office or drawing a pension, or expecting one, is legion.   Some of these belong to the landed aristocracy; a few have earned their titles by meritorious service; the remainder have no just claim, and have bought their titles and pensions. Caste does not exist in Persia. Men can readily change their social status. A ballet-dancer was the favorite wife of Fath Ali Shah. The son of a fellah may be vizier to-morrow. Hadji Baba, the water-carrier, in Morier's inimitable story, became minister to England. Lowly birth is not a bar to the highest position. Filthy lucre can purchase any title of nobility. An adventurer presenting a rifle to a prince is dubbed khan. A carpenter, tailor, or photographer is paid for his services with a title. It costs only a few cents' worth of paper and a half-hour's writing. The transaction is still more profitable for the officials if one hundred tomans are paid by an applicant for the additional honor of a rank in the army. The rank and title bring no salary or pension to the recipient; these must come as the result of another bargain. The titled nobles long since outnumbered the salaries, and a host of hungry applicants are awaiting the first vacancy. When the incumbent dies the heir must give a large sum to procure the continuance of the title and salary. This usually amounts to one year's salary. If this largess is not forthcoming the post is given to the highest bidder among the hungry expectants. Even then there is many a slip between the cup and the lip. A certain khan was informed that a salary could be obtained. He sent his present to the capital, and received an elaborate firman entitling him to the salary. On presenting it to the revenue officer he was informed that the heir had already obtained it. Vain efforts were made for another vacancy. He then asked for the return of his money, but was informed that it had been spent in procuring the firman—in other words, it had been distributed among the officials; he would be remembered the next time, in Sha Allah.*

---

* A title of some kind is more necessary in Persia because of the lack of a family name. Even Ibn or Ben ("son of") is not much used. Some are familiarly called "uncle" or "brother"; others are distinguished by

If this purchase of salaries and titles were confined to irre-
sponsible sinecures it would be bad enough ; but rank and promotion in the army are auctioned off in the same way.   A
young fellow, the son of a mirza or scribe, burglarized his
father's cash-drawer, ran off to Teheran, and came back in a
few months as a sultan or captain * in the ordnance department,
about which he knew nothing.   Civil officers, if the whim so
seizes them, make an adequate payment and are forthwith
dubbed colonel or general in the army, liable for duty at any
moment.   Having secured the position by pelf, they proceed
to reimburse themselves by *mudakhil* from the rank and file.
The money devoted to the army is not allowed to reach its
destination ; the soldiers are poorly paid, and the ordnance
and commissariat unprepared.   Apropos of this is a conun-
drum which a soldier asked of a prince : "What is it that has
a name, but no existence ? "   The prince gave it up.   "My
wages," said the soldier.   In 1826, in preparation for the
Russians, fifty thousand tomans had been devoted to the re-
furnishing of the arsenal.   When war came few bullets were to
be found, and these were not suitable for the guns, and even
the city of Tabriz could not supply lead for the purpose.   The
army is recruited from the villages and the wandering tribes.
Certain districts are obliged to furnish and support a certain
number of soldiers, and the tribes, in case of war, are called

their trade or occupation, as Saraf, banker; Farash, policeman; Ustad,
master mechanic; others, still, by their religious office, as Sheik, Molla,
or by their pilgrimage, as Hadji, Meshedi.   The official world has an in-
finity of titles conferred by the shah, indicating some relation to the
government, by the use of the words Doulah, Mulk, and Sultanah, as the
Eye of the Government, the Guide or the Righteousness of the State, the
Faithful of the Sultan.   Physicians receive their titles such as the Sword,
the Confidence, the Fidelity of the Physicians.

  * The Persians, as if in ridicule of the Osmanlis, name every captain a
sultan ; while the Turks retaliate by calling every general a pasha or padishah, the title of the king of Persia.

upon for a contingent. The officers of the army have adopted the Austrian uniform, with its short coat.* I had a good opportunity of seeing the action of the Persian army shortly after the Kurdish raid. Ten thousand troops were reviewed near Tabriz, and took part in a sham battle. Their tents were pitched near the " Prince's Garden," and the battle-scene was on the plain beyond. The sadr-um-mulk or agent of foreign affairs had prepared a large tent on a hillside. It was richly curtained, and carpeted with fine rugs, and furnished with chairs and a table covered with refreshments. The consuls had been invited to be present and to bring their friends. Mr. Abbott, the British consul, extended to us the courtesy of an invitation. For a while we watched with a glass the throng of people. They covered the plain and surrounding hills, prepared for a grand *tamesha* (show). Their number was estimated at thirty thousand. Squatted on the ground, they presented a patchwork of many colors. Their holiday coats of blue, green, yellow, and white decorated the hillsides. Richly caparisoned horses added to the scene. Their saddle-cloths were fine rugs or embroidered broadcloths. Some were wrought with silk and gold, and bordered with gilt fringes and tassels. No tables in America are more richly covered than were these steeds of the nobility of Persia. Their heads, too, were adorned with silver bands and jewels; one horse had a neck-band of solid gold, set with turquoises. The general excelled all, in that his belt of gold was set with pearls and diamonds.

The uniform of the common soldier is a navy-blue cotton cloth, with red stripes. The cavalry horses had crimson cloth

---

* Indeed, the whole official class, following the shah, have discarded the old-style long robes, and are dressed in coats and pantaloons, very much after the European style. Greater fullness in the skirt of the coat is the only marked difference; this is better adapted to their method of sitting on the floor. When Fath Ali Shah cultivated a long beard, the official class followed him in that style. Since the present shah has confined himself to a mustache, most of the nobles have done likewise.

184 *PERSIAN LIFE AND CUSTOMS*

on their breasts, and their tails were dyed crimson. The manœuvers need not be told in detail. The enemy was lying on an adjoining hill, with picket-lines out. The opposing corps attacked them. After sufficient shamming and much noise of battle, a double-quick charge was made, and the enemy's position captured. The soldiers and the band (trained in European style) struck up a song of triumph and marched back to their tents.

The Persian army numbers, nominally, one hundred and five thousand men; the actual standing army is twenty-four thousand five hundred. The soldiers are fine material. They are hardy, able to endure long marches, live on poor food, and suffer much privation. General W. von Wagner and other foreigners who have drilled them speak in high praise of them; but efforts for their discipline are rendered futile by the dishonesty of their officers. Until there is a reform of dishonest methods Persia cannot hope for true prosperity, either in its army or in its civil service.

Again, Persia would be highly benefited by a codification of the civil law, with a definite code of punishments. Too much is left to the caprice or humor of the *hakim*, who is both governor and judge. According to his state of digestion, the decision may be death or release. The most common punishment is a fine. Even murder is compounded for blood-money, with the consent of the victim's friends. A life is valued at as low as fifty dollars. Imprisonment is not for fixed times. The prisons are foul and damp. The dungeons are full of insects and vermin. The threat of putting a prisoner in the dungeon is often used to extort money. The prisoners are not separated, and often engage in vile and abominable practices. If friends bring food, tobacco, etc., the jailer shares the benefit of what is brought them. Otherwise, occasionally only, bread and water are provided for the prisoners. A common punishment is the bastinado. The feet are fixed in a board, raised in the air, and beaten until so many "sticks" are broken on them. The *lex talionis*—an eye for an eye, etc.—is sometimes enforced. Amputation of the hand, hamstringing, decapitation, shooting, pulling limb from limb, are in use. In Maragha the governor had the right hands of some thieves cut off, and the noses of some drunkards bored. The chief of police put ropes through their noses, held aloft their amputated hands, and led the men through the bazaar, as a warning to evildoers. Aziz Khan walled up fourteen robbers, two of them with their heads downward, and left them to perish. Some looties had been pursuing a system of blackmail, sending word to certain persons that if they did not give certain sums of money they would be murdered. The rogues were finally captured and imprisoned in Urumia. After being tortured for some days they were taken to the gate of the city, where a hole was dug, into which they were placed alive, two head downward and the other head upward; then lime-mortar was poured around their bodies, the head of one and the feet of the others being left above-ground, as a warning to others. When a Kurd was buried alive, head down, in the *medan* at Maragha, I asked the reason for it. A bystander said to me, "So that his spirit may not get out." The celebrated missionary, Raymond Lull, was put to death in Algeria in this manner.

In Tabriz, in 1887, a robber-chief, who had been fined several times to the amount of ten thousand tomans, and did not cease his crimes, was again captured and blown from the mouth of a cannon. His scattered fragments could be seen in the court-yard of the governor's palace.

The Babis were regarded as heretics. One of their apostles was sentenced to death by a mujtehid. First his ears were cut off; then he was struck a blow with an axe on the head, causing death. His head was then severed from his body, and an order given that the corpse be burned. This not being done, it was cut in pieces and scattered about in a field. On one occasion the tables were turned, when the Babis captured a Persian leader who had pretended to be a Babi.   They first skinned him alive and then roasted him.

Punishments are often inflicted publicly to deter from crime. I have seen the headless trunk of a criminal lying before the gaze of all in the public square.   Some notorious robbers were killed in the gardens of Tabriz after a skirmish with the police. Their bodies were brought to the square and strung up before the eyes of the people, and fired at as targets.

Torture, including the bastinado and even worse penalties, is resorted to to compel confession of crime.   I have heard of one governor ordering a lighted candle to be held under the beard, burning it and scorching the chin; of another who ordered the flesh to be pierced with holes and lighted candles inserted. These punishments are inflicted notwithstanding the fact that the shah has issued a firman prohibiting the torture of criminals.

The shah has modified some other customs for the better. The fall of a prime min'ster was, at the beginning of the present reign, a prelude to his speedy execution; but a more enlightened policy has since prevailed, and a vizier may now hope to retire and retain his head.   The title of sadr-azam or grand vizier was revived January 27, 1893, and given to the Amin-i-Sultan, Mirza Ali Askar Khan.

Another great need to insure the country's prosperity is a defining of the powers of the civil and religious authorities, securing harmony between the state and the hierarchy, that they may unitedly promote the higher civilization of Persia. Now they are semi-independent and often antagonistic.   The mollas and kadis (gazis) interpret and administer the canon law (Shari), including the Koran and traditions, as explained in another chapter.   The civil officers administer the Urf, or civil law, the will of the king.   Conflict of jurisdiction is common.   Persia is sometimes called an absolute monarchy.   It might as properly be called a limited monarchy.   It has not a

THE BASTINADO.

constitution in the European sense; but it has the canon law and constitutions as found in the Koran and written traditions, which are accepted devoutly by the mass of the people, and enforced by the mollas and mujtehids, under control of the chief mujtehid at Kerbela in Turkey, who lives beyond the jurisdiction of the shah. The priesthood in Persia, as for the most part in all countries, are intensely conservative. Projects for the improvement of the country have to run the gauntlet of their opposition, and are often baulked. Some priests have the erroneous idea that European commercial enterprises are in some way aimed at their religion. They are not convinced that a good net profit is all that European capital cares for, and that it is indifferent to religious questions. If the priesthood could be restricted, or rather if they were willing to confine their operations to the sphere of religion and morality, the government of Persia would make more rapid progress.

Another need in Persia is of popular education. Mr. Curzon expresses the opinion reiteratedly that the regeneration and civilization of Persia lie in the school. I had been led by the accounts of some travelers to expect to find schools universal, and primary education the heritage of all males. There are many schools which give a conventional training in the three R's; but in the cities readers are in the minority, and in many villages only two or three men can read, while a woman who can read is very rare. The schools are in the mosques, and the molla is the teacher. He seems to require every child to make as much noise as possible, under pain of a rap if for a moment he ceases to add to the general hubbub. Persian and Arabic are the languages taught. The Koran is read more often with the eye than with the understanding. Some familiarity with the Persian poets is acquired. Though deficient in school education, the upper classes are intelligent and quite well informed. It is sometimes surprising to find how much information in science, history, and the world's doings they have obtained without instruction or much reading. With ampler opportunities they would make rapid progress. They have the desire for education, and would gladly crowd the mission schools did the government permit. The crown prince has a school in Tabriz, with sixty scholars gathered from the best families of the city. Many of the students are preparing for public service, and are supported by the government. Persian, Arabic, French, and Russian, with the elements of the sciences, are taught. The school is in charge of the nadim-bashi or "chief of conversationalists." The medical department has several professors, who have graduated at Teheran under European instructors. Dr. W. S. Vanneman, the American missionary, was asked to give medical instruction in this school, but his other duties did not permit. The graduates in medicine are for the most part given appointments in the army. Others enter the civil service. The diplomas are issued in the form of medals of brass, silver, and gold, according to the degree. Worthy graduates also receive the title of khan.

Above all, Persia needs a moral transformation and an intellectual stimulus through those influences of Christianity which have made European and American civilizations so progressive and beneficent.

CHAPTER XI

AMONG the Persians, as among all Mohammedans, time is reckoned by the lunar year. The twelve months of alternately twenty-nine and thirty days make three hundred and fifty-four days—a difference of eleven or, in leap years, twelve days from the solar year. On this account all the fasts and feasts and anniversaries rotate through the different seasons. The only exception is the festival of the New Year or Noruz, which, being fixed at the vernal equinox, falls on a different date in each succeeding year. A child born on Noruz will not have a birthday anniversary within a week of that festival until he is thirty-two years of age.

Before the time of Mohammed the Arabs intercalated a thirteenth month every third year, thus making the calendar approximately correct. Mohammed, however, declared that it was recorded on the eternal tablets, ordained by Allah, that the lunar year should never have more than twelve months. The Persians use Arabic names for the months, and reckon the era from the Hejira, or flight of Mohammed from Mecca, A.D. 622. The notable fasts and feasts of the Shiahs,* with the exception of some established by Mohammed, are in commemoration of the twelve imams. The sacred year opens with a season of mourning for the Imam Husain. Ali had been murdered, Hasan poisoned, and Husain was on the way to Kufa to receive the caliphate, when he was intercepted by order of

* See the calendar of the Persian Year, in the Appendix.

189

Yezid, his rival, and cut down on the plains of Kerbela, together with many of his family and over seventy of his followers.   Shamr led the last onslaught.   The Shiahs, rejecting all other caliphs except Imam Ali and his descendants, yearly commemorate the martyrdom of Husain with many and varied ceremonies, which are adapted to excite anew their fanaticism.

Some say that the Caliph Mothi, son of Mukhtadir, set aside ten days for general mourning over the fate of Husain.   Others say that the celebration was established A.H. 261 (A.D. 874) by Muaz-ud-Doulah, vizier of the Dilami princes.   The "Tazia" or passion-play represents the story, and is enacted with great elaboration in the *takia* at Teheran, and throughout the country.   This play, of which a translation has been published in English, dates from the tenth century.

In Tabriz a court of the dewan-khana is covered with canvas, tiers of seats are erected, the sections are adorned with carpets, curtains, and lamps by the officials and wealthy men, and crowds throng to witness the scenes, which are enacted vividly and with lifelike reality.

The Vali Ahd defrays the expenses of the actors, amounting to fifteen hundred tomans.   The actors come from villages near Kasvin, whose inhabitants have for generations made the acting of the passion-play a profession.   After the "Tazia" each nobleman sends a present of a shawl, sweetmeats, and gold coins to the prince, as a contribution to the celebration.

During the month many of them clothe themselves in black, especially those who bear the name of Husain.   Throughout the city, on the streets, carpets are spread, and men and women seat themselves.   A molla or marseyakhan tells with pathos and art the tragic tales of the martyrs, till the people begin to lament and wail.   Weeping for the death of friends is not in accord with true resignation, but tears for the martyrs have great merit; so bereaved ones, easily moved by the affecting stories, shed meritorious tears.   Over certain doors black flags

are placed as signs that services of mourning are being held
there. By such services the people become wrought up to an
intense pitch of excitement. The first manifestation of this
feeling observable by foreigners is seen in the boys' playing
"procession." Grasping one another's girdles, they form lines,
waving sticks in the air, one blowing a trumpet, another beating a drum, and all shouting, "Shah Husain! Hasan, Husain!"
This is a childish imitation of the more serious acts of the men.

A frequent exhibition during the early days of the month is
a procession of men and women marching in irregular mass
through streets and bazaars. First come men bearing the
national banners and religious emblems, then bands of boys
chanting the mournful tale of Husain's death, followed by a
man clashing cymbals. The latter is a leader of a squad of
men, barefooted and naked to the waist. The bands are
divided into sections, and have a series of cries and responses:
"Shah Husain," "Vy Husain"; "Ali," "Help"; "Imam,"
"Martyr," etc. The cries are mingled wildly, and repeated
again and again as the procession moves on. A few stanzas
will show the nature of their songs:

> " Kerbela this day has been despoiled.
> Husain with his own blood is soiled.
>> *Chorus.* " Murder! By the hand of Shamr!
>> Cry out! By the hand of Shamr.

> " O shameless Shamr! not at all abashed,
> Ruthless against Husain you dashed. *Chorus.*

> " Surely the stones shall weep to-day!
> Seventy and two were slain to-day! *Chorus.*

> " Hasan, Husain, where like a flower.
> Yezid fell in the filth of a sewer." *Chorus.*

Some of these bands have large chains, some cat-o'-nine-tails
of iron, or straps tipped with steel, with which they lacerate

their backs. Others have large clubs, while many pound themselves with their fists until their breasts and backs are black and blue. Lastly comes a band of women, weeping and wailing, in the rear of the company of mourners.

Another scene, a type of many, comes into view before the dewan-khana or city hall, where a man is seen gashing himself wildly with an awl. A prince presents the devotee with a Cashmere shawl, thereby transferring the merit to himself—an example of the way the rich vicariously spend thousands during this period of lamentation.

These and similar scenes greet the eye until the 9th of the month, when the bazaars are closed, business is suspended, and the people prepare for the sorrowful anniversary. That night is the time for the old and the prominent men to manifest their grief. They repair to the mosques, with a large supply of candles for illumination. They anoint their heads, faces, and beards with black, filthy ointment, and make bare their feet and breasts. A molla takes the lead, staff in hand, and in irregular procession they begin a night-long lament. With singing of dirges and frantic intonations of the words "Shah Husain!" they follow the molla, who by his cry, "Well done!" encourages them. Now and then he calls a halt, and all beat their breasts with cruel vigor. A man sometimes passes around with a sponge or a piece of cotton, wipes off their tears, and presses them into a bottle, where they are kept as a remedy for disease and as a charm against evil influences. The ancients buried these tear-bottles in tombs as a proof of their affection. Some Mussulmans say that an angel collects these tears and keeps them till the day of judgment as a witness of the weeper's respect for the memory of Husain.

The dawn of the morning of the 10th (Ashura) is the signal for the young men to begin their part. By this time frenzy has been so wrought up that they are ready for the most inhuman and devilish work. They assemble at various mosques in different wards of the city.   Those desirous of acquiring special merit, or who have been hired by the rich to acquire it for them, and those who are under vows, whether rich or poor, are clothed in long white robes reaching to the ground.   The robes are consecrated for the occasion, and afterward are given to the poor.   Robed in these, and with their heads shaven, they are ready for the bloody sacrifice.   Men with knives and swords cut the crowns of the human victims.   The blood flows down in profusion over their white garments ; wild excitement takes hold of them ; swords are placed in their hands ; they start in procession through the streets, flashing their swords in the air, gashing their heads, and raising the now wild and frenzied cry, " Shah Husain! Hasan, Husain! "

Each division marches to the headquarters of the alderman of its ward.   As the large court of the kala-begi is in full view from the roof of the English consulate, we accepted an invitation there to see the climax of the celebration.   The surrounding roofs were covered with eager crowds, and the center of the court-yard was filled with women.   Soon the sound of music became audible amid the din, and the procession came in sight.   First came a company with waving banners, some with *tukhs* (steel plumes capped by balls), others with mirrors, others still with the national symbols of the Lion and the Sun. One carried a *tulug* or leather water-bottle, and others raised aloft metallic hands, representing Abbas ; for when Husain had gone on that fatal day to the Euphrates for water, his bottle was pierced with an arrow and the water spilled.   His enemies surrounded him and cut off his hands.   He put his sword into his mouth and, rushing at them, killed a number in this way. Next came a richly caparisoned, riderless horse, eloquent of the fallen Husain : on another horse two white doves were perched, representing the plumed messengers who, dipping their wings in the blood of the slain, carried the sad news to the sacred cities.   Next followed a mounted company of children strapped to the horses, their heads bleeding and their garments red from the cruel sword-cuts.   The mother who vowed to devote her child to the holy imam watches him from the throng with eager solicitude, yet with pious gratitude, thinking that now he is sure of a blessing.   It was touching to see the helpless babies so abused.   Strange carefulness was that of the men who gently stroked their infant heads with the sharp swords. Either loss of blood had exhausted them or excitement over-awed them, for they neither uttered a cry nor gave indication of alarm.

Following these was a martial band, heading a bloody corps, threescore strong, one of a hundred such corps in the city.   On they came, with a swaying, half-sidewise gait.   There were not only men, but boys of twelve and upward.   Each with one hand grasped the belt or supported the elbow of the one in front, while with the other hand he brandished a bloody sword, now and then bringing it down upon his own pate. The spectacle was horrible and disgusting.   Their scalps were haggled and mangled in irregular gashes; the crowns of their heads were weltering in gore.   The blood poured down on their faces, dyed with crimson their white robes, and made them a sight revolting and sickening, while the unceasing, monotonous cry of "Shah Husain! Hasan, Husain!" like the shouts of the prophets of Baal, deafened the air.   We almost felt as brutal as the participators to be gazing at the spectacle, much as the Roman dames must have felt, or ought to have felt, when clapping their hands as the gladiator bit the dust in the arena.

On they filed into the court-yard, to exhibit themselves before the officials.   At this juncture we noticed that men were keeping pace behind the devotees with long sticks, to ward off the blows which might inflict mortal injury.   From one fanatic they were trying to take his sword.   Some were binding up the wounds of the exhausted.   Little boys were led away bleeding.   Plenteous drafts of sugar-water were pressed to their mouths. Some were already too much exhausted, and sank out of line. Others fainted away and fell senseless. Some were fatally wounded, though the definite number of the fallen was not known. Those who die are believed to go straight to Paradise.

So the bloody corps passed from view, to be succeeded by a corps beating themselves with clubs, their children covered with chaff and ashes, representing Zainab and the children taken captive to Syria; then a group with castanets; and again a chain-gang, lashing themselves as on previous days, only intensified by the present furor, until other blood-dyed robes and swords flashing in the sunlight dazed our eyes. So it continued until noon. The same scenes were being enacted not only in that ward, but in all the twenty-four wards of the city, and with an intensified brutality when the corps from all the wards met at the dewan-khana before the mayor. Some-times, as they met in the narrow streets, sword clashed sword, and a deadly struggle ensued. But precaution was taken to avoid this. One company went to the Vali Ahd and pro-cured the release of several prisoners. When the thousands of blood-stained devotees, with numerous trains of others, had passed in review, the divisions disbanded.

Then the men took a free bath at the hammams, and were treated to food and tea. In the afternoon no one took a siesta, because Shamr, after murdering Husain, went home and slept quietly. In the evening lamps were not lighted, because the captive children were confined in a dark room. On the 11th of the month a procession of camels in the bazaars, with chil-dren in *cajavahs* or baskets, was led about, indicating the jour-ney of the captives to Syria. For several days afterward the bazaars were closed.

It is fair to say that many mujtehids and mollas of the Shiahs condemn this wild and bloody celebration as a gross viola-tion of the Koran, and regard it as an injurious excrescence,

a disgrace to Islam.   Its origin is traced to the Karabaghlis
of Transcaucasia, and thence it has spread through Persia.
Many of its objectionable features have been added in recent
years.   The Amir-i-Nizam, the first and greatest prime minister of Nazir-i-Din Shah, endeavored to repress the orgy, but
found the fanaticism of the people too much for him.

After Muharram the next six months contain frequent festivals and days of mourning.   Business is much interrupted.
Days of mourning commemorate the deaths of the imams,
their feasts, their births, etc., though Yezid's death is a time
of rejoicing.   The birthdays of Mohammed, Ali, and Husain
are specially celebrated.   They are ushered in with displays of
fireworks, and the bazaars are closed.   Salaams or receptions
are held by the shah, the crown prince, and other dignitaries.
On Ali's birthday, as well as on the evening before, guns are
fired off, and the bazaars are illuminated at night.

The 15th of Shaban (the eighth month) is a great national
festival—the Fourth of July, so to speak, for the Persians the
day of the greatest rejoicing.   Two causes are assigned for the
festivities: one the birth of the Imam Mahdi, the twelfth and
last imam, who still lives in concealment; the other the wedding of Ali and Fatima, the daughter of Mohammed.   Fatima,
it is said, had many suitors, though Mohammed declared that
he on whose house a shooting star should fall would receive
his daughter.   Ali's house was hit by the lucky star.   For
what event could pyrotechnics be more appropriate !

The government appropriates two thousand tomans a year
for fireworks.   The people, too, buy them.   Everybody carries home a bundle of sky-rockets and Roman candles or fire-
wheels.   This is done not only for amusement, but as a merit
for their souls.   Omission to do so is a sin.   If one has only
enough money for bread, let him forego the bread and shoot
the money into the sky!   Better still is it to combine the
pyrotechnics with a feast.   On the evening of this festival the

whole population, including Christians, go on the flat roofs and watch the fiery trains on every side darting through the sky.

Two weeks after this the great fast of Ramadan begins. This fast was probably copied after Lent. The Mosaic law had but one day of fasting—the day of Atonement. Mazdeism, in the fourth Vendidad, taught that, " of two men, he who fills himself with meat is filled with the good spirit much more than he who does not do so. It is this man who can strive against the fiends." An unfounded tradition states that the Ramadan fast was only intended to be for three days, and that the knowledge of which three days was lost, and therefore the whole month must be kept. The appearance of the new moon is watched for carefully, and news of its rise is telegraphed from city to city in cloudy weather. The fact of its appearing is made known to all by the firing of cannon, and morning and evening throughout the month the same signal is given. The fast must begin at early dawn, as soon as a white thread can be distinguished from a black one, and continue until the dusk of the evening will not allow the difference to be discerned. In 1886 the fast fell in June, and the morning gun was discharged at 2.45 A.M., and the evening one at 7.45 P.M. A Mohammedan near the arctic zone would long for darkness to interrupt his fast. The Eskimo, with three months of daylight, would find obedience to this command impossible. Abstinence from all food, from smoking tobacco, from drinking water, and from all sensual indulgence is required. All persons must keep the fast except the sick, travelers, and children under thirteen years of age, on peril to their souls and bodies as well. Sick persons and travelers are enjoined to render an equivalent afterward. To prepare for the day the whole population rise while it is yet dark and eat a hearty meal. On one day in 1894, either by mistake or as a practical joke, the cannon was fired two hours and a half before the time. Men and women started from their beds and rushed out to inquire concerning the time, in great perplexity, not daring to eat their morning meal. When they learned that the fault was not in their watches, nor in their having overslept, but with the gunner, they demanded his punishment, and he sought the sanctuary of a mosque. Toward evening food is made ready, and as soon as the cannon is fired a shout goes up all over the city from thousands of throats, and the hungry people fall upon their food. In summer months, with days sixteen hours long, it is a very trying ordeal, especially for the poor. The laborer, with tongue and lips parched, stomach craving, and hands weak, does a sorry day's work, and excites one's compassion and indignation. Many of the rich make the task a lighter one. Night is turned into day, and day into night. They feast on the best viands of all the year, smoke and enjoy themselves during the night, go to bed at the first streak of dawn, rise at noon, go to the mosque for prayers, promenade the bazaars, ride and chat in comparative comfort until the evening meal. Business is largely suspended. Bankers and merchants open their doors only for a few hours in the afternoon. Pressing government business is often engaged in at night. If it be asked whether the people keep the fast, I believe the answer must be that on the whole they do. Doubtless a considerable number eat in secret ; some, indeed, say that more than half do so. They are, however, wary not to be caught. In 1891 two men were discovered in the act of eating. They were nailed by the ear to a wall and spit upon by the passers-by. An Armenian villager, dressed like a Mohammedan, was dragged before the mayor on the charge of breaking the fast, and was not released until proof was furnished that he was a Christian.

The object of the fast is to subdue the flesh and lead to repentance. An expiatory efficacy is attached to it in the popular mind. Often its effect is to increase anger, profanity, and

strife.   Animals and men are more reviled and beaten in this
than in any other month.   The multitude attend the mosque
with great regularity, and read the Koran, even though they
do not understand Arabic.   The Koran is for this purpose
divided into thirty portions, one for each day.   Each is named
from the first word of the portion.   In the shops and on the
streets men may be seen busily engaged reading it.   It must
be read in a particular manner, with definite tones, accents,
and pauses.   To finish reading the whole in three days is very
meritorious.   Prescribed prayers and purifications must be
made before reading.   Tradition says that whosoever teaches
his son to read the Koran will receive a heavenly crown, and
whosoever reads only one letter does a good act, which will
meet a tenfold reward.

   Other circumstances add much to the solemnity of the fast
among the Shiahs.   The birth of the Imams Hasan and
Mohammed Tagi, on the 15th of the month, makes that day
memorable.   The death of Fatima, on the 2d, and the martyrdom of Imam Reza, on the 24th, and, above all, the assassina-
tion of Ali, move their hearts.   Ibn Mulzam, the Kharijite
conspirator, smote Ali with a poisoned sword on the 19th in
the mosque at Kufa; he died on the 21st of the month.   On
the 24th Ali's son smote Ibn Mulzam a single stroke, as the
latter had done to Ali, and on the 27th he died.   The three
days that Ali lingered between life and death are most solemn
ones.   All work then ceases.   The bazaars are so absolutely
closed that meat and vegetables cannot be purchased.   On the
night of the 19th none should sleep.   Mourning and beating
of the breasts is kept up until the 23d.   The day of Ibn Mulzam's death is one of rejoicing.   In Irak they eat sheep's head
as a sign of their devouring him.

   In April, 1893, the anniversary of Ali's death and the
Armenian Easter fell on the same day.   It was a perfect
Sabbath, but the Christians were rejoicing while the Moham-

medans were mourning. A story was circulated that five hundred Mohammedans had gone to the mujtehid and declared
that it was inappropriate that the Armenians should be feasting
while they were sorrowful. Would he not give permission to go
and loot their houses ? The mujtehid is said to have replied,
" The Christians here are but few, while their co-religionists in
Russia and India are as the sand. If we hurt the Christians
here they may retaliate in those countries."

The fast is succeeded by the *Fitr*, or *Oruj Bairam*, on the
1st of Shavval. Then the shah and governors again hold
salaam. There is much feasting, and especially eating of
dates. Mourners visit the graves of the dead, and are visited
by their friends. Duty requires every one to distribute to the
poor both money and food, and for every member of his family
five eighths of a batman of wheat.

The next important day is the *Kurban Bairam*, the Festival
of Sacrifice, on the 10th of Zil Haja. This festival was instituted in imitation of the great day of Atonement, on the 10th
of the seventh Hebrew month. During the first years of the
Hejira, Mohammed at Medina, in order to conciliate the Jews,
kept the day of Atonement. Afterward he modified it, sacrificing two rams, one for himself and his family and one for
his tribe. It is now connected with Abraham's offering of Ish-
mael, not Isaac. The Shiahs on the same day commemorate
the departure of Husain from Medina on his journey to Kerbela. The victim which may be sacrificed on Kurban Bairam
is a camel, cow, sheep, goat, or buffalo. The idea in it seems
to be commemoration, consecration, and thanksgiving, but not
expiation. In Tabriz the usual sacrifice for the people is a
sheep. The crown prince devotes a camel to be sacrificed,
and whosoever takes the head to his Highness receives a reward. This is sometimes the occasion of popular strife.

The remainder of the month is filled with memorable anniversaries, fitted to excite the people for the Muharram that

follows. There are the festival commemorating Mohammed's
declaration that Ali was to be his successor, the Khatam
Bakhsh, the accession of Ali to the caliphate, and, lastly, the
death of Omar, on the 26th. The latter is an occasion of
great joy and cursing. Omar's pate is loaded with impreca-
tions as the supplanter of Ali. A writer * describes a celebration where a large platform was erected and a disfigured and
deformed image placed upon it, to which the crowd addressed
all sorts of revilings. Having exhausted their vocabulary of
vituperation, they attacked the image with sticks and stones,
until they broke and scattered it in pieces. At times an
Armenian is hired to impersonate Omar, so that they can curse
him to their hearts' content. Enmity between the Turks and
Persians is kept alive by these celebrations. It has even been
considered a matter important enough to be stipulated in some
treaties that the Persians should cease to curse Omar. On this
anniversary, in September, 1893, the Osmanli consul at Tabriz
was riding out in a carriage. He was attacked by a Persian,
who shot one of the horses, and then, taking a horse from a
traveler, galloped away. It was at first thought to be an act
of fanaticism. Afterward it was explained that the man had
had a quarrel with his father and had threatened to do something
that would bring destruction on him and his property, according to the practice in law that a father is liable to arrest, fine,
and imprisonment for his son's misdemeanor, if the latter
escapes. This diplomatic explanation at least answered the
purpose.

* " China and Persia," vol. i., p. 364.

CHAPTER XII

IT is not my purpose to treat of the doctrines and beliefs of the Shiah Mohammedans, nor of their history, nor of the numerous sects, new and old, to be met with in the country. The Shiahs number about fifteen millions, eight millions of whom live in Persia. The Shiahs or sectaries agree with the Sunnis or traditionalists in the main articles of belief. They believe in the existence and unity of God, the revelation in the Koran, creation, fatalistic providence, angels—good and bad —the prophets, the resurrection of the body, the judgment, heaven, and hell. Their creed is, " There is no God but God ; Mohammed is the apostle of God ; Ali is the vicegerent of God." The latter clause is not received by the Sunnis, who hold different traditions. They claim that one hundred and twenty-four thousand prophets have spoken to man, and are mediators between him and God. Six of these are superior, namely, Adam, Noah, Abraham, Moses, Jesus, and Moham-med, the latter being preëminent. Ali and his descendants, through Fatima, are declared to be the rightful successors of Mohammed, the caliphs of Islam. As imams they have high dignity and honor. Abubekr, Osman, and Omar were usurpers. The twelfth and last imam disappeared, is yet alive, and will reappear as the Mahdi. Their religious rites are the repetition of the creed, prayer, alms, pilgrimage, and fasting. By the proper observance of these they believe that they receive for-giveness of sins and a title to Paradise. The ministers of their religion are called mollas. They are not regarded as priests or mediators in a ritualistic sense, but are leaders in worship, in-structors, interpreters of the sacred law and its traditions. They are not a caste, but are drawn from all ranks of the people. They receive a course of instruction under the chief mollas or mujtehids, consisting of Persian and Arabic, Mohammedan theology, dialectics, and interpretation of the law. Some stu-dents go to Kerbela for more advanced study. They are called *taliba*, and are often unruly, as students are in other lands. They have an *esprit de corps* which makes it dangerous to incur their enmity. In February, 1893, a fracas occurred between some three hundred students and the same number of sayids. The latter beat about fifteen of the former. Continued hostili-ties were imminent, and the mujtehid had difficulty in pacify-ing them, which he finally did by sending a peace-offering of sugar to the sayids. Two causes of the trouble were reported—either some students wished to take meat from a sayid butcher without paying for it, or a sayid was drunk and the students wished to punish him.

The mollas are of various grades. Some teach the primary schools in the village and city mosques; others are leaders of prayers; while others still, in various degrees of prominence, are interpreters of the law, writers of contracts, deeds, etc., and judges of civil and religious cases at law. They decide ac-cording to the Shari; that is, the Koran and its traditions. Those who attain eminence in their respective sects by reason of their learning or sanctity are honored with various titles, such as Hujat-il-Islam, Sigat-ul-Islam, Sheik-ul-Islam, and are by popular indication, without regular election, regarded as mujtehids. There are one or more of these in every city, but the chief mujtehid of all resides at Kerbela. The chief muj-tehid of Tabriz, Hadji Mirza Javat Aga, is a man of marked ability. When we called on him on one occasion he suggested for our discussion the subject of the proofs for the existence of

God.   He has much wealth, and is reported to own several hundred villages.   His influence and honor are great.   Criminals seek the protection of his gate as a refuge.   In 1882 the governor demanded a refugee.   The mujtehid declared his house an inviolable sanctuary, and refused to deliver him up. The governor appealed to the shah, and the mujtehid was ordered to answer before his Majesty.   When he made his exit from Tabriz throngs of men and women pressed about him with tears, kissing his hand and receiving his blessing.   After he had made his peace with the shah and returned, more than fifteen hundred men went out to meet him, some going as far as ten miles.   Some men kissed his feet, others the stirrups, while many animals were sacrificed before him in his honor.

The mollas are generally conservative, resisting innovation in state as well as in religious affairs.   They marry and keep up establishments in style and expense, according to their ability.   Some few mujtehids, with a pretense of sanctity, live on uncarpeted floors.   Their favorite animal for riding is the large white donkey.   The income of the mollas is derived from their fees for teaching, writing documents, and deciding cases, from the offerings and legacies of the people, especially the *khums* or fifths, which are devoted to religion.   A molla may engage in secular business.   One class of the mollas are the marseyakhans, reciters of the tales of the martyrs.   They are eloquent and effective speakers.   During the revival services of Muharram and Ramadan, sections of the bazaar are marked off and crowded with people to hear their lamentations.   They are kept very busy going from house to house and mosque to mosque.   They may be seen hastening on quick-pacing horses to their next appointments, making hay while the sun shines.

The mollas wear a peculiar dress.   Their robes are long and flowing, bound by a large girdle in thick folds; their cloak or aba hangs low; their turban is large and full.   Girdle, cloak, and turban are often of light colors, frequently white.   Their shoes are of the old style, sandal-like, turned up at the toes and pointed, and with heavy heels.

A semi-religious order are the sayids, direct descendants of Mohammed. When we consider the number of children that Mohammedans have, and that descent through both male and female lines is counted, we are not surprised that after twelve hundred years there is an immense multitude of them. But there are also many false sayids. An official told me that when he was young he had a seal made with "sayid" engraved on it. Afterward he changed his mind and destroyed it. Had he retained it his children would have regarded themselves as sayids. Their privileges are exemption from taxes, support from the *khums* or fifths, and other alms of the faithful, and, if so inclined, the privilege of blackguarding and browbeating their brethren whose blood is not so holy. Many of them are wealthy and honorable men engaged in all avocations, but it is a mistake to have such a privileged order in the kingdom. Their dress is much the same as that of the mollas, except the turban, girdle, and sometimes other parts of the costume, which are dark blue or green.

Another peculiar set of men are the dervishes. They are orders of religious mendicants of many kinds and degrees. The ordinary one seen in Persia is a strolling story-teller, with long disheveled hair, a close-fitting skull-cap, sometimes embroidered with verses from the Koran or the names of the imams, and bound with a fillet with hanging tassels. His girdle is a bundle of rough threads; his cloak a fanciful patchwork, an embroidered cloth, or the skin of a beast, with its hoofs or claws hanging down. He has for his *kashgul* or collection-box a large Indian nutshell, curiously carved, and in his hand a mace or cane. This may be a heavy stick of iron, a tomahawk, or an immense club of uncouth shape or with a knob driven full of spikes. The dervishes have altogether a very romantic appearance. They are generally good-natured

souls. They tell their stories on the street corners and in the
bazaars, and collect the pennies; they squat down in a little
tent before the gate of some rich man; they stroll from village
to village; and wherever they are, their cry, "Ya hak, Ya
hak!" ("Oh truth, Oh truth!") is heard. They are not highly
respected, but are in a manner looked upon as holy, and never
ridiculed.

Having thus briefly indicated the doctrines and religious
orders of the Shiahs, I proceed with some details regarding
their chief religious rites. A new convert must first repeat the
creed: "There is no God but God; Mohammed is the apostle
of God; Ali is the vicegerent of God." After that he is circumcised. The Mohammedan boy is often circumcised on the
eighth day. Sometimes it is delayed for some years. It is
made the occasion of feasting and rejoicing. At the age of
twelve the youth must begin the exercise of the rites of religion. One of the important rites is prayer. Five times a day
are appointed for prayer—dawn, middle of the morning, noon,
middle of the afternoon, and sunset. Morning and evening
the muezzin mounts a minaret or the roof of a mosque, and
gives the azan or call to prayer: "God is great! I testify
that there is no God but God; I testify that Mohammed is
the apostle of God, and Ali is the vicegerent of God. Come
to prayer! Come to security! Prayer is better than sleep."
The muezzin may be an educated molla or an ignorant man.
A wealthy neighbor had the call given from his housetop by
an illiterate scavenger or porter, who had simply memorized
the Arabic words, and was paid for his trouble with some
loads of wheat. The preparations for prayer are somewhat
elaborate. Certain ablutions are preparative. The ablutions
are performed, not by dipping the hands in a basin, but by
pouring water from a ewer or from the palm of the hand.
The Sunnis and Shiahs wash the hands differently. One rubs
toward the elbow, the other downward. They can be distin-

guished from each other by the direction of the hair on the arm. The toes are also carefully rubbed with water, the ears moistened, and the teeth cleaned. A spot of ink, or other defilement, may invalidate the prayer. When preliminaries have been finished the worshiper takes his position on a prayer-rug, with head uncovered and shoes removed, faces toward the Kebla, the Kaaba at Mecca, and places a tablet of pressed earth from Kerbela before him, and holds a string of beads of the same earth in his hands. These beads number ninety-nine, according to the attributes of God. A long one at the end is called the molla; two double ones are called the caliphs. With the beads he keeps tally of his petitions. The tablet is placed before him because Mohammed enjoined that the worshipers should bow their heads to the earth. The prayer is said according to a fixed rote, every motion being prescribed. With the repetition of certain words the devotee raises his hands to heaven, with others his eyes; at one time he kneels, at another prostrates himself with his forehead on the earth; again he touches his knees, toes, palms of the hands, and forehead, to indicate his absolute submission. He must not look backward during the exercise. He may, however, keep an eye on those round about him, and on his goods lest they be stolen, or ejaculate a curse on his apprentice, or tell a passing customer to wait a little while and he will attend to him. He may interject a greeting to a guest or an order for tea, provided he proceeds without mistake. The prayer consists of certain suras of the Koran in Arabic, which are understood by few in Persia, the same words being repeated day after day. A translation of the prayer, with pictures of the worshiper in each posture, can be seen in Hughes's " Dictionary of Islam."

Their conception of prayer is that it is the rendering of worship or the paying of a debt of service to the Creator. It is a duty which the faithful are under obligation to perform. The ideas of confession, petition, and intercession are not present to their mind. The prescribed prayer is called the *namaz*. There is also the *dua*, which is more in accordance with true prayer, being an expression of their desires to God.

Persians have a custom of saying frequently, " In sha Allah " ("If God wills "). With some it becomes a thoughtless or irreverent interjection, or a vain repetition of the divine name. A goodwife was in the habit of saying, " In sha Allah," in a pious way. Her husband ridiculed her. One day he said, " Let us have a dinner of rice and mutton." His wife answered, " In sha Allah." He went and brought the things from the market and gave them to her, saying, " Make ready and let us eat quickly." She answered, " In sha Allah." When ready the wife said, " Let us sit down and, in sha Allah, eat our dinner." The man said, " Of course we will; why do you always say, ' In sha Allah ' ? " Just then the police entered and took him to prison. Being released, he knocked at his door. The wife said, " Who's there? " He answered, " It is I, in sha Allah."

All places are regarded as suitable for prayer. When the call sounds the man stands up among his guests, or in his shop, in the midst of the noise of manufacturing, or on the house-top, or on the street corner. The workmen throw aside the pick and shovel and begin their devotions. The gospel idea of closet prayer is unknown to them. At first acquaintance a Christian is an enigma to them, never being seen to engage in prayer. A native, describing a Christian lady, said, " She does not revile, she does not steal or lie, yet she has no religion."

In addition to the daily prayers there are services in the mosque. These are usually held on Friday or *Juma*, the meeting-day, the Sabbath of Mohammedans. There is a partial cessation from work on that day. Government offices and some of the bazaars are closed, but the mass of the people continue working. A considerable number assemble in the mosques. The molla or peesh-namaz leads the prayers and repeats passages from the Koran in Arabic. Sermons are not infrequently preached in the vernacular; at times fervent and eloquent, at other times deep and incomprehensible, consisting of the recital of traditions, or of exhortations of a practical nature.

No village is without its mosque, no city without a considerable number of them. Those of the present age are generally rude structures, without architectural features worthy of mention. Some of the ruined mosques are of great beauty. Some now in use have large and well-formed arched roofs, and hold large audiences. Several new mosques in Teheran are built in elegant style. Few mosques in Persia have minarets. The furniture of the mosque is simple. The congregation sit on the floor, which is covered with a rough reed matting or with carpets. Women sit apart and are veiled. Christians are rarely allowed to enter a mosque, their presence being considered defiling. The ground consecrated to a mosque is forever sacred, and not to be devoted to secular uses. If the basement or first story is reserved, a dwelling can be built on the place where a mosque has stood.

Burial of the dead takes place with a prescribed ritual. A death in the house is announced by a molla from the housetop, by repeating certain portions of the Koran. In the case of a great man this is done twice, but news is not sent to distant friends. They may remain for months and even years in ignorance of the death of a mother or a child. No one will be the bearer or sender of evil tidings. The custom is to bury very quickly. A man who died at four o'clock in the afternoon was buried before dark. Doubtless many are interred alive. In the city of Maragha the body of a woman had been prepared for burial according to custom. Moistened cotton was placed in the mouth, the nose, and the ears; the body was bathed three times, the last time in camphor-water; the eyes were bandaged ;

the body was wrapped in the *kafan* or shroud, and would have been borne quickly to the cemetery had not darkness intervened. At dawn the body was found to be in a different position, and shortly afterward the friends were astonished by the question, "Why are my eyes bandaged?" Her bandages were loosed, she was restored to health, and shortly afterward gave birth to a child.

The injunction of the Koran to wash the body under a covered place is not always obeyed. There are families whose trade it is to attend to this last office for the dead. Two sticks about a foot long are put under the arms of the corpse. These are to prop it up when it rises from the grave and is catechized by the angel Gabriel. After he is satisfied that it is the body of a true Mussulman strength will be given to sit upright. Burial without these sticks is considered very heterodox. Some ignorant people are loath to part with a limb, lest they appear maimed at the resurrection. A certain Meshedi put his nail-parings carefully away in a paper. One day the boys found them and scattered them. He was very angry and dismayed, and said, "What now will I do in the resurrection?" In shaving the head a tuft of the hair is left, that by it a Mussulman may be recognized.

The friends assemble at the funeral with such expressions as, "May God be merciful to *you!*" "May *your* life be prolonged!" "Our life is from God!" "It is the will of God!" "It is the act of God; we must be resigned!" Tea and coffee are served, and sometimes pilau and other viands at great expense. Hired mourners are in attendance. The molla recites a dirge, telling them to weep not for their friends, but to weep for Husain and the slaughtered innocents. The tender hearts of the bereaved are easily moved, and their tears and their beating on their breasts are a merit as being for the martyrs. Neither the men nor the women wash their faces or comb their hair until the first days of mourning are over.

The men open the seams of their coats, as if rending their garments, and put dust on their hats. A bereaved woman sometimes tears her flesh with her nails, pulls out her hair, uncovers her head, and sits in the hot sun screaming. The length and loudness of the wailing are supposed to indicate the depth of the sorrow. For two weeks wailing is so loud that the neighbors a block away can hear it. The women, her companions, sometimes weep with her, sometimes scold and upbraid her, sometimes try to assure her that the death is not a fact. The putting on of the oldest clothes is a sign of mourning.

The body is at times covered with a shawl, at times placed in a coffin. The latter is rudely made, with black cloth nailed over it. A child may be borne on a pillow, others on a bier. The bier is carried by different sets of bearers, the passers-by acquiring merit by helping. Women do not go to the grave. The procession is irregular; every one moves at his own gait, and as fast as possible. Riding is a disrespect to the angels who walk before the corpse. I once noticed a waiter with lighted candles borne in front of a Mohammedan funeral procession. They said it was simply to honor the dead. Prayers and reading of the Koran are part of the ceremony at the grave. They are also repeated on the eve of Friday, and on special mourning-days. On these occasions the people and mollas crowd the cemeteries to pray, mourn, and eat pilau and taffy. The grave of a man is dug three or four feet deep, that of a woman two feet deeper. The face is placed toward Mecca. Some bodies are laid on the ground and incased in brick, and reserved to be removed to some shrine. Thousands of corpses are taken to Kerbela or Meshed, to rise with the imams. Such caravans are frequently met on the highways. Dr. Perkins tells of an Englishman traveling, who saw some oblong boxes in the caravansary and told his servant to arrange them and he would spread his bed on them. He might have spent the night reposing with the dead had not his nostrils aroused him to the true state of the case.

Little attempt is made to beautify graveyards. They are desolate, without tree, grass, or flower. In the midst of the cities they are trampled down by donkeys and men, and when somewhat obliterated, often opened again for another interment. There is occasionally a large monument or a tomb of an imam-zada; other graves are marked with rude stone slabs. On these are inscriptions from the Koran or the poets, and sometimes the name, age, and date of death. Some have signs of the man's trade, as an anvil and hammer, a pistol, or a cup and pitcher. In old cemeteries are some immense blocks of porphyry, five or ten feet long and a cubit in height and breadth. They seem quite ancient, and no such large stones are now brought for any purpose. They are often taken for use in bridges and tanks. They may belong to the Mongol period. One in the bridge over the Kuri Chai is said to have an Armenian inscription. Some old cemeteries have rudely carved rams or rams' heads. Oil is sometimes poured out as an offering upon them. A Mussulman told me they were so made because Abraham offered up a ram. That would indicate that the dead are a sacrifice to God. Sir Ker Porter discovered one at Old Julfa, with an Armenian inscription, and he thinks they are of Christian origin.

Mohammedans of Persia seem to have great faith in written prayers, either as petitions or charms. Many are written and put in leather or cloth cases, and suspended from the neck or tied to the arm of a child to protect it, or to a horse to keep it from stumbling. In cholera times printed prayers were posted on the walls. Women will frequently desire to have a prayer written for barrenness. Once I was conversing with a village soldier, who asked me if I knew anything of science, saying that he was in love, but opposed by his father; would I not write a prayer for him, that his difficulties might be overcome? The desire for written prayers is a source of considerable revenue to the mollas. In the Russo-Turkish War the mujtchid of Kerbela issued a decree that the war was a holy one (*jahad*). The *taliba* or students entered into the war. First they prayed over some pease and cast them in the direction of the enemy, indicating that they would be driven out. When the *taliba* were defeated they fled home, saying, " Self-preservation is the first law."

A remarkable innovation has been introduced by some. On one occasion I was visiting the house of a wealthy Persian. We entered a room, and there was unveiled before me an almost life-size picture of Ali, with his two sons, Hasan and Husain, seated on either side. Ali was represented as crowned with a halo, clothed in camel's-hair cloth, and having in his hand the double-pointed sword which an angel is supposed to have brought from heaven. Before this picture they prostrated themselves, kissing it and paying it profound adoration, while they mumbled their prayers. This marks a striking change among Mohammedans. Mohammed would almost rise from his grave to rebuke it. Not satisfied with the older representation, in which the face was veiled, they have made an opportune discovery in a remote part of India. This is a portrait of Ali on canvas, showing his sacred features. By order of the shah this picture was solemnly conveyed to Teheran and received with great honor. An order of nobility was instituted in commemoration of the discovery, and the imperial sanction was given to its use in the devotions of the faithful.

By some, Ali, Hasan, and Husain are regarded as the first of all creatures, the supreme intercessors, sinless, and endowed with the divine light. Ali voices his power in the thunders; his gleaming sword is seen in the lightning's flash. On him rests the hope of salvation. Devotion to him is the first duty of the believer.

The third meritorious act, according to the Mohammedan

faith, is almsgiving. There are two kinds—the *zakat*, which is enjoined, with directions as to what portion of each product should be given; and *sadakat* or "righteousness," which is voluntary. The faithful are commanded to give one fifth of their income. The underlying idea is the merit of the donor, that he may acquire a claim on God's mercy. He does not give because need or suffering appeals to him. It makes no difference if the beggar is an impostor, or will use the alms in wickedness. God, it is believed, will count it equally to the credit of the giver.

The usual forms of alms are in support of religion, the maintenance of the sayids, and of the poor. Occasionally a man builds a mosque, a bridge, a free water-tank, or makes provision for free ice-water in the bazaar. Sending portions of a feast to the needy is common. While Islam enjoins ample charity, yet much of it is wasted on professional beggars, useless dervishes, and lazy sayids. Hospitals, asylums for the blind, the aged, orphans, or lepers, are unknown, and famine calls forth little systematic beneficence.

The professional beggars are frequently pitiable spectacles. Women may often be seen sitting in the street on a winter day, their teeth chattering, and their babes unprotected. Men with only a bit of sackcloth over their loins, and almost nude boys, make appeals. To clothe them is useless, as they will return in their rags the next day. Many are frauds. I once saw a man lying in the street apparently nearly dead. He declared that fever was burning him up, and cried for help. I had him carried to the dispensary. The doctor examined him and found his pulse and temperature perfectly normal.

It is considered very meritorious for a Mussulman to pay the expense of the burial of a dead believer. Two beggars agreed that on alternate days each should feign himself dead, and the other collect alms for his burial. They had remarkable skill in stiffening their limbs and bringing a deadly pallor to their countenances. After many successful efforts they were one day informed that a great man was approaching. Having made all preparations, a piteous tale of distress was poured into the khan's ears. He recognized the men, and immediately agreed to bear all the expense of the burial. He ordered his attendants to dig a grave and light a fire, that hot water might be prepared for washing the body. The accomplice besought him not to trouble, declaring that he had vowed that he would himself perform these last rites for his friend. Unheeding, they made all the preparations, and only when the scalding water was falling on his pate did the dead man abandon his ruse. The noble then gave the beggars a present and sent them away.

The Mohammedan considers it a sin for the least scrap of bread to be destroyed. He will stoop and pick it up. He never wishes to cut down a tree after it has blossomed in the spring, because its fruit will sustain life.

Another religious observance of prime importance is fasting This is considered under Ramadan, in the chapter on the Sacred Year. The pilgrimage remains to be described. A pilgrimage or hadj to Mecca is obligatory on every Mohammedan once in his lifetime. Only poverty, sickness, or unsound mind can be a ground of excuse from this duty. The Shiahs have multiplied their places of pilgrimage. Some of them, by good policy, fall within the borders of Persia. These are Meshed, the tomb of the Imam Reza, and Koum, the tomb of Fatima. Even more important than these are Meshed Ali, at Nejef, and Kerbela. The journey to these shrines from most parts of Persia is long and difficult. The pilgrimage to Mecca can be made more easily by way of Tiflis, the Black Sea, and Suez, and to Meshed by the Caspian steamers and Transcaspian Railway, and the new wagon-road to Meshed. The idea underlying these pilgrimages in the minds of the people is the obtaining of forgiveness and merit by the hard ship and expense they entail, by doing honor to the sacred persons and places, and by performing the rites prescribed. Men who have made unlawful gain have a strong conviction that it will become lawful to them by undertaking a pilgrimage.   There is a rule, however, that the pilgrimage is not effective unless a man has settled up all legal claims against him.   Hence a servant about to start will come to his master, whom he probably has robbed, and say, "Aga, if I have offended you, if I have caused you loss, forgive me, make it *hallal*" (or lawful).   If the master says, "No matter, it is well! " the account is squared.   A rich man will make a show of settling all his old accounts or extortions, that he may appear before God clean.   When a prominent official was going on the hadj to Mecca he caused it to be announced in the mosque before hundreds of people that he wished every one who had a charge against him, or from whom he had taken unlawfully, to come and he would pay it.   The people said this promise must be a lie, as he had taken hundreds of thousands of tomans.   There was an Armenian who had a bill for purchases against the nobleman.   He went to his palace and waited for three hours.   After trying various methods of getting the money he finally said to the official, " Now, your Honor is going to appear before God, and what will you answer if you are asked, 'Have you paid Baron A—— his money?' It will be unlawful for you to go on my money.   I do not make your journey *hallal*."   With this artifice he obtained the settlement of his account.

People at times go on a pilgrimage from motives not religious.   Childless women go with their petition, or invalids hoping to be healed, being tied for some days in the portico of the shrine.   Men often go for the opportunity of seeing the world, or to get out of the country for a time.   Others combine trading in merchandise with the pilgrimage.

The pilgrims start so as to reach Mecca in the month of

Zil Haja, for the *Kurban Bairam.* They gather from a district, to the number of several hundred, a well mounted and outfitted caravan. Each one passes one end of his turban or scarf beneath his chin, and takes in his hand a staff of bitter almond. As the bands go out of the city, with songs and music and flying banners, their friends accompany them for a distance. Shopkeepers and passers-by come up to them, kiss their hands, and receive their peace, wishing them a safe journey. Others sacrifice sheep before the caravan, while the pilgrims distribute safety-money to the beggars. Rich men go with great pomp and display. A Tabriz merchant made the pilgrimage with two wives, four children, one hundred and fifty servants, and one hundred extra pack-animals. His encampment, when he pitched his tents for the night, looked like a small town. Such a man must also distribute a large amount of food to the poor each night, so that his expenses are very heavy. When the pilgrim returns from Mecca he is known by the honorable title of Hadji, or from the other shrines by a title derived from the place, as Kerbelai or Meshedi. If he dies on the journey his spirit goes directly to Paradise; if he dies at the shrine he is still more blessed, for his body will rise with the prophets and imams on the day of resurrection.

It is considered meritorious for a man of means to pay the expenses of a poor man on the pilgrimage. The shah at times provides for indigent mollas a purse for this purpose. I have heard that one day a molla came to the shah for a present of one hundred tomans for the hadj. An official who disliked mollas asked him why he came there drunk. The molla protested that he was not drunk. The official affirmed that it was proved by the fact that his pockets were full of stones. This the molla denied. The official immediately proved to the shah (by sleight of hand) that the pockets were full of stones, and the molla was sent away in disgrace.

Besides these great shrines there are hundreds of small ones, scattered all over Persia. Some of them are tombs of the imam-zadas, or descendants of the imams; some of them are the scenes of supposed miracles, some of them the inventions of crafty priests. A shrine in Karadagh, which was visited much for the healing of the sick, originated in the following manner: One morning a man told his neighbors that during the night a heavenly light—a manifestation of an imam—had appeared on a certain hill. The report spread, and people began flocking to the shrine. It was a time of an overstocked melon market, and the bazaar was distant. The story brought a throng of purchasers near, and the man sold his melons at a good profit. Then he told the people of his deceit, but they declared his confession a lie and held to the fable as truth.

Just outside of Urumia a shrine has been built. A sayid dreamed that an imam appeared to him, informing him that gold was hidden in a cemetery to be used for his honor. Several nights afterward the man dreamed the exact place, and with the supposed find built a shrine. The interest on the investment came to him speedily, as one whom the imam honored with a vision.

The belief in dreams and visions of the Prophet or the imams is wide-spread. It is sometimes turned to good account. A pasha in Turkey had built a mosque, but had borrowed eight hundred tomans for the purpose from an Armenian. The debt remained unpaid. Finally the Armenian gave thirty tomans to a friend of the pasha to persuade him to pay it. One morning the friend came before the pasha much agitated, saying he had had a vision in the night. An old man with flowing robes, long white beard, and bald head had appeared to him and asked, "Who built this mosque?" He answered, "The noble Azat Pasha." "Why," said the old man, "have you so long allowed the Armenians to own part of it? If you don't pay them quickly I will smite the ground with my staff, and the mosque will tumble." The warning of Elijah had effect, and payment was made the same day.

A belief in miracles, as showing God's power and the imam's influence, is a present factor in their religious life. Let me give a few instances of this. In 1882 a band of pilgrims reached Kerbela after dark. The gates were closed and the guards refused to open them. The pilgrims prayed, the gates of the city flew open of their own accord, a lame and a blind man were healed, and there were heavenly manifestations to both Sunnis and Shiahs. At the news of these signs Tabriz was excited. There were great rejoicings. The bazaars were illuminated and cannon were fired, because God had shown his favor. In 1883 a Turkish pasha tried to persuade the keeper of the shrine of Husain, at Kerbela, to give him a carpet which was kept there. Finally he sent soldiers to take it. The keeper told them he had sent it to the Mosque of Abbas. The soldiers attempted to enter there, fell down on the threshold, and, spitting blood, died on the spot. In 1894 a Mussulman in Baku went to a Russian house of prostitution on a holy night in Muharram. An unique and unheard-of punishment overtook him, and was regarded as a sign of the displeasure of the imam. It was telegraphed to Persia and was the cause of awe to multitudes. In Zenjan there was a tree revered for its age, its size, and its growth, without being watered. A storm blew it over, and a spring gushed forth and continued flowing. It was regarded as a miraculous blessing.

Many of the sheiks and pirs among the Kurds, Ali-Allahis, and others, pretend to cure diseases, barrenness, etc., by touch and prayer. A reputation for holiness and power to work miracles is a great source of gain, as well as fame, to them. A sheik thus wished to increase his reputation and influence. He gave out that on a certain day he would kill and raise to life one of his pupils. A great crowd assembled. According to previous arrangement, a drug which would put him into a heavy sleep had been given to the pupil. He was commanded to enter the room and die. Then word was given to the people. They entered, found him lifeless, and prepared him for burial. The grave was dug, the body deposited, a little earth placed upon it, and the people were told to come in the morning. At sunrise a crowd assembled, the earth was removed, and the body called upon to rise. No answer came. He had not correctly calculated the time when the effects of the drug would pass off. The pupil had awakened in the night, and, after trying to escape, had died. The sheik was arrested for fraud.

A belief in charms and talismans (Arabic, *talisim*) is almost universal. The names of the Prophet and the imams are engraved or written on stones and made into necklaces and armlets. Written prayers, verses from the Koran, and even the whole Koran, printed in miniature and inclosed in a case, are fastened to the arm or hung on horses. Necklaces and beads of Kerbela earth are carried about on the person. Some of this earth is put into loads of goods to protect them from robbers. All these charms are supposed to keep from disease and accident, and especially from the evil eye. The belief in the evil eye (*nazar*) is wide-spread. Not only is there supposed to be danger from the glance of a malignantly disposed person, but even words of praise are dangerous. No mother wishes her child to be praised. She is afraid it will bring him ill luck, and she will answer with something disparaging. She will prevaricate about the number of her children, for fear of a spell. She will dress her boy in girl's clothes, or in other unbecoming style, fearing that if he looks handsome the evil eye may strike him and even cause his death. I have been shown a charm which was cracked. The owner affirmed that some one cast on him the *nazar;* it struck the charm and cracked it; otherwise it would have injured him.

The owner of a large garden received us on his veranda.

I noticed a little piece of wood, with writing on it, attached
to a post. To draw him out I asked about it. He answered
that it was a prayer, a verse from the Koran, to prevent the
evil eye. He said that a man once came in and saw a fine
tree full of fruit, praised it, and then the tree quickly withered
up. Another came through the covered hall, admired it, and
it fell down. A charm of great potency is supposed to be the
name of the mother of Moses. They regard it as unknown.
I have a number of times been asked for it, and answered
according to the Bible. They were surprised and incredulous
that I should know it. They believe that by saying it a locked
door will fly open, and other signs be wrought.

The power of spells was tried in the Babis' war, at Zenjan.
It is narrated that a figure in woman's attire came out with a
black pitcher and began to sprinkle water near the Babi quarter.
The Babis went out and found that it was a man in disguise.
He said that six of the mollas had read prayers and repeated
spells over the water for forty days and given him twenty tomans to sprinkle it, that the Babis might be dispersed.

There was a noted highway robber, Lala Beg, whom the
government had made many vain efforts to capture. One
time he killed eight soldiers and fled. They thought he used
magic to protect himself. The Zil-i-Sultan commanded Rukn-i-
Doulah to capture or kill him. A sayid promised to throw a
spell around him, and in consideration of this received five
hundred tomans. The prince, one hundred and fifty soldiers,
and the sayid came upon the robber. He was sitting in a
field eating his breakfast. The soldiers were afraid to approach, fearing his magic. The sayid called out to him, " O
giaour, infidel, we must either kill or capture you!" His
words were scarcely finished when Lala Beg cried out, " O
sayid, you call me an infidel! I don't wish to give you pain,
because you are a descendant of the Prophet. Look between
your eyes! " The gun gave a report and the sayid dropped,

smitten through the brain. His magic was vain for his protection.

There is a wide-spread belief in signs, lucky and unlucky
omens, indications of the stars, etc. As in ancient Chaldea,
so now in Persia, astrology is a flourishing science. The
munajim or astrologer has a recognized place. He is found
in the palace, he is consulted by the poor. The lives of some
men are directed by him in all their details, and nothing is
done unless the omens are favorable. By a glance at the
Persian almanac we can understand some of the details of their
trade. They have the years divided into a series of twelve,
with Jagatai Turkish names, respectively the year of the mouse,
ox, leopard, rabbit, whale, snake, horse, hog, hen, sheep, dog,
and monkey. Every year has its special attributes. For example, in the year of the rabbit rain will be abundant. A
child born in the first third of it will be quick and truthful, in
the middle will be stupid, in the last third will be wise. Directions are given as to what to do at the beginning of each
month, that it may pass in safety and without sickness or misfortune. When the new moon of Ramadan is first seen, immediately look at vegetables or running water, or at a turquoise
or agate, and at nothing else. After a view of the new moon
of Safar, look at a mirror, at gold or silver; of Ramadan, look
at a ring, a sword, armor, fire, or the Koran; and so the lucky
omens are given for each separate month. There is a table
telling by what sign to find anything. To let a hat, a whip, or
a pen drop, to hear a crow or a bat, see a snake, burn one's
clothes, have a bad dream, or a nose-bleed, or a cat jump into
the lap, to weep or laugh in sleep—it is indicated for each
day of the month what each of these events signifies, of weakness or strength, sleeplessness, trembling, or success. It tells
on what day and month to be bled or have a tooth pulled, or
to write a prayer that a scorpion may not sting, or to put on a
new coat, go to the bath, go on a journey, or when to see the

governor or the king. One day is good to put a child in a
cradle, another to begin nursing it. One is good for getting
married in, another for watering the garden ; one day is lucky
for nothing whatever. It is made plain what results, good or
evil, come from the twitching of the eyelids, or of any other
member. Sneezing once is unlucky, sneezing twice is lucky.
Three lamps in a room are bad luck. The number thirteen
is unlucky. In counting they say, "ten, eleven, twelve, it is
not thirteen, fourteen." If a man is going out to business or to
the mosque, and one asks him where he is going, he considers
it a bad omen and returns, or sits down for ten minutes and
starts again.

Fortunate is the great man who can have an astrologer
always with him, to observe the stars and cast the die on the
brass instrument, with its thousand curious signs. The astrologer is master of the secret science. He can tell when to start
on a journey, what physician the sick should call, and whether
his medicine will be profitable. He can tell who is the thief,
and frighten the criminal into returning the booty. In some
places there are fal-khanas or houses of divination, where priests
are ready, for a consideration, to tell fortunes. Sometimes
the holy books are consulted. I heard of a case where, on
opening the book, the finger rested on the words, "This year
thou shalt die." Fear accomplished the portend, and death
shortly occurred.

The astrologers understand a good deal of astronomy.
They make correct calculations of eclipses and understand
them. Ignorant people, however, have curious notions concerning them. One man gave as the reason of an eclipse that
the sun had sinned and God took its light till it repented. I
saw an eclipse of the sun on May 17, 1882, from the roof of
Fiske Seminary, Urumia. Many of the bazaars were closed.
The populace were excited. They betook themselves to prayer
in the mosques. Their loud supplications could be distinctly

heard.   One Mohammedan went immediately and paid a Jew a debt.   Many thought it portended war or trouble to the king.

Much superstitious fear was awakened by the appearance of the brilliant comet of 1880.   It was brought into connection with a prophecy uttered by an Italian priest, who set the time for the world's destruction in December.   It was published in Turkish and Persian newspapers, and created a sensation.   This fear was not confined to Mohammedans, but extended to Armenians.   One Armenian priest ordered his people to put off their jewelry and ornaments and betake themselves to prayer and supplication.

The action of the people in an earthquake was interesting to observe.   In May, 1883, at night, several shocks disturbed the sleeping city.   At noon of the next day a severe shock caused every one to flee into the yards.   Nearly every house in the city was cracked, some roofs fell in, and walls were overturned.   Eleven houses fell in Bagh-Meshed.   Many articles in the bazaars were overturned.   Vases were knocked from the mantels, dishes fell with a crash to the floor, and dust and plaster covered everything.   The dogs set up a terror-stricken whine.   Men ran in all directions, sometimes against one another.   Bankers, in their haste, abandoned their money-bags, and some women managed to get away with them. People might be heard standing in the middle of their yards calling to God for mercy, and wailing and crying with terror. Others ran into the open fields beating their breasts.   The Armenian priests consulted their books and said that there would be another one at 11 P.M., and that it portended the death of kings and great wars.   An astrologer from Teheran sent an assuring telegram that the earthquake would continue for forty days.   A Tabriz molla predicted a shock on the following Sunday at 2 P.M.   People were in terror; many quit sleeping in their houses, and camped in the gardens.   The crown prince tented in his park. Ladies were so much scared that they imagined half a dozen shocks a night. One man said that his wife's heart beat so hard that he could not tell whether there was a shock or not. On Sunday the bazaars were all closed. But the prediction failed, and the molla was arrested for frightening the people. One Persian explanation of the earthquake was that the ox which, with twenty-one horns, supports the earth was enraged and was tossing his horns.

There are many other religious practices or superstitions among the Persians. I shall mention one more. Their idea of ceremonial defilement has a special bearing on their relation to foreigners and native Christians. Their law of clean and unclean meats is copied after that of the Jews. An exception is made for camel-meat. Oysters, lobsters, hare, and pork are abominations. Once I was narrating the parable of the prodigal son. Before I had finished a man stuck his fingers into his ears and went away, saying that it was defiling to listen to me. His ground of offense was that I had mentioned swine and had said that the father had embraced the boy who had been feeding them.

In avoiding social relations with other races the Shiahs go beyond the Koran and their Sunni neighbors. "The people of the Book," including the Jews and Christians, if not Zoroastrians, are "clean," and they are so regarded by the Arabs and Osmanlis. But the Persians regard the touch of a Christian as defiling.

According to their strict notions it is a pollution for a Christian to enter the house of a Mohammedan. Ambassadors from Europe, when first received, were not permitted to enter the residences of the officials. Mr. Anthony Jenkinson came to Persia with a letter from Queen Elizabeth. When he departed from an audience with the king a servant followed him till he was beyond the court, sprinkling sand on the path he walked over, showing the idea they had of his uncleanness.

The shah-zada (governor) of Tabriz did not receive the French embassy of 1841 until several days had passed, because there was much rain, and the dampness would make the intercourse with Christians more defiling. This dread of contamination in time of rain is still prevalent. Armenians used to be prohibited from going on the streets when it was raining, and only in 1880 the governor of Ardebil annulled the prohibition in that city. As late as 1889 some Armenians in Maragha were beaten because raindrops from their defiled garments fell on Mohammedans.

The touch of a Christian makes food unclean to him. Hence a Mohammedan will not buy meat slaughtered or touched by a Christian, nor any kind of moist food. Some village children, with clothes in tatters and covered with dirt, were given a few grapes by a foreigner. Their parents would not permit them to eat of the fruit until it was washed. If the strict Shiah is under the business necessity of entering a Christian's house he will not drink tea from his cups or even in his house unless it is made by a Mohammedan servant. He will not smoke the pipe after a Christian, nor accept his hospitality in any way. Indeed, Mohammedans have been abused and beaten for taking service with a Christian. Even at the present day most of the servants of Europeans belong to heterodox sects. A Mohammedan who was traveling with Christians asked for a drink of water. In reply he received a blow on the face, with the remark that he was worse than the Armenians, because he traveled with them.

Vessels, also, if used by a Christian, are defiled and unfit for use. A copper vessel may be purified by immersing it in water and praying over it, or by repeating the creed; but an earthen vessel must be broken. Water-sellers will sometimes give Christian travelers a drink for more than the price of the mug, and then break it. They have been known even to break the bowl from which water was poured out on a Christian's hands to wash them. Wash-water poured out where the sun cannot shine makes the place unclean forever. On such an occasion the owner of the house consulted with a molla as to what he should do. The latter told him that he must rebuild the house. He therefore demanded the price of the house, saying that he must tear it down. One man excused himself for giving his room to Christians, saying that the house was old and he intended to tear it down anyhow. Dr. Perkins with his dead child was compelled to sleep in the street. An American scientist, ignorant of the language, approached a lunch-stand, and putting out a piece of money reached for some *kabab*. The restaurateur gave a shriek of dismay, fearing his viands would be polluted in the eyes of all other customers. The same traveler drank water by having it poured into his hands. On account of this feeling the traveler in many parts of Persia must take his cooking and drinking vessels along with him, not knowing at what place they may be refused. Often, indeed, many of these difficulties are overcome by a little extra money. A Persian proverb says: " By giving money the molla can be cast out of the mosque." The love of money overcomes many an orthodox Shiah's prejudices.

This defilement is supposed to reach not only foods and drink and the vessels that contain them, but to contaminate other things as well. A street urchin with not a clean square inch on his body has been known to ask alms of a Christian and wash the money before putting it in his pocket. At a reception an officer dropped his cane. An Armenian nobleman politely picked it up and handed it to him. The latter, with disdain, sent the cane out to be washed before he would use it. A story, probably exaggerated, was told of a nobleman who went to a reception and gave his arm to a Christian lady to promenade. When he returned home his khanum had the sleeve of the coat taken out, washed, and pressed. A Mussulman who was having a suit made by an Armenian tailor told him not to press it,

as that would necessitate dampening it, nor to thread his needle
by putting his thread to his mouth, nor to cut the thread with
his teeth. A shoemaker was told not to blacken his shoes,
but let his Mussulman apprentice do that. It is for this reason that a Christian is rarely permitted to enter a mosque or
shrine. A sayid had a prayer-room where for years the story
of the martyred imams had been told. He was much chagrined because the Armenians bought the neighboring house
and so his room became unfit for sacred use. Strict Shiahs will
not sell a Christian a Koran, or anything containing a verse
of it, nor will they allow him even to touch it. For this action
they quote the verse of the Koran: " Let none touch it but the
purified." They even prefer that no translation of the Koran
shall be made, though a Persian interlineary has been published.
The more bigoted will not give the Christian the polite greeting, " Peace be to you! " The infidel has no peace; to him
he says, " May God keep you! " It shows how this fear of
defilement is in their minds, that when a man in Kurdistan
became demented his craze was that he was ceremonially unclean, and he wished continually to wash himself.

Sometimes the nature of these customs provokes retaliation.
An English consul in Tabriz went to call on a Persian. They
shook hands, and then the Persian reached his hands out of
the window to be washed. When the consul left he parted
with the same greeting, and he then walked to the fountain in
the courtyard, ordered his servants to bring a towel and soap,
and washed his hands thoroughly in the presence of the Persians. But this bigotry is fast passing away. Already more
than half of the people are ashamed of such ideas. Most Persian gentlemen receive the Christian, especially if he be a foreigner, with courtesy and true politeness, extend to him the
hand of fellowship, serve refreshments to him, visit him, and
accept his hospitality in return. The court of the shah gives
countenance to no such antiquated notions. Foreigners guard

against offending the sensibilities of the strict, and such prejudices are fast sinking out of sight.

With respect to its morals Persia takes a low rank.   In
social life, polygamy, concubinage, temporary marriage, and
free divorce manifest their demoralizing effects.   Sensuality is
strongly developed.   Impure thought and conversation prevail.
Their stories and poetry abound in obscenity, and many of
their picture-books are unfit to look at.   The sensual doctrine
of a heaven where every man will have seventy houris suits
the popular taste.   Though much freedom is given by law to
the passions, yet unnatural vices prevail.   Sodomy is common
among the vicious class and the wealthy; even Armenian and
Nestorian youth, following the lead of some of their bishops,
are guilty of it.   Theft and highway robbery are common,
burglary rare.   Gambling prevails among the upper classes.
The profane use of the divine name by men and women alike
strikes the ear continually.   Cursing is a public nuisance; the
donkeys are driven through the streets with oaths.   Yet reviling, though so common, excites many quarrels, and is resented
with intense passion, especially the reviling of another's religion.
It is severely punished.   Wife-beating is common.   Human life
is held cheap, and many go about with daggers in their belts.
Almost every traveler carries a gun with him for protection.
Oppression and injustice are widely prevalent.   But the characteristic faults of the Persians are deceit and its twin vice,
dishonesty.   All departments of life are so filled with deceit
that one becomes incredulous of every statement until it is confirmed.   Xenophon says that the ancient Persians were taught
three things: to shoot with a bow, ride a horse, and tell the
truth.   For the first they have substituted the rifle and retain
their skill, as also in riding; but truth-telling is a lost art.
Falsehood is so natural that it is hard for them to tell the truth
even when it is to their advantage.   Mar Yohannan said that
"people lie as long as they can find lies to tell, after which

they may from accident or necessity once or twice speak the truth." Professor Browne translates a tradition that certain persons demanded of the Imam Jafar-i-Sadik, "Will your followers commit crimes and do unlawful actions?" He answered, "Yes." "Will they be guilty of fornication and sins against nature?" they asked. "It is possible," he replied. "Will they drink wine and commit murder?" they inquired. "It is likely enough," said he. "Will they utter a false-hood?" they interrogated. "That," said he, "is impossible." The imam evidently had a sense of humor. A preacher spoke from the text, "Lie not one to another." After the service a young man came up and introduced his brother as a "dread-ful liar." The narrator remarks that the latter might have re-turned the compliment without adding in the least to his former reputation. Yet a phrase constantly on the lips of a Persian is, "The liar is an enemy of God."

One reason why Persians are false is because they are taught the doctrine of *tagia*. According to this doctrine it is right to deny one's faith for the sake of safety. It justifies pretend-ing to be, and acting like, a Sunni when on the pilgrimage to Mecca. It widens into the idea that deceit for a good purpose is proper, and resolves the good into what is advantageous.

Many Persians have a great fear of false oaths taken for-mally upon the Koran. Their dread of a curse acts as a restraint upon them. By custom an oath is to them an end of strife. Informal false oaths are an habitual occurrence. Most shop-keepers think it necessary to swear by all the imams as to the price they paid and the gain they are making on a transac-tion. Seals can easily be got to a false document. In the Babi wars the Persian generals did not hesitate to give their seal and oath on the Koran, guaranteeing the safety of those who should surrender, and yet they slaughtered them after they had laid down their arms.

As to dishonesty, it is sadly prevalent. We have probably
greater rascals in America, who wreck railroads and embezzle
millions; but in Persia the proportion of dishonest people is
inconceivably large. Deceit in bargaining, overreaching, re-
pudiation, bribery, and venality are usual factors. An honest
man—the noblest work of God!—is rare. Diogenes would
light his lantern and search a long while for him. Servants are
a very unfaithful class. Besides his salary the cook reckons
on such perquisites as fees from the shopkeepers, the difference between silver and copper currency; he will, moreover,
charge more than he has paid, and collect commissions from
peddlers and others who sell to his master, or to whom he sells.
In addition he may take things to his home or sell them in the
market. One servant inquired, on being hired, how much rice
was used in the house, wishing to gauge his *mudakhil* or illegit-
imate income. An English consul, tired of having his horses
starved and the feed sold, adopted the habit of coming out
and standing by while they were being fed. The hostler made
a trap-door, so that he could let the barley fall down below
and take it away afterward. In building-operations all sorts
of tricks are practised. Even the picks and shovels must be
counted every night, or they will be missing in the morning.
The Persians are so unable to trust one another that few great
companies are formed, and thus many things that might be
done with large capital must remain undone.

The conscience of the Persian is not often of the tender
sort. If it is, the law (Shari) affords an easy way of quieting
it. Restitution is rarely thought of by the penitent. I knew
only one man to restore the value of stolen property. A fellah
entered in great agitation and put two reals into my hand, saying that he had stolen a shovel two years before, and his conscience was not easy. The mollas claim the power of purifying
dishonest gains—making them *hallal*. A conscience-smitten

man went to a molla in a small city and said he wished to
have his unlawful money cleansed and his conscience eased.
The molla said, "All right; give me ten tomans and I will do
it for you." He said to himself, "How will giving him ten
tomans cleanse the remainder?" He went to another molla.
He would do it thoroughly for twenty. Finally he went to the
mujtehid, who said, "Give me all your property and I will
cleanse it for you. I do not say whether I will give it back
to you or not. Make an entire surrender and I will cleanse
your money and your conscience." He wrote a list of all he
possessed, even to his clothing. It amounted to one hundred
and fifty tomans. Then the mujtehid said, "Now give me a
note for the one hundred and fifty." Having received this, he
added, "Now go and get me fifty tomans, and next year you
may pay me fifty more, and the following year fifty, and your
property and your conscience will then be purified." Afterward the man narrated the transaction to a Nestorian, who told
him to repent and restore to those whom he had defrauded,
and hereafter use a just weight and measure. He returned
to the mujtehid and told him that his wife objected to the arrangement, and got his note returned to him.

It is supposed that if the man from whom money has been
stolen will say willingly, by subterfuge or otherwise, "It is excused," "It is lawful," it becomes so. Dr. Browne translates
an amusing story illustrating this. "The mother of a thief was
dying," he writes, "and she enjoined her son to obtain for her
a lawful shroud. He sallied forth at night, attacked a traveler,
and found in his saddle-bags a piece of linen. Seeing this, he
exclaimed, 'Praise be to God, who has not suffered me to return disappointed and ashamed to my mother!' Then he began
to beat the owner of the linen, saying, 'Make this linen lawful
to me with thy whole heart.' On his return he told his mother
that the man had more than a thousand times said with tears
and groans, 'I make it lawful to thee.'"

The Persians have, nevertheless, some good traits of character. They are charitable, hospitable, contented, industrious, temperate, and not bloodthirsty nor quarrelsome. Their gentleness, affability, and courteous manner, though at times insincere, cannot be gainsaid.

CHAPTER XIII

THE Ali-Allahis are a sect which is widely scattered in Islam, and is regarded as heterodox, and consequently is despised and slandered by both Shiahs and Sunnis. They conform externally to most of the rites of the Mohammedans around them, but have esoteric doctrines and practices, the secrecy of which leads to much surmise as well as suspicion. Nothing definite is known of their system, unless the supposition is correct that they have affinity with the Nusairiyeh of Syria. The tenets of the latter were revealed by a pervert, Suleiman Effendi, in a book published in Arabic, and found in English in the "Proceedings of the American Oriental Society." Whether the information I have received of the Ali-Allahis is authentic or not I have no means of verifying; but I have little doubt there are large grains of truth in what follows, which will aid the future investigator to arrive at a full understanding of their tenets, while my experience among them will afford reliable views of their village life.

I first became acquainted with the Ali-Allahis when on a visit to Ilkachi, one of their villages, at the time of Noruz. Pir Semmet Aga, their sheik, had invited us to the wedding-festivities of his son. We found him dressed in long flowing robes of the old Persian style, with a felt skull-cap and bare feet. The people regarded him as holy and worthy of high reverence. They came into his presence to kiss his hand, offer him gifts, and sacrifice sheep and oxen in his honor.

They brought their sick to him to be prayed over and healed. Some poor men came with an offering of bread, and, kneeling and prostrating themselves, kissed his feet. He took the bread, blessed it, brake it, and distributed it to them, as a consecrated thing. He regarded himself as sinless and endowed by God with original righteousness; but a proper definition led him to admit his sinfulness.

On the day after our arrival we accompanied the pir and his people to their cemetery. It was the last day of their year, and according to custom they were going to repair the graves. The pir headed the procession. At the graves he read from the Koran and intoned some prayers, after which taffy and sweetmeats were eaten. He was specially interested in testing the correctness of the direction of the graves by a compass which I had. They called it the *Kebla-nama*, i.e., indicator of the Kebla at Mecca. A question of his shows how prevalent are mistaken ideas. He asked me if it were true that in America we disposed of the bodies of the dead by putting them in a liquid which dissolved them, and then poured it all out on the ground.

Above the cemetery and on the hill beyond are two shrines, one for men and one for women. The one for men is the larger of the two. It was built, so they declared, by the widow of a humble saint in a single night, without assistance from any one. Before that a light had burned there, an emanation from the presence of the husband's ghost. The age of the tomb was reported as several centuries. I asked a long-haired, wild-looking dervish how old it was. He said, "Before Abraham was, it was." Further questioning brought out the fact that he meant before his son Abraham was born. We entered and examined the shrine. It had an altar for sacrifices and niches for burning candles. The people prostrated themselves and kissed the railing, thinking that their prayers would be especially acceptable through the merit of the saint.

In the evening the villagers began to welcome the Noruz (New Year). Some fired off guns and lighted bonfires on the flat roofs. Young men let down ropes on their girdles through the skylights. To these girls tied sweetmeats, or sometimes caught hold of them and were drawn up by the boys. It is perhaps this frolicsome play of village life that gives rise to stories about orgies of Venus being kept among Ali-Allahis. The festivities were prolonged until after midnight. In the early morning they began their round of New-Year's visits and congratulations. From five hundred to eight hundred persons came to pay their respects to our host. Many of them brought an apple, an orange, or a colored egg, presenting it to the chief in both hands as a mark of respect. We joined in the rejoicings and had a long day of visiting and feasting. Sweetmeats were served in every house, though tea and coffee were not so much seen as in the cities. We breakfasted with the civil head of the village (kand-khuda), the father of the prospective bride. The Ali-Allahis have not the idea that the Shiahs have that eating with non-Mussulmans is defiling. They are friendly and cordial in their intercourse with Christians. At breakfast we sat around a *kurisee*. This is a table about a foot high, which in winter is placed over the *tandur* (underground oven) or pan of charcoals, and overspread with comforters to keep the heat from escaping. Around it, and partly under it, the family sit in the daytime and sleep at night. Though the time for fires was passed, the *kurisee* served the purpose of a table. On it the cloth was spread, and the company sat on the floor around it. In front of each person were put several sheets of bread, which served as plates and spoons. The bread, in color, size, and shape, resembled a half of a sheepskin. Each one tore off a piece of bread, and with it helped himself from any dish, and ate the bread and its contents together. Our bill of fare seemed excellent for simple village life. Besides ordinary dishes such as mutton, eggs, rice, cheese, and curds, we had cabbage-dumplings, grape-molasses, taffy, rose-leaf preserves, watermelon preserves, fig-sauce, and cream from the cow, the sheep, and the buffalo. Buffalo's cream is a great delicacy. In the evening we had a dinner of boiled mutton and rice dressed. The natives used hands for spoons and fingers for forks, and rolled up their sleeves to facilitate eating. We were furnished with wooden spoons, but sometimes, as a special mark of favor, a piece of meat would be selected and passed to us by some one in his fingers, an act of courtesy it can hardly be said we enjoyed.* We drank sherbet out of a large punch-bowl, and it required some exercise of muscle to properly balance it.

We had scarcely rested from the New-Year's festivities when we were awakened by the preparations for the wedding. Village custom allows much freedom to the boys and girls, especially among this sect. This young couple had grown up together and had reached an understanding among themselves. But they could not openly have anything to do with the arrangements. The youth told a friend, and that friend told the pir. He proposed to the girl's father, who, after considerable delay, consented. After the old folks had settled the preliminaries a molla was called, who drew up the contract, in which the couple affirmed their desire to be married, and the man promised, if at any time he divorced his wife, to give her a sum of money. The amount varies from a few tomans to thousands, according to the rank and wealth of the parties. It is much less when the contract is made with a widow or a divorced woman. The contract had been made in the autumn. Then the girl was veiled and her charms concealed from the groom and all his relatives. Village custom had not required this before that time. After a period his aunts and sisters

* In England, during the shah's visit, a Persian of distinction is said to have honored a lady of high degree by taking a chicken, tearing off a piece with his fingers, and passing it to her ladyship.

came in a body, caught the girl, and unveiled her. But the prospective groom could not yet see her face.

The wedding-day had been set for Noruz and had now arrived. From early morning till late at night friends came to the groom's house with presents of fruits and candies, and especially of silver coins, which were presented stuck in an apple or pomegranate. This money was intended to pay for the outfit which the groom had purchased for the bride. Toward evening friends of the bridegroom arrayed him in his wedding-apparel. They then formed a procession, put the presents on trays, raised them on their shoulders, and marched with music and dancing to the bride's house. She did not appear, but the presents were sent upstairs for her to examine. Every man who carried a tray was entitled to a present from the bride's mother. She distributed to them thirty or forty pairs of stockings. She wished to acknowledge our gifts in some Persian way, but we assured her the privilege of being present was our portion and reward.

The feast which followed seemed almost like a sacrament. An invocation was made to Ali, the all-powerful Ruler. Responsive prayers were uttered, and almost total silence prevailed. A candle was now placed in the center of the room. The food was first set before the light as a manifestation of God. The men kissed the bread which was passed to them, and repeatedly brought their hand to their heart, their chin, and their forehead, in token of reverence. There was much mystery and solemnity about it all. After the feast their custom is to rise and sway from side to side, and whirl around and around, saying, "Yahoo, yahoo!" until an intense religious frenzy seizes them, and they fall down exhausted, frothing and foaming at the mouth. This part of the celebration was omitted at this time, and instead of it we were invited to read from the *injil* (gospel).

On the next evening the bride and her friends formed a procession and marched toward the groom's house. He first came out to meet them, then suddenly turned and ran back. The champion of the bride ran after him, trying to overtake him and seize his hat. He is entitled to a forfeit before he restores it. Then the groom went to the housetop and threw apples at the bridal procession as it entered the yard. If his betrothed has not lifted her veil for him secretly, he may try to punish her by hitting her. With the arrival of the bride the wedding festivities are over.

During these days we had many conversations with the pir and his people concerning their religion. They call themselves the Ahli-Allah ("followers of God"). They are called popularly Ali-Allahi ("believers in the divinity of Ali"). Some have supposed that they were once Christians, who, when conquered by the Arabs, substituted the name of Ali for Jesus, and afterward forgot their origin. There is little proof of this supposition. There are at least seven sects of them in Persia— Davudis, Yedelar, Sheik-Ibrahimis, Atash-Begis, Alavis, Abdul-Begis, and Benyaminis. These are followers of different men bearing these names, but supposed to be manifestations of the same person, and, according to some, incarnations of God. The Ali-Allahis number several hundred thousand in Persia. The Gurian tribe of Kermanshah belongs to them. One of their traditions is that Nusair or Davud, a disciple, said to Ali, "You are God! " Ali said, "Do not say so." Nusair repeated it. Ali struck him and he died. Then Ali brought him to life. Nusair stood up and said, " Did I not rightly say, ' You are God ' ? Else how could you make me alive? "

I received the following information concerning the beliefs of the Persian sects:

They reverence Mohammed little more than any other prophet. He may be called their John the Baptist, the forerunner of Ali, their great prophet. They call Ali the Light of God manifested in the flesh. They pay honor to him which is due to the Creator alone.   Prayer and sacrifices of fruits and animals are offered to him.   He is the Redeemer.   God is believed to have made frequent manifestations of himself in the prophets.   Ali was the highest manifestation of that divine personality which dwelt in Abraham, Moses, David, Christ, and Mohammed.   Christ and Ali are therefore essentially the same person.   They therefore welcome Christians as elder brethren.   Many of them listen with pleasure to the gospel, as the Word of God.   They have little regard for fasting, alms-giving, and the Mohammedan ritual of prayer, but have great veneration for shrines, and have certain prayers of their own, in Turkish, which are repeated many times a day.

Light is their sacred emblem, their symbol of the divine in-fluence.   God is the central light, from which the universe of spirit and life emanates, or is reflected as a candle in a room whose walls are covered with many mirrors.   At their feasts, as we have seen, a portion of each dish is set before a lighted candle.   Some of them hold to the pantheistic conception that not only prophets and imams, but all angels, men, and the vital principle in animals and trees, have emanated from God and are of his essence.   Associated with this idea is the doctrine of transmigration, and the final absorption of all in the bosom of the Infinite.   The wicked are thought to enter into donkeys, mules, and other beasts of burden.   Apropos of transmigration, an anecdote was told me of a murshid who, one day setting out hunting, caught a fox and tied it to his saddle. Before he could mount, the horse took fright and ran back to the village.   When the people saw the fox in the saddle they cried out, "O murshid! appear to us in whatever guise you will, but do not come as a fox!"   Some of the Ali-Allahis, however, hold the Mussulman doctrine of judgment and para-dise.   Others of them, again, deny the existence of Satan. Evil is a principle in the heart of man, they affirm.   Most men

are regarded as sinners, but the prophets and the pirs or elders
are sinless.

Two of their rites come very near to the sacraments of the
Old Testament. Circumcision is performed by the barber, in
the presence of the assembled relatives. The other rite greatly
resembles the Passover. It is frequently celebrated, and at no
set time or place. Whoever wishes it at his house consecrates
a lamb or sheep for the occasion. The victim is brought into
the yard of the pir, and is sacrificed to Ali by a man who has
been formally appointed to this service. It is then cooked,
blessed, and divided by the pir among the men, and eaten
with bread, in great solemnity. At the same time a selection
is read from one of their sacred books. After the reading,
raisins and nuts, which have been set aside as thank-offerings
for the harvest, are distributed, and sherbet is drunk. This
sherbet is grape-juice, boiled down to the consistency of
molasses, and mixed with water when desired for drinking.
Their story is that the sect originated with forty persons, one
of whom was Ali. God sent them a grape from heaven. Ali
pressed the juice of it and the forty drank of it. From this
arose the custom of drinking the sherbet.

The sacred books to which reference has just been made are
in Turkish, and are understood by the people. They were written by the last of their divine incarnations, Sultan Nahani, a pole
of the universe, three or four centuries ago. They are for the
most part poetic, religious autobiography, and hold a higher
place in their regard than the Koran. Many of their sacred
books were lost in the Russo-Turkish War. The author is supposed not to have died, but to have become invisible.

They have a service for the consecration of children. The
father presents the child before his fifth year, holding a nutmeg
in his hand, in the presence of the pir. After a ceremony the
nutmeg is divided and given to the assembled company. The

eldership among the Ali-Allahis is hereditary, or at least is confined to the priestly family.   Polygamy is rare ; but marriage is
not restricted by laws of consanguinity.   The Pir S. was a cousin
of his successor, A.   S. married A.'s sister.   Their son married first one, and after her death another of A.'s daughters,
and A.'s son married S.'s daughter.   Their object in this is to
preserve the sacred seed.   The results are plainly seen in physical, racial, and even in social deterioration.

CHAPTER XIV

SOCIAL AND FAMILY LIFE

THE Persians are eminently a social people. They are vivacious and entertaining, fond of jokes and story-telling, and ready in repartee. They are much given to visiting and feasting. This is remarkable, since the great bond of society with us is entirely wanting: the social intercourse of men and women is not permitted, and the idea of it shocks their sense of propriety. Men visit with men, women with women. Dancing amazes them beyond measure, and seems an immodest license and a perversion of liberty.

The Persians are a polite people. They have elaborate rules of etiquette, and many set phrases and compliments suitable for every occasion. Visits are made at the festivals, both for congratulation and condolence, and often for the transaction of business. The physician is honored with an hour's social chat before the ailments of the caller-in are mentioned. He is expected in return to make himself comfortable in the parlor for a prolonged tea-drinking before being inducted into the sick-room. Time is of little value. Social calls are often of three or four hours' duration.

The greatest social event in Persia is the festival of the New Year or Noruz. It commemorates the entrance of the sun into the sign of Aries at the vernal equinox. It is the most fitting and beautiful time for the New Year. Then the sacred year of the Jews and of some European nations began. March 25th was the first day of the year in Scotland until 1600, and

243

in England until 1752. At this season, Persia, throughout most of its borders, begins to put on its robe of verdure, flowers begin to bloom, and the farmer takes up his work in the fields.

Some Persians affirm that the world began to move in its orbit on that day. Others place the origin of the festival in the time of Jemshid, the founder of Persepolis. He introduced the solar year, and celebrated its first day as a splendid festival. The sculptured procession on the great staircase at Persepolis is supposed to represent the bringing of presents from the various provinces at Noruz. This is the only festival of ancient Persia that has not been displaced by the sacred seasons of Mohammedanism. The Persians never fail to enter into its enjoyment, except when the movable lunar calendar of Islam brings some religious ceremony at the same time. From 1893 to 1896 Noruz falls in the great fast of Ramadan. The festivities with which ancient kings celebrated it are curiously described in the "Arabian Nights," in "The Enchanted Horse." In the introduction to this story it is said: "Noruz, or the new day, is a festival so solemn and so ancient throughout the whole extent of Persia, taking its origin even from the earliest period of idolatry, that the holy religion of the Prophet, pure and unsullied as it is, has been hitherto unable to abolish it; although it must be confessed that it is a custom completely pagan, and that the ceremonies observed in its solemnization are of the most superstitious nature. Not to mention large cities, there is no town, borough, village, or hamlet, however small, where the festival is not celebrated with extraordinary rejoicings. Those that take place at court surpass all others by the variety of new and surprising spectacles, so that nothing that is attempted in other parts of the world can approach or be compared with this sumptuous magnificence." A thousand years after Haroun-al-Raschid the festival still holds its place. To an outside observer its ceremonies do not seem as "pagan" as some of those connected with Shiahism.

Prior to the festival of Noruz the dervish pitches his white tent before the door of some nobleman, and sits there and yells, " Ya hak! " ("O truth! ") until his claims to charity are satisfied. The letter-carrier presents himself to receive an *anam;* the cook expects a new coat; the mirza, and even the physician, are remembered by their patrons; and the alderman receives goodly donations from his constituents. During the last week of the old year the bazaars are profusely decorated. Gay cloths, carpets, and shawls are exhibited in the shops. Pictures, mirrors, mottoes, bunting, and embroideries are hung up. Arches are constructed, spanning the streets with pendent ornaments. Villagers crowd in front of the open shops, and groups of boys stroll about to see the sights. Every one buys a collection of nuts, raisins, figs, dates, dried apricots, grape-juice paste, etc. These fruits must be of seven kinds, the name of each beginning with the letter S. The collection is called the *yeddi luvn.* Many send to their friends a plateful, with the compliments of the season. The last Wednesday, called Akhir Chahar-Shenba, is a gala day. It is the children's festival, but the whole population is ready for a frolic. Clowns in fantastic costumes and ludicrous masks, and strolling minstrels with tambourines and cymbals and leading a monkey, perform and collect shahis. Boys crowd the streets, and women gather on the housetops, to see the shows. School-boys enter into the spirit of the day and make a mock visit to their principal. One of them, arrayed like a Kurdish sheik, in long flowing robes, great turban, and a cotton beard, and with attendants armed like Kurds, but with canes for swords, presents himself and declares that a fine has been levied upon the school. He receives a present, and they all go off to expend it on some of the good things in the bazaars.

As the great day approaches, every man says to himself, " Well, to-morrow is Noruz. I must get my head shaved, go to the bath, dye my hands, nails, and beard with henna, put on

a clean skull-cap, and see if the tailor has my new coat ready.
I must buy some sugar and tea, tobacco and candy, and then
I shall be ready for all comers."

In the capital the festival is ushered in and celebrated with
elaborate ceremonies by the shah and his court. The crown
prince in Tabriz keeps the day with similar rejoicings. At the
astronomical termination of the year a tray of the seven fruits
is brought before the prince. Some of these are eaten. Incense is burned, according to a custom of the fire-worshipers.
One hundred and ten guns are fired off, with reference to Ali,
who is said to have been named successor to Mohammed on
this day. Consuls, nobles, and high officials, clothed in their
uniforms and decorations, pay their salaam to his Highness and
partake of a feast. Luck-money, coined with the name of the
shah, is distributed to all. Some of these gold and silver
tokens are sent to the mujtehid and other ecclesiastics. They
presage a fortunate year for the recipient, because the king
thus indicates his royal favor. After the salaam there is a
military review in the *medan* or public square. The trumpet
is sounded; the officers on their gaily caparisoned horses present themselves with their companies. Each soldier receives a
token of fourteen shahis in value. After the review, wrestling-
contests and ram-fights enliven the scene. In some villages
buffalo-fights are a part of the programme. These powerful
animals, sometimes made ferocious by partial intoxication, make
a rough contest. In other places, such as Hamadan, the day
is ushered in with a display of pyrotechnics. From the housetops thousands of rockets and "fusing-jugs" are set off.

The festivities extend over two or three weeks. The bazaars are generally closed and business suspended. All are
bent on pleasure. Merrymaking reigns supreme. Days are
designated for visiting particular classes or wards of the city.
On the first day the official class exchange visits, while the religiously inclined give the honor of precedence to the mujte-

hids. On succeeding days the crowd moves from ward to ward. Calls are often an hour long. About breakfast-time (noon) a group of friends may unexpectedly enter, and a new supply of pilau must be served up quickly. Families that have suffered bereavement during the preceding year do not make visits, but receive them, serving to their guests bitter coffee and omitting all sweetmeats.

Noruz is a pleasant time to renew old acquaintances, make new ones, and to visit both rich and poor without interfering with their business engagements. I shall give an account of the visits made during one Noruz season, since they afford the best opportunity to become acquainted with the social customs of the people. According to a custom in visiting men of rank, we sent a request to the governor-general, the former Amir-i-Nizam, that his Excellency might appoint a convenient time to receive us. The governor's house, in a group of government buildings, was built in semi-European style, with windows on all sides and faced with red brick. He had two large reception-rooms, one furnished in Persian, the other in European style. The Persian room had portières over the doors, and was carpeted in the usual manner, with a large center-piece, two *kenarehs* or side-strips, and a *kala* or head-piece, the four rugs neatly covering the entire floor. The *kenarehs* and *kala* were of soft *kecha* or felt, half an inch thick, and the color of camel's hair, with a simple figured border.* Over these was spread, for their protection, a breadth of cotton cloth, called *ru-farsh*. At the upper corners of the reception-room were divans, consisting of mattresses and pillows, and covered with the finest Senna rugs. On one of these divans the governor sat to receive Persian visitors; the other was reserved for men

* The best of these *kechas* are manufactured at Yezd and Hamadan. A traveler mentions one the dimensions of which were one hundred and twenty by eighty feet. It was transported from Yezd on a line of camels for the palace of the minister of justice at Teheran.

of high rank, while other guests sat on the carpets around the sides of the room.

We had removed our galoshes and hats on being ushered in. The governor, in stockinged feet and with hat on, received us cordially, rising and shaking our hands. To his "Salaam alakum!" ("Peace to you!") we responded, "To you peace! May your Excellency's feast be blessed!" He replied, "May your favor be increased!" After being seated on chairs we inquired concerning his Excellency's "noble condition." He replied in the customary phrase, "Al hamd ul Ullah!" ("Praise God, I am well!"); but on second inquiry he declared that he was feeling ill, and most of his conversation in the midst of tea-drinking was about his ailments. He ended the interview by saying that he had a *peeshkesh* for the doctor, which proved to be ten imperials.

Afterward we called on the beglar-begi or mayor. He is of the Dumbli family, which have ruled in Azerbijan before the Kajar dynasty. He has great wealth, being lord of many villages. All the guests in the saloon rose and remained standing while he led us into a room furnished with tables and chairs. A special feature of the room was the great number of gilded and illuminated firmans and honorary degrees from the shah, framed and hung on the walls, or placed in the niches. According to custom, tea was brought in in tiny glasses having handles of silver, and placed on glass saucers. The cup-bearer served each person on an individual waiter of silver, and in the order of the rank of each one, as judged from the position of their seats. He first offered tea to his master, but he, with a wave of the hand, declined to be served until after his guests. The tea was piping hot, without cream, and as sweet as a syrup. On the waiters was a little bottle of Shiraz lemon-juice and sliced *naranj* (grape-fruit) for flavoring it. After a time the attendants reappeared. One bore a salver on which were tiny coffee-cups in holders. The latter resembled in shape an egg-

HOUSE DECORATIONS.

cup. They are sometimes chinaware, and sometimes Zenjan-silver filigree, of exquisite workmanship. The other attendant bore a coffee-pot; he lifted one of the coffee-cups, placed it in the holder, and filled it about two thirds full of very thick, black, sweet coffee.*

The *kalean* or water-pipe was brought in and passed to us. We declined with the phrase, "It is not our custom." The host took a few whiffs and passed it to the guests in the saloon. Finally we said, in the customary form of adieu, "Will you command our dismissal?" He replied, "Do you withdraw your graciousness?" If the host wishes to shorten the visit he can hasten these courses.

A visit to the *kalantar*, the chief alderman, showed us some different phases of Persian life. An hour's ride on horseback brought us to his place in the suburbs. He had extensive grounds, beautifully laid out with fountains and flower-beds and shaded avenues. In his greenhouse were orange and lemon trees bearing fruit. One of his rooms was papered with chromos, another with cuts from the illustrated papers. He had a large household of retainers. The *kalantar* was fond of religious discussion and familiar with the Bible. He had written a book in defense of Islam against Christianity. His opinion was that Paul undermined and corrupted the religion of Jesus. He found in the prophecy of Habakkuk of the Holy One from Mount Paran, who drove asunder the nations, a prediction of Mohammed. Conversation on religion is habitual among the Persians.

Here there were set before us some choice sweetmeats. Among the favorite confections is *gaz*. It is made from the juice of the tamarisk-tree and has a delicious flavor, which is

---

* Sometimes sherbets are substituted for the tea or coffee. These are drinks made of lemon, plum, cherry, rose, cucumber, or other fruit-syrups. Simpler forms are *skanjabi*, made of vinegar and honey, or *ayran*, a kind of buttermilk.

increased by being mixed with pistachios. Another favorite is
fig-paste, called "ease of the throat."   This is variously fla-
vored and colored.   Among the candies popular in Persia are
sugared burned almond, pomegranate jelly cut in little squares,
khulva, a taffy of molasses and nuts, rock-candy, and *peshmak*,
which is made of sugar and butter, crystallized like snowflakes
or thistle-down, and formed into pyramids, cones, and other
shapes.   A very rich pastry sprinkled with sugar, but without
fruit, is much prized.   Their cakes, made of rice-flour and nuts,
with sheep-tail fat and saffron flavor, are rarely agreeable to
foreign taste.   Year by year confections are being improved
by contact with Tiflis and Constantinople.   The best sweetmeats are now made in the houses of the wealthy, and some
of their ladies are expert in the art.   At Noruz and other festivals great *khonchas* * of candies are sent in by the clients of
the great, and the center of the parlor is occupied by a large
display of them.   It has lately become the custom to rent a
large amount of confections for an occasion, only those being
paid for which are eaten, and the rest returned.

These visits, together with others to mollas, merchants, and
physicians, gave us considerable knowledge of the life of well-
to-do Persians.   The impression was gained that their manner
of living is very comfortable.   Their wealth is not great, but
they have the conveniences and luxuries which the country
affords, or which they think it necessary to import.   Their
houses are neither of marble nor of cut stone, nor do they have
many of the charms of beautiful architecture.   But the wealthy
class in the cities have pleasant rooms, excellent food, fruits
and flowers in abundance, troops of servants waiting their
every beck and call, stables full of valuable horses, incomes
easily earned, plenty of leisure for an afternoon siesta and for

* A *khoncha* is a wooden tray, about two feet by four, which is carried
on a man's head when a wedding-dowry or a present of sweetmeats is
taken through the streets.

social intercourse, many holidays and a disposition to enjoy them; and withal they have no reason to envy the far more opulent but possibly less contented plutocrats who under steam pressure and with lightning rapidity are "bulling and bearing" one another in the marts of civilization.

New-Year's calls on the poor of Persia revealed a striking contrast. We knocked at the outer door, that the women might have a chance to conceal themselves. Bending low, we stooped down and passed under a long arched way, and entered a little yard with mud-plastered walls. The *cahva-khana* or hall opened into a half-underground room, in one end of which was a poorly made window, covered with oiled paper, its cracks being similarly pasted over to keep out the wind. Its flopping, ill-fitting door was low, while the sill was very high, in order that the shoes may be taken off in the hall and not obstruct the opening and shutting of the door. The rafters overhead were unceiled. The furniture consisted of common carpets (*ghelim*), a mirror brought with the wedding-outfit, a copper basin and ewer, a small tea-urn and some glasses, and a *kalean* on the lower niches. On the upper niches were a few bottles, and on the once whitened walls had been pasted some cigarette-papers, caricature prints, and verses from the Koran. The host greeted us with a hearty "Welcome! You have done me a great favor." We replied, "May your festival be blessed, may your house be blessed!" He answered, "It is a present to you." The other guests rose, placed their right hands first on their hearts, then to their foreheads, and bowed low. We knelt on our knees on calico cushions, the weight of the body resting on the heels. The host, though his circumstances were straitened, was bright in conversation. A small boy dressed like a grown man entered, and we inquired, "Who is this?" "He is your slave," he replied; which meant, "He is my son." A dish of wheat was growing on the window-sill, a symbol of the renewal of the year. A fish was swimming in a pan, which called forth a remark from him that fish always look toward Mecca at Noruz. He placed before us a few candies, some boiled eggs, and pickled grapes. He had the samovar already boiling, and sat down beside it, washed the cups and saucers, and placed tea before us. We did not decline to drink, for the poor man would feel aggrieved. He honored us specially by almost filling our tea-glasses with sugar, though he himself sipped his tea through a small lump which he held between his teeth and retained to sweeten succeeding sups. What does a poor man have besides the things within sight? His goods consist of a few rude dishes of native pottery, a jar or two of pickled herbs and dried vegetables, a flour-bin, some copper pots, and a chest of clothing. With his wages of a dime a day as a laborer or servant he must provide for his Khadija and Ismiel, Husain and Fatima. He thanks God for the blessing of such a family; but how do they live on such a pittance? Most of it goes to buy bread, which, with some salty cheese to give it taste, or a glass of weak tea, constitutes his breakfast; his luncheon is bread and sour milk, garlic or onions or some cheap fruit; for dinner a stew of meat and vegetables, highly seasoned with red peppers and onions —a large quantity for a little meat—makes his bread palatable. Lack of employment or high prices reduce him to bread and water. In winter a few shahis' worth of charcoal lasts the family a long while under the *kurisee*.

In sleeping rich and poor alike lie on the floor. The bedding, which consists of a short mattress, a round pillow, and coverlets, is folded up and placed in a recess by day. In summer many of the people sleep on the roofs, rising when the sun disturbs them.

The social habit, which is so universally exemplified at Noruz, is a striking trait of the Persian character. One of the social institutions of great attraction is the tea-house. The tea-houses are of various grades. Some are rudely furnished, with merely a raised platform which surrounds the sides of the room, and is covered with matting or carpet. Others have an air of comfort imparted to them by divans, mirrors, chandeliers, etc. With tea at half a cent a glass, and one pipeful of tobacco sufficing for a crowd, it is no wonder loafers seek them and business men make appointments in them. The common pipe, cigarettes, and the *kalean* or water-pipe are much used. In the latter the smoke passes through the water and is drawn into the lungs. Lemon-juice and other flavors are sometimes mixed with the water.

The ordinary *kalean* is about two feet high. It consists of a vase capable of holding about a quart of water, a top about the size of a goblet, in which burning charcoal and dampened tobacco are placed, a wooden tube which supports the top on the vase, and a mouthpiece or stem about twenty inches long. The support and stem are turned on the lathe, in various ornamental designs. The vase and bowl are of glass, stone, china, brass, or silver, and are set with turquoises or other jewels, and carved, enameled, and decorated with pictures of the shah, flowers, and similar objects.

Another place of social resort and gossip is the bath-house. Custom and religion require frequent ablutions. For the men, whose dyeing of the hair and nails with henna, scraping the flesh with tufa, etc., the bath is a frequent necessity, and no less so for the women, whose hair-dressing, dyeing of eyelashes, etc., require so much time and attention. The bath-houses are below the level of the street, so as to be supplied with water. The arched domes are lighted through slabs of alabaster. One may know when he is near the bath-house by the long rows of colored towels hung on the street walls. The fuel used is weeds, thorn-bushes, straw, dried manure, bones, carcasses, or any other rubbish, and the odor inside and out is sometimes very offensive. The atmosphere of the vaulted room is very hot, as in the case of the Turkish bath. The water in the plunge-tank is changed only once in two or three months, and is consequently a prolific breeder of disease.

The Persian has few kinds of amusement. His theater is the "Takia" or passion-play of Muharram; his lyceum lecturers are the dervishes on the street corner, and the poets and marseyakhan in the residences of the rich. Singers, musicians, and dancers are adjuncts of weddings and other feasts. The Persian gentleman does not dance. A prince, seeing some European noblemen dancing, expressed his surprise, saying, "Why do you exert yourselves so much? In Persia we hire people to dance for us." No violent games of ball and no severe gymnastics are in vogue, except for the *pehlavans* or wrestlers. Horse-racing and hunting are favorite amusements; chess, checkers, and backgammon are old and standard games. Cards are being introduced throughout the entire country, and gambling is unhappily prevalent.

The custom of giving presents is universal. A person returning home brings a *sogat* or present to each of his relatives and friends. The custom is so binding that some men unwillingly go in debt to avoid a breach of it, and others stay away from home from inability to do what is expected of them. Gifts of dainties from the table, of the first-fruits from the orchard, and of loaves of fresh bread are sent from friend to friend. Formal tokens of commendation from a superior are greatly prized. The shah yearly sends a *khallat* or robe of honor to each governor on the renewal of his appointment. Its bearer is an important official. He is met by the governor at a villa called *khallat-pashan*, where the latter puts on his robe. Its style and elegance indicate the degree of appreciation intended to be shown. It is a high honor for a royal person to give another a robe which he himself has worn. When the crown prince wished to show his appreciation of Dr. Holmes by presenting him with a robe of honor, he first wore it himself a few days.

Certain other presents may be regarded as taxes. Such are the large amounts sent by the governors to the shah at Noruz. Of a similar nature are those sent to local officials by subjects and by foreign residents, as a recognition of obligation for civil protection. On the receipt of such a gift it is customary to give the bearer a sum of money, showing appreciation of the gift and its sender. Fees, tips, and *anams* are very common. *Peeshkesh* is a gift to a superior, and is generally made with the idea of procuring an equivalent in cash, favor, or influence. Bakshish is a freewill offering to an inferior.

The social life of men outside of their own harems is in a sphere separated from women, and the account of their social life as hitherto presented has been confined to the relations of men. I will now turn to woman and her relations in the family life.

The most striking fact in the condition of woman in Persia is her seclusion. Her dwelling is shut in from the street and the view of the neighbors by high mud-walls. In the houses of the rich the privacy is made more complete by having two apartments, the *berun* and the *anderoon*. The latter is reserved exclusively for the women and children, and is also called the harem or forbidden place. Eunuchs act as guardians and stewards of this family. The wife never sits at a feast with her husband's guests, nor receives male visitors. The latter must not even inquire about her health, or refer to her. The husband, if occasion calls for it, speaks of her as "the mother of Ismiel" or "of Hasan," or uses some other circumlocution. Another man may refer to her as "the mother of Zebedee's children." If a man enters the gate unannounced he must cry, "Women, away! " that they may have time to conceal themselves. It is a misdemeanor for one to open a window overlooking his neighbor's yard. A Mussulman requested me to raise the wall surrounding the school, because the boys could look from the roof upon his women. A pigeon-trainer was accustomed to go on his roof to follow the birds, and so over-looked his neighbor's yard. He was warned not to do so, and on repeating the offense was shot dead. So carefully do they guard their Bathshebas from the sight of any David.

The street costume for woman is a contrivance for maintaining her seclusion even when she is out of the harem. It consists of *shelwar*, chudder, and veil. The *shelwar* is a combination of very full trousers and stockings, fitting tightly on the feet, and gathered at the ankles. The chudder is two yards square, of cloth, and is put on over the head and envelops the whole person. The veil is of muslin or linen, and completely conceals the face. Before the eyes is a lace-work, through which a woman can see her way, but not even a glance of her eye can be seen. This street costume is made of only two or three fabrics, either blue, black, or barred; so that among the many uniformly dressed women a man could not recognize any one of his own wives. As the women glide through the streets they lift their veils to get a fresh breeze or to see the pitfalls, but if a man appears unexpectedly the veils go down with a jerk. If a lady of high degree is riding through the streets an attendant goes before and commands, " Men, turn your eyes away! " Common mortals should not look upon the shadow of a princess. Even old hags who are washing clothes by the watercourses, and beating them upon the stones, attempt to arrange their veils and chudders so as to conceal their features. The wife of a Persian official who had been brought from Constantinople, and who was used to the freer ways of that city, went out in Tabriz in her foreign costume. The mujtehid sent his servants to warn her to cease to do so or she would be beaten. Even young girls must put on this street costume. Concealment is thus complete only in the cities. In the villages women are allowed more liberty, and among the Kurds and wandering tribes a still greater degree of freedom is accorded them. Liberty among the nomads is associated with greater purity and less scandal. Indeed, the disguise of the city dress gives facilities for secret intrigues. The Turks and Arabs require no such absolute concealment of the countenance, nor does the law of Islam command it.

A wife is in subjection to her husband—a subjection so abject that she does not even dream of the possession of those rights which have been and are being granted to women in Christian lands. She occupies the position of slave to man's pleasure and comfort, and aspires to nothing more. She does not sit down to eat with her husband, but eats after waiting on him. If perchance she accompanies him on the street, she walks some distance behind him. Wife-beating is very common, and is allowed by law and custom. Despising his wife as a woman, and having inbred ideas of her inferiority, the husband corrects her and punishes her as a child. But custom does not make such treatment pleasant. A Persian woman said to a foreign lady, "You are not married. Then happy are you, for you have no one to beat you." In a village where some men had gathered around me, and the women, all chattering at once, were making a great hubbub around Mrs. Wilson, a man attacked the women and struck them with his cane, saying, "Get away; you are making such a noise you confuse our conversation. You can't understand anything, anyway." If one protests against the beating of women as a barbarous practice the reply is, "How else shall we rule them?" Even when a Persian gentleman would by instinctive feeling be polite to a lady, he is restrained by the thought of his own dignity, saying, "Oh, she is only a woman; it won't do to show respect to her."

We can readily imagine that women thus secluded, and at the same time wilful and ignorant, with only the physical life developed, might make it difficult for the men to manage them without resorting to physical force. The tales of the East show us that women, even under Islam, assert themselves and repay the lords of creation in their own coin.   Such is the lesson of the following tale:

" There was a man who had a wife who was the plague of his life.   At last, vexed beyond endurance, he put her in a deep well, determined to leave her to her fate.   Three days afterward he repented and let down a rope to release her.   In lieu of her an immense dragon came out.   Instead of devouring the man it overwhelmed him with thanks and promises of favor for delivering it from such terrible company.   To recompense him, the dragon entered into a plot that the woman should remain in the well, but it would wind itself around the daughter of the king, and when no astrologer or charmer could release her, the man should come, and at his bidding it would leave, and the king would give him a large reward.   But one condition was laid down : that if ever the dragon wound itself around any other princess, the man should not molest it, on pain of death.   The plot was carried out ; at the man's bidding the dragon fled, freeing the princess, who was given in marriage to her deliverer, with an abundant dowry.   But soon the dragon captured a Frank princess.   Then the king of Frankistan, having heard of the fame of this man, sent an embassy to Persia requesting that he be sent to her relief.   After many excuses and much delay, the man, at the king's command, departed for Frankistan, filled with fear as to what might be the result if he broke his contract with the dragon.   On the way, however, he hit upon an expedient.   So, having reached the presence of the Frank princess, he said to the dragon, ' I have not come to release the princess, but only to tell you that that woman has got out of the well and is coming to attack you as quickly as possible.'   The dragon had such a vivid recollection of its former experiences that it fled in haste.   It knew that it was ' better to dwell in a wilderness than with a contentious and angry woman.' "

The limitation of woman's occupation in Persia is narrow, comprising little beyond the care of children, housekeeping, and domestic service, weaving of carpets and some other fabrics. What shall the large class of widows do for their support? Unless sons have grown up to support them they can find few ways of livelihood besides becoming concubines. Some old women can find employment in baking and washing from house to house, while others take their places on the street to beg, perhaps with a child in their arms.

The occupation of wealthy ladies is seen in the following account of a visit to some of them: "We were served to a succession of sweetmeats, sherbets, tea, and coffee. We refused only the water-pipe, and the ladies condoled with us on our loss, for it is their chief amusement. We ask how they spend their time. They answer, half sorrowfully, 'We do nothing but sleep, eat, and wonder what we will have for the next meal.' Embroidery and sewing they have some taste for, and they confessed to some skill in making certain dainties." The women, with few exceptions, are unable to read. Their capacities are undeveloped, their faculties dull from disuse. Their inattentive minds and unpractised memories require constant repetition on the part of an instructor. Those who are naturally bright are poorly informed. They are classed with the children under the one word *ushaklar*, and the proverb has currency, "Their hair is long, their wit is short."

There has of late been some advance in the education of women. The wives of some enlightened officials and mollas can read. Some are learning music and other accomplishments. Babism is said to desire women to throw aside their veils and appear in public. Kourret-it-Ayn ("Consolation of the Eyes"), a beautiful and accomplished woman, impersonated this idea. She met the mollas in open controversy, and by the charms of her person and the eloquence of her address

greatly assisted her cause.   She was killed, with other Babis,
at Teheran.   The styles of female attire may be seen by any
traveler in the bazaars.

The indoor dress consists of a number of full divided skirts,
or bloomers, reaching to the knees, and, according to the new
style, plain black or white pantaloons.   The sack or *kalija* is
loose-fitting, often not buttoned in front, with very long sleeves,
which are fastened to the wrists with many loops and knots.
Sometimes there is a cuff, elaborately trimmed.   The head is
covered with a square of cloth, tied under the chin, conceal-
ing the ears and falling down on the shoulders.   The common
head-dress of the poorer class is muslin or calico, the skirts are
of the latter material, and the sack of woolen goods.   Many
of the poor even have, as a part of their wedding-outfit, a *kalija*
or Kerman shawl, which, with no change of style, lasts for a
lifetime.   The rich ladies delight in gorgeous-colored silks,
satins, and velvets, often inwrought with gold or silver thread,
or else elaborately embroidered.   In Teheran there are French
dressmakers to invent beautiful costumes.

The shoes are sandals, usually of red or yellow sheepskin,
with pointed, turned-up toes, and an iron plate on the heel.
In walking the heels flop and clatter, and the step is with a
gliding motion, to prevent the shoes from slipping off.

The women are brunettes, of medium stature.   Heavy eyebrows and a high forehead are much admired.   The head-
dress is adapted to the latter.   The eyebrows are painted
black and extended so as to meet.   The hair is straight; it is
banged and hangs down the back in many small plaits, reaching sometimes to the ground.   To the ends are attached rib-
bons, with jewels, coins, or gold or silver bangles.   Long hair
is greatly prized, and any lack of it is supplied by the artificial article.   The hair is washed and combed at the public
bath, and receives no further attention until the next visit to
that popular institution.   The Persian woman delights in orna-

ments. On her head she wears a string of pearls, or bangles of gold and silver coin. Amulets, bracelets, necklaces, earrings, finger-rings, and even nose-rings are worn. Many of them are of great value and beauty. A moon-shaped face and stout figure are most admired. Fatness is in favor. One woman asked for medicine to make her fat. She was answered, " Why, your figure is good." She replied, " No; my husband threatens to divorce me because I am not fat."

A Persian woman's idea of life centers in and is bounded by her family. The girl looks forward to marriage as her sole destiny. There is no phrase in the native tongue corresponding to "old maid." To remain unwedded seems to a Persian woman a sin, a thwarting of the divine purpose of her nature. She is intensely domestic. Barrenness is considered the greatest curse. About the only subject on which a woman will venture to address a stranger traveling in the country is with a request for some medicine, or a written prayer, to relieve her barrenness. The fashionable but unnatural desire to limit offspring does not exist among them. But while the birth of a son is to the mother the greatest blessing, the birth of a daughter is an occasion of sorrow. There is no feasting, no tea-drinking, no joyous congratulation, as in the case of a son. Of the coming of a girl they will remark, " She is the gift of God—we must be resigned to his will." One reason for this feeling is that a daughter will be lost by marriage, while a son will be the stay and support of the parents in their old age, and his wife will become their servant.

The parents of a girl largely determine when and to whom she shall be married. They may betroth her in infancy. One writes: "There is a place upon the Kurdish Mountains where they sell the girls at birth, the family of the bridegroom taking the girl to bring up. I saw a bride of seven years whose parents had sent her to Urumia from Tabriz." A mature girl may be married without having seen her future husband. In this particular, however, the young man's position is even worse. The girl can see him as he goes about in public, if they live in the same place; but the man must rely on the reports of his mother or female relatives. Two men were quizzed at random one day about their marriages. One said he had never seen his wife before the wedding. His parents arranged the affair with her parents, who lived in another town. He was greatly chagrined, when she was brought, to find her only seven years of age. After a while he sent her home. The other said that special favor was shown him. He was allowed to conceal himself in the house and to look out of a window at her while she was at work with her mother in the yard. He was satisfied with her. Often the husband sees his bride's face for the first time looking over her shoulder into a mirror, which is a part of the bridal outfit. The man, if deceived or disappointed, can easily divorce his wife. What is the remedy of the girl? According to law she cannot be compelled to marry without giving consent. If she says "No," even at the ceremony, the marriage cannot proceed. But she can rarely exercise this veto, and is often married against her will. A girl thus forced into an unhappy marriage acted like a lunatic and gave great anxiety to her mother-in-law. Finally a foreigner supposed to have some acquaintance with medicine came that way. The case was narrated to him, and he was appealed to for a remedy for her sickness. He asked to see her alone. She frankly confessed to him that she was feigning madness because she had been married against her will, and she wished to be sent home. This ruse was played by the princess of Bengal, in the "Arabian Nights," when she wished to avoid marriage with the sultan of Cashmere.

The law of Islam allows the faithful Mohammedan four lawful wives and as many slave-women or concubines "as his right hand possesses." Full marriage is legalized before a molla, who writes a contract, which is certified by two male witnesses, or by one man and two women. This contract is called *kabin*. In it is stated the amount of her dowry, to be given in case of divorce. The necessity of paying this sum is a restraint on divorce. The secondary contract is for concubines, and is called *segah*. A third kind of contract legalizes, and in their eyes hallows, temporary concubinage. The latter is called *mutaa*, and is contracted before a molla for a definite time, long or short, and with stipulated wages. This perverts conscience and gives license and the sanction of religion to sin. For example, in the rice-fields of Mezanderan a man engages as concubines for the season as many women as are required to harvest his crops, abandons them during the winter, and the next year contracts with the same or different ones, as the case may be. For the legality of *mutaa* they quote the tradition that Mohammed gave such a license to his soldiers when going on a campaign.

One would suppose that the laws gave abundant scope to the lusts of men; but Persians do not regard their harems as secure without many safeguards. The penalty of adultery is death for the wife. Popular feeling against it is strong. A Persian narrates that a certain khan had conceived a passion for a woman and sent to take her. " Her husband, aware of it, collected his friends, attacked the khan's house, looted it, dishonored his person, and then blackened his face, put a paper cap on him, mounted him on a bare-backed ass, and expelled him from the city."

Polygamy does not lack defenders among those who practise it. A Mussulman who was asked what he thought of polygamy replied, " It is like eating; you do not confine yourself to one kind of food, but set several kinds on the table." Another Mussulman answered him, " But if the different kinds of food should begin to fight and tear up the table-cloth, what would you think? " The following quotation, translated by " Dacian,"

of Constantinople, expresses the opinion of a celebrated Mohammedan apologist who is occupied in writing a commentary
on the Koran:

"Glory to God a thousand times that I am an adherent of
a religion which draws a wall about no section of my liberty,
and imposes upon me no bondage in the matter of my desire.
I take a woman to wife. She is of medium height. If my
whim inclines to tall ones I get one of that sort too. Afterward, if I like, I get one of the fat sort. Besides these, I may,
if I choose, pick out one or more of some other style also.
All these I may have for wives for myself alone. If I tire of
any one of them, and she of me, and we agree on both sides, we
can separate. She then can suit herself exactly in choosing
another man, and I can pick out another woman. Thanks
be to God I am not a Christian, that I should be bound as a
slave to one woman, or any woman be bound to me! Do you
want to hear more? It makes the English mad to hear it,
but I am a bigoted Turk and do not care a fig for the English.
Besides all these, I can get myself just as many fine slave-girls
as I wish. In fact, whatever my whim calls for I am free to
have. But my religion does not command me to do all these
things. The question whether I will mate with a single woman
and be companion to her alone, it hands over to my generosity. Ah, it is a beautiful religion. It is a religion which trusts
to my generosity. It does not judge me to be without feeling, and therefore to be fit only to be loaded with the fetters
of bondage."

It is due, however, to many Mohammedans to say that they
are not as licentious as their law allows them to be. Many of
them, from preference, have only one wife. Others take a
second wife only when the first is childless. A man who mar-
ries a new wife every year—for such there are—is despised
even by his co-religionists.

Divorce is at the option of the husband, for any reason **or** without reason. The cause may be the sickness, blindness, or barrenness of the wife, or the anger, passion, or any whim or fancy of the husband. Sometimes a new wife demands that all the old ones shall be sent away. The ambition to marry a princess leads to the same result, as a man of inferior rank cannot have other wives as companions of a princess. The divorced wife takes possession of the girls, and the husband of the boys. If a woman wishes to leave her husband she can do so by going to the *gazi* and turning up her slipper. This remedy is rarely resorted to, as she must go out penniless. She prefers to provoke her husband beyond measure, that he may send her away with a dowry. In a well-known case a wealthy man paid large damages to release his daughter from an unhappy marriage.

If a man in a fit of anger says to his wife, "You are divorced," divorce is not accomplished unless he repeat the words three times. He can recall a divorced wife without further ceremony unless he has fully divorced her the third time. In that case he cannot take her back unless she has meanwhile been married to another man. Mohammed Khuda Banda, Mongol shah of Sultanieh, had a beautiful wife, of whom he was very fond. He had already divorced her the second time and received her back. In another hour of anger he banished her the third time. On coming to himself he sought for some excuse or authority for relaxing the law. For this purpose he called together the mollas of the province, to the number of seventy-eight; but not one was found of the Sunnis who would change the interpretation. At last he heard of one who was of a contrary opinion. Being summoned, he interpreted the law according to the wishes of the shah, secured his favor, and converted the dynasty to Shiahism.

These twin curses, polygamy and loose divorce, are disastrous to family life. Polygamy brings untold misery. On her rival's coming, the former wife may at first try to endure her lot. Her better nature may strive for the mastery, and she may come, as one did, and request that a prayer be written for her, "that she may not hate her rival." But abuse and apprehension of divorce develop all the baser qualities of her nature. She pilfers her husband's property, laying up in store against the day of her departure. This gives rise to the proverb, "A man's worst enemy is his wife." Full of jealousy, she poisons her rival or chokes the rival's child. On a certain occasion I asked a number of Mohammedans how great a percentage of wives would use foul play with the other wives and their children. They gave the shocking estimate that ninety or one hundred per cent. would do so. To spite her husband the first wife may commit adultery, so that they say, "The dog is faithful, the woman never." And, with some reason, her heart is a whirlpool of bitter passion, and she makes the house a bedlam. Let us hear the testimony of a Tabriz molla on this point, given in a discourse in a mosque. "They tell us," said he, "that there are dragons and scorpions in hell. I am not afraid of them. I have a worse hell on earth. My two wives, with their jealousies, quarrelings, their demands for dress, etc., give me no peace. I could well leave them for other torments." So, smarting in the fires he has kindled for himself, he pays the pittance of contract-money and turns the wife loose to misfortune and that which is worse. The woman in her trouble exclaims, "When the gates of hell are opened the Mussulman men will go in first." No wonder that she contrasts her lot with that of the Christian wife and mother, and says, as one did, "Your Prophet did well for your women; ours did not. I shall have words with our Prophet, when I see him in the next world, for giving men permission to have a plurality of wives." "I am the twentieth wife," said one. "Some have died and some have been divorced." Even the paradise set before her is a sensual one, in which she will find a place subordinate to the houris, the thought of which must

PERSIAN GIRL.

fill her heart, not with joy, but with jealousy. Yet there is much true domestic happiness in Persia. Though mated unseen, they not infrequently are well suited to each other, and when drawn nearer by the common love of their children they enjoy family life.

Notwithstanding the unequal provisions of the law of Islam, the women are bigoted and faithful Mohammedans. They look upon their condition as their fate, their kismet! They are devoted to their fasts and their prayers, though they must pray in a low voice and cross their hands before them, not stretch them forth, as men do. If opportunity offers for a pilgrimage, the journey of two months, with all its difficulties, seems as nothing to them in view of the merit and honor. They regard themselves alone as enlightened, and all the rest of womankind as in spiritual darkness. They despise Christian women as unclean, and, even if astonished at their education, will say, "What a pity that so refined and cultured a lady should go to hell!" A village woman said to a missionary, "You have fine clothes, you are beautiful, you can read, your works are good, you tell no lies, you only lack one thing: turn and become a Mohammedan!"

CHAPTER XV

THE mass of the population of Persia are peasants, including in this term farmers, gardeners, and shepherds. The peasants are robust and temperate. As a class they have few wants and fewer comforts. Their food is simple, their clothing cheap and scanty, their houses very rude, their minds uncultivated. Very few of them can read. The primitive flint and steel still light their fires and pipes. They have little ambition to rise in life. They are acquainted with the rites and traditions of their religion, and are faithful in the performance of its ceremonies, but neglect the weightier matters of truth and righteousness.

The contrast between Persian and American farmers is greater than between the city laborers in the same countries. The American farmer is really a landlord. His house and barn are palaces compared with those of the Persian peasant. His superior comforts in life, conveniences for labor, and intellectual advantages are beyond all comparison. Persian farmers are not the owners of the land they cultivate, and have no expectation of becoming proprietors. For safety their houses are all collected in villages and are crowded together. The stable is just beside the living-room, with one yard for both. The roof of the stable and the corners of the yard are filled with stacks of hay, thorn-bushes, and manure fuel. The latter is prepared by being kneaded, formed into cakes, and stuck upon the walls to dry. In all villages it is ever present

to sight and smell. Some of it is moulded into bowls and
covers for the *tandurs* and skylights. The village streets are
narrow, crooked, and as filthy in rainy weather as an undrained
barnyard. Fleas, flies, sand-flies, mosquitoes, body-lice, and
sheep-ticks are common nuisances.

A glimpse of the life of the farmers' wives, as seen on the
Ujan River, is presented by Mrs. Wilson as follows: " In one
room the whole family of father and mother, sons and daughters, brides and grandchildren, live together in such harmony
as may be where there are rival wives and different sets of children. A swinging hammock holds the youngest baby, and the
other children, half naked, filthy, and often sore-eyed, seem to
receive little care, though mother-love is strong and tender here
as everywhere. The clothing of men and women is a common blue cotton cloth, made up with little difference in style,
except that the woman's costume reaches only to the knees,
leaving limbs and feet bare. But the head-dress is distinctive:
only men wear hats, while women have handkerchiefs of red
—the favorite color—and in the street are enveloped in the
chudder of checked white-and-blue cotton. My costume in
every particular was a wonder to them. They asked me to
take off my shoes and ' be comfortable ' (?), to wear my hair
in tiny braids down my back as they do, and especially to take
off my hat and cover my face like a woman. In answer I told
them, ' We are ashamed, not to uncover our faces, but to expose our bodies.' And they looked down at their open breasts
and uncovered limbs as though they had received a new idea
of modesty. An all-sufficient explanation of my appearance
was simply to say, ' It is our custom.'

" One morning I saw a family at breakfast. A great pot of
soup made of sour milk and herbs was lifted out of the deep
oven and poured into bowls, which the men shared together,
two at a bowl, dipping in their bread and big wooden spoons
alternately. When they had finished the women used the same

bowls and spoons, and ate the remainder. The soup seemed savory as Jacob's, and good appetites are born of constant work and fresh mountain air.

"After breakfast the women do the daily baking. The yeasted bread is rolled into balls on a sheepskin, then rolled and tossed deftly till it becomes a long thin sheet, spread on a cushion, and slapped on the sides of the oven till baked, and is crisp and good when fresh. Thirty or more of these sheets are baked every day, and it is no easy task bending over the hot furnace preparing them. Next the house is swept and the dishes washed, though not wiped. Perhaps there is a special job on hand of salt-grinding, and two women sit at the mill turning the heavy stones, each taking hold of the wooden stick which serves as a handle. There is always knitting or carpet-weaving for regular occupation. Over a huge wooden frame are stretched rough brown threads to serve as a warp, while on a bench in front the weaver sits deftly putting in the bright colors. An inch a day along the line of the pattern is perhaps all she accomplishes, but it is the one artistic pleasure of her life. At noon is milking-time, and the village herd comes in from the fields. For each owner to select his own among this bleating crowd seems well-nigh impossible; and when we asked how it was done one man said, 'If a man has ten children doesn't he know them all?' The women sit on the ground to milk, while the children, like Homer's flies that 'buzz about at milking-time,' hover near to stick in their dirty little fingers and get a taste of the warm foam."

The farmers go out long distances to their work. The most primitive methods are employed by them. Two kinds of plows are used. The smaller one is simply the fork of a tree; the point of the larger one is covered with iron. They do not overturn the soil, but only loosen it to a shallow depth. For some crops the ground is plowed three times. After harrowing, small ridges or ditches are made to divide the field into sections, in order to facilitate irrigation. These are made by two men, with the use of a large hoe. One man pulls the handle and moves the soil, and the other, with a rope, lifts the hoe and places it for the next pull. The seed is carried in a sack on one arm and scattered with the other. There are no fences; the fields extend for miles without interruption, save for the watercourses and trees planted beside them. The reaper bends over his work with a short sickle in one hand, while in the other sometimes a stick a foot long is fastened with bands of leather or a glove, so that he may grasp a larger bundle. The traveler is accustomed to salute the harvesters with the greeting, " May God give you strength!" They answer, " Your coming is pleasing; may Allah keep you!" He replies, " May your harvest be blessed!" They respond, " May your life be prolonged!" If the traveler be a prominent man they bring a sheaf and set it before him on the road, or a sheep with a knife held at its throat, ready for sacrifice should he give the word. The proper acknowledgment is a bakshish. The sheaves are taken to the threshing-floor on donkeys. A wooden rack is placed on top of the pack-saddle, that a larger load may be bound on the diminutive animal. Ropes made of wool or of the fibers of a thorn-bush are used to tie on the loads. Hay is also tied into bundles in the same way. On some plains carts drawn by oxen or buffaloes are used for transporting the crops. They are heavy structures about fifteen feet long. The bed is six feet wide at the back, and gradually narrows until it reaches a point at the end of the tongue. The wheels have clumsy spokes, on the ends of which heavy arcs of wood are nailed. Other wheels are solid circles of wood, without spokes, and with broad iron tires.

The threshing-floors are just beside the village, and close to one another, for safety and convenience. A plot of land about twenty-five feet square is leveled off and hardened. A staple is fastened in the middle, and to it a pole is sometimes attached.   Oxen, tied to the staple or pole, tread upon and thresh out the grain.   The oxen are often muzzled.   The people say it is right to do so, lest the oxen surfeit themselves to their own injury.   Several kinds of threshing-machines are used.   One kind consists of a roller, about five feet long, with teeth or iron spikes spirally arranged on it.   It revolves as the oxen draw it.   Another kind is in the shape of a paddle, four or five feet long and two feet wide in the broad part.   Under it are fastened about thirty rows of flintstones, which protrude below the surface.   The front part is turned up like a sled-runner, and a man stands on it and beats the oxen.   By either of these methods the straw is thoroughly cut up and the wheat loosened.   With a wooden pitchfork, the prongs of which are tied on with twine, it is cast before the wind, and the chaff is blown aside.   The cut straw is stored away for fodder and plastering, but bricks are made without straw.   Harvesting is done by men, the seclusion of women generally precluding them from working in the fields.   I have, however, seen a woman standing by the threshing-machine, holding a babe in one hand and beating the oxen with the other.   In Mezanderan the women work much in the rice-fields.   Occasionally a farmer has a "bee," when the neighbors assist him with heartiness, and the host provides roast sheep and boiled rice for the company.   Of the crops little more need be said. The yield of grain is from three to twenty fold.   The cotton plant and pod are smaller than the American.   Its cultivation was greatly increased during the Civil War.   That event is remembered as the time when cotton reached its highest price. The cotton is taken from the stock and pod by hand.   It is then put in an oven and dried.   After this it is laid on a wicker platter and hammered.   Then it is passed under a cylinder, turned by a crank by a man sitting on the floor, and the seeds separated.   The latter are fed to animals.

A peculiar crop is the harvest of thorns.   On the uncultivated

land and on the fields after harvest spring up great quantities
of camel-thorns. These are diligently gathered, and brought
on donkeys' backs to be used with dried manure in baking
bread, burning limestone or brick, and heating the bath-houses.

The landlord sometimes lives among his *ryots* or peasants,
occupying a castle, around which his villages extend. More
frequently he is an absentee—a khan, a mujtehid, or a merchant—living in some near or distant city. A considerable
number of villages belong to the crown, and are called *khálisa*.
Over each village is placed an agent, who collects from the
peasants first the rental for the landlord, secondly the annual
tax, and thirdly a good reward for his own trouble. These are
paid in cash, or more frequently in kind, with a certain number
of *kharvars* of grain and loads of straw. Land is assigned to
the farmer on shares, with no certainty of his having the same
plot the next year. The proportion paid by the farmer depends on seed and water. When using his own seed he gives
one third in rental; when the owner furnishes the seed he gives
two thirds of the crop. The agent is frequently extortionate,
and the farmer desirous to escape with a light tax; so there is
continual quarreling, beating, and cursing. One method of
keeping the grain from being tampered with until it is divided
is by a wooden seal about two feet long, the impress of which
is left on the pile of grain and must be found undisturbed in
the morning. When oppressed or beaten the poor farmers have
little hope of redress. They sometimes rise *en masse* and go
to the nearest governor to petition for relief. As a last resort
they abandon their village. Gathering up their few utensils
and clothes, piling them on their oxen and donkeys, and driving a few sheep before them, the family seek subsistence under
a new landlord. At times a whole village is thus depopulated.
They have never owned the land upon which their houses were
built, and the bare mud-walls have little value. Sometimes
they have a right to take away the timbers of the roof and the

doors.   This emigration might be called a Persian strike, and
it is effective in injuring the landlord, if not in bringing him to
terms; for in a sparsely populated region it sometimes perma-
nently diminishes the value of the property, while the amount
of the taxes remains the same as before.

The Persian farmer rotates his crops.   He fertilizes with
manure, ashes, and refuse.   Earth from old walls is highly
valued as a fertilizer.   Irrigation greatly enriches the land.
Grain is sometimes stored in pits which have been plastered and
lined with brush and straw.   The khans often keep storehouses
of wheat, waiting for a rise in price.   Lack of snow or rain
in winter quickly sends the price higher, and many begin to
create " corners " and bring on a bread-famine.   The Amir-i-
Nizam, when governor of Tabriz, won the gratitude of the people by bringing to the city year by year the government supply of grain, which had been received as taxes, and selling it
at fair prices.

The flocks and herds of a village are pastured in common,
in charge of a herder and some boys.   The watch-dogs are
fierce yellow curs, a terror to a stranger.   Sometimes yokes are
put on these dogs, to prevent them from jumping walls and
trespassing on vineyards.   Servants have been known, after
purloining grapes, to mangle some bunches with their teeth, in
order that the canines might bear the blame.   The flocks
consist of sheep and goats, herds of cows, buffaloes, horses,
donkeys, and camels.   Sheep and goats are greatly valued
for their milk.   Of it most of the butter, *yogurt*, and cheese is
made.   Mutton is more valued than beef.   The latter is tough
and tasteless, the former savory and free from offensive odor.
The Persian sheep is noted for its large tail.   It is a mass of
fat of ten pounds' weight.   The yarns of some travelers to the
effect that the tails of these sheep are supported on a little
wagon to prevent their dragging on the ground are, I need
hardly say, apocryphal!   The tail-fat, roasted with the mutton,

is considered a delicacy; when so rendered it fills the place which lard and cottolene occupy in Western households. The United States minister to Persia, Mr. Truxton Beale, imported some of this breed of sheep into California. The cows are diminutive in size and give a scanty supply of milk. There is a popular notion that if the calf is taken away the cow will become dry. Hence the hide is stuffed with straw and placed beside the cow at milking-time. Oxen, buffaloes, and donkeys are almost exclusively used for farm-work. Oxen are sometimes shod and as many as six pairs hitched to one plow. The buffalo is extremely ugly, black, almost hairless, and very powerful. The donkey has great endurance, lives at small cost on straw, weeds, and thorn-bushes, and is withal the best friend of the Persian farmer. Horses, mules, and camels are little used in farming. Of the camel's hair the villagers make thick ropes, rough cloth and rugs, and even the finest quality of shawls. The feeding of the camel is interesting. It eats hay, thorns, thistles, and the roughest of stubble; but its peculiar food is a ball of barley or other flour, about the size of a croquet-ball, which is prepared and thrust into its mouth. It is susceptible to cold, and should be used on the road in northern Persia only about seven months in the year. When old or disabled its flesh is eaten. Sometimes it becomes crazy, and is then very dangerous. When so, it will tear and grind a man to mincemeat under its knee. It is tamed only by starvation.

Irrigation occupies much of the attention of the farmers. Every river, creek, and spring is utilized. At some distance up a stream a channel is dug and the water taken off on a high level. The watercourse follows the crooks and turns of the valley, going far up into the gullies, preserving an approximate level, sending out its branches, and distributing its supply over the low ground. The only principle of mechanics utilized is that water flows downhill. For flour-mills the stream is kept on a high level and made to run down through a trough and so turn the wheels. In summer good-sized rivers are completely utilized and their lower channel left dry. Where only a tiny spring flows, it is collected in a pond and let out with a flush. In gardens large reservoirs of masonry are built for the same purpose. Besides all these, fountains are opened up with great labor and expense. Wells are put down to tap the underground sources, especially in the upland valleys. These wells are joined by a tunnel, called a *karis* or a *kanaut*, through which the water flows, until it finally comes to the surface of the ground on the lower plain. The opening is called the *chesma* or eye. These wells are sunk two or three hundred feet apart, and often are as much as three hundred feet deep. They not only serve to collect water, but especially to make it possible to remove the earth from the subterranean channel or tunnel. The length of the latter is from two to ten miles. The ground is generally a loose sedimentary deposit, and a few men, with a short shovel, a leather bucket, and a wind-lass, easily excavate the channels. The earth is left around the mouth of the well, making little mounds, which are one of the special features of Persian landscapes. The wells are left open, and are dangerous to herds and hunters. The tunnel, not being arched, is liable at any time to cave in and tempo-rarily stop the supply of water. Many of these tunnels pass under one or more villages before coming to the surface. The value of a fountain is often the equivalent of the village, which without this supply would revert to the wilderness. Water privileges are a continual cause of quarreling. Near villages, and among close neighbors, irrigation strifes are common, and even murders are committed over well contentions, as the ser-vants of Abraham and Lot disagreed. Since their crops de-pend upon it, they hotly and persistently maintain their rights.

There are no artesian wells in Persia. Dr. W. W. Torrence procured a concession from the shah to bore artesian wells. He organized a company, which was incorporated by the

State of Maine. Seventy camel-loads of machinery were brought five hundred miles, via Bushire, to Teheran. The privilege was granted of boring a well on the American Mission premises, on condition of a perpetual water right being granted for irrigation purposes. A well was bored to the depth of nine hundred feet. But the breaking of parts of the machinery necessitated sending them to Baku for repairs, and thus delayed the boring. Finally the company exhausted its capital and suspended operations, without accomplishing any results. It was a great misfortune for Persia, since artesian wells would be a sure means of preventing famines, as well as of increasing the arable area of the country.

CHAPTER XVI

BUSINESS LIFE

"WHAT do the people in Persian cities do for a living?" is a question frequently asked. The open bazaars furnish the answer. The bazaars are not merely places of barter, but constitute an extensive manufacturing establishment. Many of the shops are factories, and, though each one is on a small scale, they collectively carry on large industries. The condition resembles that of an American city before the advent of steam and the establishment of great factories. There is no machinery; the furthest advance is in the use of sewing-machines, treadles, and imported hand-tools. All the methods of manufacture are open to the view of the passer-by. Some tradesmen are seen carding wool and making *kecha* or felt matting; others are pulling cotton fiber and making quilts. In the timber bazaar men are sawing boards with long hand-saws; a little farther on carpenters are making them into doors and windows; others are sawing out the teeth of wooden combs. In the next shop the blacksmith is blowing his bellows and welding hinges and latches. Rows of hatters are seen shaping *kulas* and stretching them on moulds, and exhibiting their stock of different styles and thicknesses of felt, broadcloth, fur, and lambskin. The confectioner is seen pulling taffy, and crushing rice-flour with a great sledge-hammer; the restaurateur chopping meat and mixing with it garlic and onions, to make savory cabobs; the baker is kneading dough, heating the oven, and throwing on pegs the sweet-smelling *sangaks*, while

278

he talks across the ten-foot street to the chandler, who is pouring candles into moulds before the gaze of all. Scores of saddlers, braziers, turners, tailors, silversmiths, and other artisans are busy at work, stopping their work only to wait on their customers. They are perhaps making some goods to order, but especially are preparing a stock for all the surrounding towns and villages. Some articles, such as woolen, cotton, and silk goods, are woven on hand-looms at home; carpets are made in the villages; dyeing is done throughout the city; but the great factory is the open, busy bazaars. In them contests of capital and labor do not arise. Each shopkeeper is a small capitalist, and has a few apprentices, whom he feeds and clothes, and each of whom hopes soon to set up a separate shop. The artisans have guilds, and sometimes work in combination to regulate the price.

Bartering in the Persian bazaar is a complicated process. Scarcely a shopkeeper makes even a pretense of having a fixed price. He asks more than he expects, allowing a wide margin for "jewing." If he should get what he asked he would regret that he did not ask more. I have known a carpet-dealer to refuse to sell a rug at his own price, and demand more, because the buyer immediately agreed to take it. Let us suppose that a customer stops before a shop and inquires the price of an article. "Seven krans," says the seller. "It is dear," replies the buyer; "what is the real price?" "No, it is not dear. See how pretty it is—there is not another like it. What will you give for it?" The buyer replies, "I'll give two krans." "What!"—with indignation pulling back the article —"do you think I found it? Many days' work have been put on this. It is *antika*" (antique, superior). "But your price is very high. Give it to me for two krans." "Impossible!" says the seller. "Look at it—it is excellent. For your sake I will favor you with it for six krans 'black' [copper] money." "Do you think I am a fool? Haven't I two eyes? In the

name of our religion I will only give you a manat for it. This
is my best offer!"   "Do you wish me to suffer loss?   By the
Prophet, by the hand of Abbas, I paid five krans for it.   Give
me an abbasi profit."   "You are lying.   I have no time to talk
all day.   Give it to me for four krans; I am going."   "It is
a present to you; give me five krans and it is yours!"   "No!
Four krans."   "No!   Five krans"—with an oath.   The
buyer moves slowly a few steps away; the seller pretends to
put up the article.   Each one expects the other to renew the
dickering.   Finally, it may be, the seller yells after the customer,
"Aga, look here."   "Well, what is it?"   "Give me four and
a half and take it."   "No!"   "Well, give your money."   And
the four krans are paid over in "black" money, with which
the buyer had loaded down his pockets beforehand by changing his silver or "white" money, to save the difference in the
coins.   The proverb of Solomon thus receives daily illustration: "It is naught, it is naught, saith the buyer: but when
he is gone his way, then he boasteth."   Every one will call to
mind the negotiations of Abraham with the children of Heth,
which exemplify another kind of Oriental overreaching.

In bartering the Mohammedan has an advantage over an
Armenian or foreigner, not only because his co-religionist is
willing to sell to him cheaper than to others, but because, in
the case of vegetables, meat, or anything that is moist, and
sometimes in the case of dry articles of food, a Christian is not
permitted to touch them.   A Christian picked up some tea in
his hands to smell.   The shopkeeper objected.   The buyer
said, "All right, weigh what I have in my hand," and he paid
him two cents for it.   For this cause there are no Christian
bakers, butchers, or fruit-dealers in Persian cities.

A numerous class of merchants are those who go from city
to city.   One of them starts, let us suppose, from Ispahan, with
the goods and wares of that city—its brass-work, enamels, and
tiles.   He goes to Kashan, sells what he can, and replenishes

his stock with velvets and silks. Here and there he gathers embroideries, carpets, and curios. At Tabriz he remains awhile trading, and finally sets off for Constantinople. There he disposes of his Persian stock and buys European goods, and soon returns to make a profitable exchange in the Persian markets.

Wholesale trade is largely confined to imported goods, such as cotton and woolen piece-goods, notions, tea, sugar, etc. Goods are sold on long time, at large risk, and therefore at high prices. The retail price is in some cases one hundred per cent. in advance of the original European price. The customs-duty on merchandise, according to treaty, is five per cent. Large partnerships or companies are not usual, because of lack of confidence. Lately some companies have been formed, especially among the Armenians, for export trade. Many of the latter spend the autumn and winter in Persia, purchasing the crops of cotton, silk, furs, opium, nuts, raisins, and dried fruits, and then spend the spring and summer in Russia in selling them.

In commercial affairs the Persians use the Arabic notation for indicating the date, the number of yards, the weight of the bale, etc.; but for money a peculiar system is used, based on the denar. Its multiples are indicated by signs, built one on the other, after the manner of stenography. This notation reads from right to left, while the Arabic notation reads from left to right. This method is called the denar system. (See Appendix.) Fifty denars equal one shahi, twenty shahis equal one kran, ten krans equal one toman. The Imperial Bank and many Armenian merchants are now introducing the decimal system.

Persian bankers or *sarafs* are numerous and capable. Their transactions are confined to loans and exchange. As the Koran forbids the taking of interest, the amount is added to the face of the note at the first. A banker, even when wealthy, is accustomed to sit on a cushion in a little shop, with an iron box behind him, a mirza or two beside him, and a pile of copper shahis in front, for money-changing. Exchange in Persia is regulated by Europe and India. The price of the Russian ruble is telegraphed to Tabriz, and forms the basis of calculation. Paper rubles are an article of purchase and sale, though not a circulating medium. In 1883 the shah prohibited dealing in paper money. The wording of his edict, as given by Curzon, was that "the people are very foolish who take dirty pieces of paper for gold and silver, and in future all Russian rubles will be confiscated." But trade in them still continued. One reason was the great scarcity of Persian coin. In buying a bill of exchange the Persian banker would give part of its value in Persian or Russian silver, and the remainder in rubles, notes, and Russian and Turkish gold. Coin was at a premium of six or seven per cent. Goods were sold and accounts kept by merchants on the basis rightly called *churuk* or "rotten," and payments were made by drafts cashed at the above discount. Cash, when obtained, was a rare and curious spectacle. The main currency was Russian ten, fifteen, and twenty copeck pieces, of an antiquated coinage, counted as 6⅔, 10, and 13⅓ shahis. These were often counterfeit, worn, punched, or *tezabi* (reduced in weight by acid), and subject to discount according to their condition. The task of counting a thousand tomans in such currency was very irksome. The Persian sits on the floor, counts in handfuls of three or five coins each, setting aside one coin as a counter when the fiftieth hand is reached, and finally reckoning up the counters. On reaching thirteen, the unlucky number, he is accustomed to say, "It is not thirteen," and complacently throws down the next hand. He keeps repeating the previous number, lest it slip from his memory. In Urumia, at the time referred to, silver medjadeyas and rupees were also in circulation, besides old Persian coins. The latter were rudely stamped, with rough edges and varying shapes and values. The privilege of minting was granted to individuals on the payment of a tax. In Azerbijan alone there were mints at Tabriz, Ardebil, Khoi, Urumia, and Soujbulak. Old copper coins were still more unshapely than the silver ones. Some of them, such as a coin of Soujbulak, were of as small a value as one fifth of a cent.

The mint at Teheran, established in 1878, removed some of these difficulties. The new coinage is quite regular. The old coinage was withdrawn from circulation by a peculiar Oriental device. By royal firman five of the old copper shahis were declared equal to two of the new ones, so that all copper coins in the hands of the people suffered much depreciation. Russian silver, too, was discounted by the shah's order, and disappeared from circulation in Persia. At present, under a silver standard, copper currency rates at 95 per cent., and gold at from 180 to 210 per cent. Labor is paid, and retail trade carried on, in copper currency; taxes and customs are paid, and general business is conducted, with silver coins, of the value of one or two dimes. Persian gold coin has practically disappeared from circulation.

The ordinary rate of interest is from 12 to 18 per cent. Rates run as high as 48 to 120 per cent. The Kurds often borrow at 10 per cent. monthly compound interest, and after a few years must surrender their villages to satisfy a claim which was originally small.

The depreciation of Persian currency has been steady.* Sixty years ago the gold dollar would bring three and one third krans in exchange, twenty-five years ago five krans, in 1891 seven or eight krans, in 1893, at the abolition of free coinage in India, nine krans; after the repeal of the Sherman Bill the gold dollar equaled more than the toman.

---

* In Sir John Malcolm's time the toman was equal to the pound. Curzon says that in the middle of the seventeenth century the toman was equal to three pounds ten shillings, and in the preceding century to four pounds ten shillings.

In the banks, stores, and government offices, and in houses of the nobility, are a class of men employed as clerks, secretaries, and accountants. They are called by the general term "mirza." The mirza is master of the pen. He can write correctly, and with the observance of the numerous forms necessary in addressing the various grades of society and official life. His education is primary. His outfit consists of a kalamdan and a roll of paper. The kalamdan is a pen-case about eight inches long and one and one half in width and height, which is carried in his girdle or pocket. It is usually made of papier-maché, ornamented with pictures of flowers and animals, men and women. The contents of the case are a small inkholder of brass or silver, some pens, a penknife, a piece of bone, a small spoon, and a pair of scissors. The pens are stiff reeds, of the same kind that were used for writing on papyrus or parchment. The goose-quill, though it has been used in some countries since the sixth century, has not been adopted in Persia. The steel pen is being introduced, and has already modified the writing of Syriac and Armenian, and will doubtless modify the Persian character. The penknife and bone are used for sharpening the pen. The point of the reed is laid on the bone to be cut to the proper bluntness. The scissors are necessary for trimming the paper, as etiquette and good luck require. Some lint or cotton is put in the inkholder and saturated with ink. The spoon is used to pour water on it and mix it.

The mirza sits on the floor, sufficient unto himself. Sometimes he has a small table, about a foot high, in front of him. In writing a letter he takes a piece of unruled paper in his left hand, supports it on his forefinger, and writes from right to left, curving the lines upward. He then reverses the paper and writes upon the wide margin, at an angle to the other lines and from the bottom upward. The sender certifies it by sealing it with his signet. This is usually made of brass or stone, with the name and title engraved upon it. Formerly a letter was folded until it formed a flat roll half an inch in width. It was then closed with a band of tissue-paper, on which the seal was affixed. Now letters are put in envelopes, large or small, according to the rank of the person addressed. In keeping accounts the mirza makes the entries, not in columns, but successively on a line, and joins by a vinculum the name, item, and amount.

One part of Persian business life which merits special description is the construction of buildings. It is a difficult task, owing to a variety of causes. Available materials are poor; honest contractors are not to be found. Master masons have an unenviable reputation. Sharp must be the unsophisticated foreigner to escape being fleeced. Even experienced natives are completely hoodwinked. Buying materials is bewildering. There is no regular market-price. Tedious caution is required to reach the lowest price. The custom is to contract in the winter for materials to be delivered in summer, both for cheapness and to insure their preparation. This is done at considerable risk. When the materials are being brought, other vexations begin. There is an interminable tramp of donkeys, loaded with stones, brick, or lime. Each load must be counted or weighed, and receipted for. Time and patience are consumed. In the weighing constant efforts are made to cheat the purchaser. If he does not weigh the lime it will be light weight; if he does it will be mixed with earth. If he does not give a receipt for the bricks each time they are sent he will be charged with more than he has received. If he appoints an overseer he will be either careless or a rascal, and will either allow the account to get mixed up and give the seller an opportunity to outwit him, or he will accept a bribe and wink at fraud. When the work actually begins one is amazed at the slowness of the fellahs or laborers. Their picks fall so very deliberately and accomplish so little. Two fellahs fill a hod with earth and lift it on the shoulder of the hod-

carrier, who meanwhile stands idle, as they do, also, till he returns. In mixing mortar four or five men do the work of one.
The bricklayer has a gang of attendants. Some bring brick,
others mortar; one apprentice throws each brick to him, and
another passes him the mortar by the handful. The bricklayer,
as he works, sings all day long, with variations, calling for
materials: " My child, give me mortar. Throw me a brick, my
son; let me see a brick; let it come to me. Brother, throw
me a baby brick [i.e., a half-brick]. Give me mortar, O my
father." An army of men seem to be accomplishing nothing,
though the overseer is urging them to activity, and riling their
tempers and his own all the time. But these workmen have
much excuse for laziness, in view of their wages. The fellah
gets from six to nine cents a day, the hod-carriers and water-
carriers twelve to sixteen cents, the carpenters eighteen to
thirty cents, the mason eighteen cents, and an apprentice five
or six cents; while from the wages of each one the contractor
or master mason "eats" a half-cent a day.

The first thing noticeable about the buildings is the width of
the foundations. They are from three to five feet thick, made
of rough, uneven stone and a mortar of lime and sifted earth.
The stones at the edge are placed with care, sometimes with
a layer of brick between them, and the middle is filled with a
conglomerate of small stones. The cellars are arched. The
mason draws a circle on the wall at one end, using simply a
string and a bit of charcoal. The apprentice mixes a dishful
of gypsum (*gach*). The mason throws some handfuls of it on
the wall, and presses some bricks upon it in the form of the
arch. They adhere immediately, and one row after another
is put on until the cellar is arched over. The top of the arch
is filled in with earth, and plastered over with mud or lime-
cement to make the floor. The walls above the foundation
are built of sun-dried brick. The process of manufacturing
these bricks is very simple. Earth is mixed with water,

kneaded by the feet, moulded into brick, and dried for two days in the sun. When water and earth are at hand the cost of the bricks is from seventeen to twenty cents a thousand. They are laid with a mortar of mud and water. The poorness of the material, and the possibility of earthquakes, are the reasons for the thickness of the walls. The outer surface of the wall sometimes has a facing of kiln-burned brick. More commonly there are pilasters, with the intervening spaces arched and whitened. Unhewn trunks of poplars or sycamores are used as rafters. They are grown by irrigation and used when five to six inches in thickness. Over the rafters thick laths are placed, and on these a reed matting, together with several inches of earth and two or three coats of straw and mud-plaster. This roof must be renewed every second or third year.

I once noticed the raising of a heavy beam. It was a hard task for them, as they rarely handle such heavy timbers. The workmen were Mohammedans, and as they gave the signal to pull all together they shouted, "Ya Ali, ya Ali!"—calling to their help their Imam Ali. Beforehand they carefully closed the gates of the lot, that no one might enter. I inquired the reason for this action. They said they did it lest people should enter and cast the evil eye on them and some accident happen.

The interiors of Persian houses are generally whitened with plaster of Paris and ornamented with cornices. Some rooms have figures in stucco-work on the ceilings and in the *takhtchas* (niches). A few rooms are elaborately frescoed with a scroll-work of branches and flowers, birds and animals, in relief and colors.

The foreign trade of Persia is carried on for the most part with England and Russia. In the south the important trade-routes are through the Persian Gulf ports, Bushire and Bandar Abbas, by the Karun River, and by Bagdad and Kermanshah. The northern route by Trebizond and Erzrum is much used. The Turkish government allows goods *in transitu* to pass in bond, securing to itself certain fees, and to the country along the route considerable profit. Russia puts a duty on goods *in transitu*, in order to reserve to itself the trade of northern Persia. Its manufactures are entering in increasing quantities via Julfa, the Caspian ports, and by the Transcaspian Railway. Taking into account the whole of Persia, England has the bulk of its trade, both as to value and tonnage. It is interesting to watch the rivalry of these two great powers in Persia in matters of trade and politics.

Great Britain entered on a new era of activity at the time of the appointment of Sir Henry Drummond Wolff to the post of minister at the court of the shah. The first indication of this was the negotiation of a treaty, by which the Karun River was opened for navigation. The Karun is navigable for one hundred and fifty miles, as far as Ahwaz, and thence to Shuster, after transfer around the rapids. The New Oriental Bank established agencies in Teheran, Tabriz, Ispahan, and Bushire. During and after the visit of the shah to Europe (1889) a series of projects were set on foot. The Imperial Bank of Persia was authorized, with ordinary banking rights, and given the power to issue paper currency, together with the privilege of working mines. It was understood that the conditions of the concession were the payment of forty thousand pounds in cash and six per cent. of the net annual profits to the shah. The Imperial Bank sold its mining rights to a Mining Corporation, organized largely from the same stockholders, for a sum nominally eight hundred thousand pounds, of which one hundred and fifty thousand pounds were paid in cash, and the remainder in one hundred and thirty thousand five-pound shares of the Mining Corporation stock. A Road Company also was organized, to make highways from Shuster to Ispahan and Teheran. Concessions were granted for electric-light plant, for artesian wells, for the manufacture of matches, the control of the tobacco trade, and the establishment of lotteries. Russia secured the exclusive right to make railways for a period of years, established a consulate at Meshed, and joined that city by a wagon-road to its Transcaspian Railway. French engineers appeared on the scene to open a highway from Trebizond to Tabriz. Internal monopolies were projected; one was for the control of the brick trade, another for that of lime, another for the manufacture of crockery. It seemed that a new era of commercial enterprise was dawning upon Persia, and that the resources of the country were soon to be developed.

For a while progress was promising. The Imperial Bank established its branches throughout the country. It purchased the Persian branch of the New Oriental Bank—a fortunate event for the Persian depositors, as the New Oriental Bank made an assignment shortly afterward, causing great loss in Japan and India. A paper currency, secured by a reserve, was issued in the English and Persian languages, the first paper money issued in Persia since that of the Mongol khan was rejected with rioting. This new issue has not met with favor.

The engineers of the Mining Corporation opened up operations. Petroleum was found, according to report, at Doliki, iron at Hormuz and Karadagh, asbestos in Kerman, besides soft and hard coal, lead, copper, manganese, and borax. The mining of copper was successfully begun. In Afshar, Azerbijan, the prospectors discovered indications of mercury. Several bottles of it were collected, and served to stimulate the price of stock. After spending two seasons prospecting, the field, however, was abandoned, and the company went into liquidation in 1894. The engineer, on returning to England, was sentenced to imprisonment for false pretenses.

Work was begun energetically on the highway from Shuster to Ispahan, but difficulties not anticipated, and the opposition of the inhabitants, retarded it. Navigation of the Karun was rendered unsafe by the tribes along the banks shooting at the

sailors as at a target.   The project for a wagon-road from
Trebizond never passed the initial stage.   French engineers
spent some time in Tabriz, the guests of the foreign agent;
but later he turned the foreigners out of his house, and called
the mollas to read prayers to purify it from the pollution of
their drunkenness.   No railways have gone into operation as
the result of Russian concessions.

In addition to these business enterprises, certain swindles,
such as the Anglo-Asiatic Syndicate and the Persian Lottery
Company, were floated on the English public, and brought large
profits to their projectors.   One Persian official was sued in
the English courts for the recovery of forty thousand pounds.

Of all the concessions, the one which authorized the Imperial
Tobacco Corporation has proved most historic.   By this concession the entire purchase, sale, and export of the tobacco-
crop of Persia was granted as a monopoly.   The conditions
of the concession were reported as the payment of forty thousand tomans in cash, and eight per cent. of the annual profits
to the Persian government.   Major Talbot, the concessionaire,
sold his rights to a company chartered by Parliament under
the title of the Imperial Tobacco Corporation.   It was pro-
claimed in Persia in February, 1891, and its plans were stated
to a mass-meeting of Teheran merchants, under the direction
of the minister of commerce.   Mr. Ornstein, the director-gen-
eral, with a full staff, many of whom were from the Turkish
régie, arrived in April.   It was understood that three hundred
Europeans and ten thousand Persians would be employed in
the factories and agencies of the company.   Unprecedentedly
large salaries were paid.   Rumor said that much "boodle"
reached the hands of officials and priests.   The outlay excited
the wonder of the people.   Soon those who felt themselves
neglected in the distribution of the bounty began to express
opposition to the company.   Two thoughts were emphasized
by the opponents—first, that the price of tobacco would be in-

creased, and, secondly, that it would be defiled and rendered
unfit for use by passing through the hands of infidels. The
political and commercial rivals of England were not slow to
encourage the discontent. It was pointed out that the Persian government had been outwitted; that the terms of the
concession were too favorable to the monopoly. Agitation
was begun, too, against the prime minister, the Amir-i-Sultan,
a man of ability and great influence with the shah. The
"Akhtar," the Persian newspaper of Constantinople, attacked
the concession and was suppressed. Secret tracts were circulated through the kingdom. Anonymous petitions, asking for
reforms in the finances, the abolition of polygamy, religious
freedom, and a representative system, were distributed. The
mails were searched by the government, and prominent men
were implicated in these movements. One of these, a molla,
Jalal-i-Din, was arrested, and hastened, under guard, beyond
the frontier. Prince Malcolm Khan, Persian minister to England, addressed a telegram to the shah, denouncing the prime
minister. For this and other offenses he was summarily re-
called and his titles and decorations taken from him. He refused to appear before the throne, and has since remained in
exile. Mustashar-i-Doulah, ex-consul to Calcutta and foreign
agent for Azerbijan, was also ordered under arrest. The police
sealed his house, set a guard about it, and, notwithstanding
his venerable age, imprisoned him. All his papers were examined. He was deprived of his titles and pension, and taken to
Teheran to answer to the charges. The Babis were implicated
in these petitions, and about forty arrests were made among
them in Teheran.

The greatest agitation was led by the mollas. As interpreters of the canon law they frequently have come into conflict
with the civil officers; but their power had been curbed and
their jurisdiction limited during the preceding decades. Now
the mollas stood forth as the champions of the people, in a

cause appealing to their pockets, their prejudice, and their sense of justice. The popular cries were: "We are to be taxed for the benefit of foreigners! They would increase the price of the poor man's pipe!" Considering their universal and constant use of tobacco—next to bread their great necessity—it was not strange that excitement grew apace. As early as May 19th, Hadji Sayid Ali Akbar, a molla of Shiraz, began to declaim against Europeans, and especially against the monopoly. The government ordered his arrest and expulsion. The mollas assembled the people in the mosques and incited them to resistance. A mob collected to prevent the arrest of the molla, at the same time making threats of attacking the Christians. They were quelled by the fire of the soldiers. Some were wounded, and two women and a child were killed. A still greater agitation occurred in Tabriz. Here, by a strange oversight, the monopoly had failed to cultivate the good-will of those in authority. In the crisis the governor-general, Amir-i-Nizam, and Hadji Mirza Javat Aga, the chief mujtehid, two of the ablest and most powerful men in the kingdom, combined against the monopoly. The first manifestation of popular feeling was the sacking of the house of the Persian agent of the monopoly. Placards were next posted threatening some members of the royal family and the general of the army. Threats were made that if the shah did not abolish the monopoly appeal would be made to Russia, and they would give their allegiance to the czar. A special messenger was sent from the capital to quiet the priesthood and people. Intense agitation continued for months. Finally, as the only preventive of open rebellion, it was decided to partially abolish the monopoly. It was canceled for the province of Azerbijan, though the tobacco-crop of the year was purchased in other parts of the country.

Meanwhile there was an incipient rebellion in Kaladash, in Mezanderan, headed by the mollas. A regiment was sent against the malcontents. Some severe fighting occurred; several hundred of the rebels were killed, with eighty of the soldiers. In the beginning of October the bazaars at Meshed were closed, and there were three days of excitement. In December, Molla Hasan Shirazi, chief mujtehid of Kerbela, the Sahib-i-Zaman or Lord of the Age—the pope of the Shiahs—issued a decree stating that, "to-day the use of tobacco is prohibited in every form by the Lord of the Age." His interdict, addressed to all the faithful, was to be in force as long as the monopoly should continue. He grounded his decree on a phrase of Mohammed: "Every man is master of his own property." The monopoly contravened this dictum. The effect of the interdict was magical. The nation laid aside their pipes. Some persons maintained that the decree took away their desire to smoke. Women, even in the shah's palace, ceased to use the weed. The soldiers declared that they would obey their mujtehid rather than their general, and that if ordered to shoot they would shoot the latter. One company, in an emergency, pretended that their powder was wet. The opposition daily gathered strength. Placards were posted in the capital, urging the Moslems to engage in a holy war, and threatening the lives of Europeans. There was great danger. Many confined themselves to their houses. On December 27th the shah recognized the wisdom of yielding to the popular demand, and issued a proclamation to the effect that his Majesty, "extending his favor to his whole people," would abolish the monopoly for the internal trade, and that it would only remain in effect for the export trade. But no half-measures would satisfy the excited priests and people, who were now assured of their power. On January 4, 1892, a mob surrounded the palace of the shah and of the Naib-i-Sultanah, minister of war, and demanded the entire and complete abolition of the monopoly, with the expulsion of its agents from the country. The minister of war first tried pacification. It was reported that the queen mother came out of her house, bearing a Koran, and asked the mob to disperse. It finally became necessary to order the troops to attack the mob. They fired upon them and scattered the rioters, killing some of them. Afterward, it is said, two hundred or more of the rioters were secretly arrested, beheaded in prison, and their bodies thrown into a well. During the following days troops patroled the city for public safety, and the Christian population was in special danger. Revolution was imminent. The hearts of the people were alienated. The shah appealed to the Russian minister to quiet the disturbances. The latter called the leaders of the mob and advised them to cease rioting. The shah and his ministers assembled in council to carry on negotiations with the mujtehid. It was evident that Persia is a hierarchy as truly as she is a monarchy. Canossa was not far distant. The manager of the corporation gave the following account of the negotiations: "The chief mujtehid imposed the following conditions for the maintenance of order: (1) that the families of those killed should be indemnified; (2) that protection should be granted to all those who took part in the demonstration; (3) that all European institutions and undertakings in Persia should be abolished. Should these conditions be refused, the mujtehid threatened to appeal to the Russian minister for their enforcement. On the Persian government representing that it was quite impossible to comply with the third request, it was, after some difficulty, agreed to compromise on the basis that the *régie* or monopoly be abolished altogether. The chief mujtehid, however, made demand that I should myself state that the *régie* had been abolished, and offer to return all tobacco at purchase price. I refused to comply. Thereupon the British minister represented to me that we were in the presence of revolution, and that my refusal might endanger the lives of the European colony. I therefore consented."

The government sent the following notification to the manager: "As the result of the extraordinary events that have taken place the government of his imperial Majesty has helplessly and regretfully canceled the monopoly of tobacco which had been granted to your company," and closed it with a promise of indemnification. Then the manager issued an order informing the people of its complete abolition, and announcing to vendors that they could come and buy back their tobacco. As soon as the mujtehid of Kerbela was assured that the monopoly was a thing of the past, he issued a decree canceling the interdict; then the faithful resumed their pipes, assured that it was the will of Allah that their tobacco should not be defiled by infidel hands.

The indemnity was settled at five hundred thousand pounds payable in London, with the condition that the property of the company in Persia be turned over to the Persian government. In the House of Commons it was pointed out that the expenses of the corporation had been fifty-five thousand pounds, and the assets turned over to the Persian government had been one hundred and thirty-nine thousand pounds, so there remained a good margin of profit for the projectors. The necessary indemnity money not being at hand, the Russian government offered to advance the sum, with security on the customs. At this England took alarm, and an arrangement was made whereby the Imperial Bank of Persia loaned the amount to the Persian government at six per cent. payable in forty years, and secured by the customs of southern Persia. Thus Persia entered the ranks of debtor nations.

The affair was a disastrous failure, and British prestige received a severe blow. The London "Times" said: "It illustrates our inferiority to the Russians in the art of dealing with Orientals." To Persia the financial loss and even the temporary disloyalty were slight calamities compared with the retardation of its internal development. Such monopolies cannot be approved, though it would be better to have development

by monopolies than stagnation and decay. By this disaster to
the government the wheels of progress were turned backward.
Foreign capital became alarmed and withdrew from the task
which native capital is not willing or able to undertake. Many
projects were indefinitely suspended. The priesthood at the
same time received a new accession of power.

Foreigners were rightly apprehensive for their personal safety.
The European employees of the corporation left the country
as quickly as possible. The very sight of them seemed to
irritate the populace like a red flag waved before a mad bull.
Threats of violence against them and other foreigners were
uttered constantly, and bitterness was manifested against all
Christians. On June 16th this placard was posted on the
streets of Tabriz: "Aga Shirazi thus commands: The Protestants must depart from the city in twenty days. If they do
not we must make the *jahad* [holy war] against them." This
proclamation was torn down by the governor, and in the midst
of the excitement the mujtehid * hastened to ascend his pulpit
and declare it a forgery. We were assured that the placard
was a political move, and was not aimed at the American Mission. By a strange coincidence it was posted the day on which
several missionaries were leaving Persia, and shortly before
the teachers and scholars of the boarding-schools dispersed to
their homes for vacation, so that some received the impression that the Protestants were fleeing from the country. The
monopoly agitation undoubtedly made the position and work
of all Christians and foreigners less secure.

In connection with this agitation it is interesting to recall
that in Mohammed Shah's time a rumor spread among the Persians that the infidels used not only the blood but the bones
of animals to clarify sugar. Strong protests against the use

* Mujtehid Hasan Shirazi died at the beginning of 1895, in his eighty-
fourth year.

of sugar began, in consequence, to be heard on all sides. To quiet the outraged sensibilities of the people and put himself right before them, the shah ordered that no more loaf-sugar should be imported. After that time imported sugar was declared to be clarified solely by steam.

CHAPTER XVII

MODERN missions in Persia were begun in the sixteenth century by Roman Catholic monks among the Armenians at Ispahan, Tabriz, Nakhejevan, and Erivan. For a time they were quite successful, but afterward the work declined. Some of the results remain at Ispahan and in Transcaucasia. An effort among the Nestorians in the eighteenth century was more successful. The metropolitan of Diarbekir quarreled with his patriarch and was consecrated Catholic patriarch of the Chaldeans. Several bishops and congregations in Salmas and in Urumia followed the metropolitan and submitted to the pope. The largest of these congregations was at Khosrova, Salmas. There, as well as at Urumia, large missions of French Lazarists and nuns were established in 1841. Subsequently stations were opened at Teheran and at Tabriz. The bishop resides at Urumia, having the rank of ambassador from the pope to the shah. There are from eight thousand to ten thousand Roman Catholics in Persia.

The earliest Protestant missionaries were Moravians who, in 1747, came to evangelize the Guebers. They were, however, unable to remain, owing to the disturbed condition of the country. Henry Martyn was the pioneer of this century, and in his " Memoir " are narrated his discussions with the mollas of Shiraz and Ispahan. He left as his legacy the Persian version of the New Testament. Some efforts were made to reach the Jews and Mohammedans, through the work of the missionaries of the London Society for the Jews, and also through the Basle Society, but their labors were afterward abandoned.

The first permanent Protestant mission was established, in 1835, by the Rev. Justin Perkins and Asahel Grant, M.D., in Urumia, by the American Board. It was called the Mission of the Nestorians. Its founders and their successors were men eminent for piety and devotion, as well as for ability. They labored for twenty years to reform the Nestorian Church from within, aiming to bring about a revival of spiritual and evangelical religion. This purpose was abandoned with regret when circumstances required the organization of the Evangelical Church. This was effected in 1856, with one hundred and fifty-six communicants—a number which had increased to seven hundred and sixty-three in 1870. In 1869 plans were made for the enlargement of the mission, whose name was then changed to the Mission to Persia. Shortly afterward it was transferred to the Presbyterian Board of Foreign Missions, at the time of the Reunion. In 1871 Teheran was occupied, as was also Tabriz in 1873, and Hamadan in 1881; and the mission was then divided into the Eastern Persian Mission, comprising Urumia and Tabriz, to which have been added Salmas station in 1885, and Mosul, in Turkey, in 1892.

In 1869 the Rev. Robert Bruce, D.D., began mission work in Ispahan, which was subsequently taken in charge by the Church Missionary Society. Later on Bagdad was occupied. This is known as the Central Persian Mission.

In addition to these missionary posts there is stationed at Urumia and Kochanes (the seat of Mar Shimun, the Nestorian patriarch) the special mission of the Archbishop of Canterbury. It is extremely ritualistic, refuses the name Protestant, and has for its avowed object the strengthening of the Nestorian Church to resist the influence of the Roman Catholics on the one hand and of Protestants on the other. It has a strong force of missionaries—"brothers" and "sisters"—who wear the garb of their order, and are under temporary vows of celibacy and obedience. How far it will succeed in its object is not yet evident. In lawsuits against the Catholic Mission, to recover church properties, the Anglicans have been unsuccessful. They have hampered the evangelical work in many ways, but the annual additions to the Protestant communion show no diminution. In the controversy engendered by their presence its members have been developed in moral stamina and confirmed in doctrinal stability. The Anglican missionaries are indoctrinating their students with high sacerdotal ideas, and will probably build up a party in the Nestorian Church intermediate between the evangelical and the papal communions.

Whatever may have been the purpose of these missions, it is evident that the restrictions of the government have largely hindered all of them from evangelizing Mohammedans. Mrs. Bishop criticizes the church as slothful in its efforts to evangelize Persia. She says: "The absolute fact is that Christian nations have not shown any zeal in communicating the blessings of Christianity to Persia. The populous shores of the Persian Gulf, the great tribes of the lower Tigris and Euphrates, the Ilyats of Persia, the important cities of Shiraz, Yezd, Meshed, Kashan, Kum, and Kermanshah, are untouched by Christian effort. Propagandism on a scale so contemptible impresses intelligent Moslems as a sham, and is an injury to the Christianity which it professes to represent." On the other hand, ex-Minister Benjamin commends the missionaries for their prudence in yielding to the injunctions of the authorities and in not assuming an aggressive attitude. I cannot enter at length into this question, though I shall mention two facts which show the attitude of Persia with reference to Christian propaganda among Mohammedans. One is the celebrated case of Mirza Ibrahim. The latter was a convert from Islam who was baptized in Khoi, and driven out by his family. He was arrested in Urumia while telling others of his new-found faith. When brought before the *suparast* and governor he boldly confessed Christ and maintained the truth of the gospel. He was beaten, threatened, and imprisoned. He was offered money if he would forsake his faith. Finally he was taken to Tabriz under guard and imprisoned, and his appeals to the shah for release were vain. After suffering the horrors of a Persian prison for almost a year he was choked to death by his fellow-prisoners, with the connivance of the authorities. A number of criminals, one after another, took him by the throat, saying, "Declare that Ali is true and Jesus false." He answered, "No; Jesus is true. Jesus is true, though you slay me." After his martyrdom the grand vizier observed, "Our law is that the pervert shall be put to death; it was a mistake to imprison him—he should have been executed immediately."

The attitude of the government is clearly seen in its treatment of the German missionaries, the Rev. Mr. Köhle and Dr. Swenkle, who came to Persia in 1894 to evangelize the Jews. While *en route* to their field, Urumia, they had conversations with certain Mohammedans, whose acceptance of the truths of Christianity deeply impressed them. They wrote an account of their experiences, which was published in Germany and fell under the eyes of the Persian government. A decree for their expulsion was issued, and ten days granted them in which to sell their effects. The German minister plenipotentiary strangely consented to this summary sentence, simply requesting an extension of time to thirty days. He might have enjoined the missionaries to confine their work to the Jews, and maintained their right to do so on an equality with the citizens of other countries. Within the month Mr. Köhle died of typhoid fever, and Dr. Swenkle withdrew.

Turning now to the non-Mohammedan races, we find in various parts of Persia scattered remnants of fire-worshipers, Jews, Armenians, and Nestorians. It is the settled policy of the shah's government to grant full protection and liberty to missionaries laboring among these races. Missionaries have cause for gratitude to God and to the shah that they have been well protected while living in the midst of a fanatical Mohammedan population.

In the minds of some people there is a stigma of proselytism attaching to missions among Oriental Christians. The necessity for such work is twofold. It is necessary for the sake of these churches. The Armenians and Nestorians are living in spiritual darkness and need a new setting forth of the gospel for their enlightenment. Their clergy do not teach or preach to the people, and Christians of other names are under obligation to them, as to other races. Again, the influence of Christianity on Mohammedans will never be felt until the Christians dwelling among them realize the duty of manifesting Christ in lives of holiness and righteousness, as well as of witnessing for his truth. Only a revivified and reformed church can impress Islam with the superiority of the religion of Jesus. These scattered communities have been preserved in God's providence in a remarkable manner to be a future leaven of the gospel. They occupy strategic positions in the heart of Islam, and for that reason it is wise to put forth an amount of energy and labor in their evangelization which is largely disproportionate to their numbers or importance among the races of the world. The same reasoning applies to the work among the Jews of Persia, and we have the sure word of prophecy that their turning to Jesus will be as life from the dead.

In a certain sense all residents in Persia from Christian lands are missionaries, either for good or for evil. Diplomatists and tradesmen, as well as missionaries, are continually making impressions on the Persians by their conduct and manner of life. These impressions are sometimes curious and amusing. In a conversation with some village soldiers one asked me if I knew of dog-worshipers. I told him I had heard of fire-worshipers, cow-worshipers, etc., but not of dog-worshipers. He said he had seen some in Teheran. Some foreigners there had fed dogs at their tables, washed and clothed them, fondled them in their laps, and took them riding in their carriages; were they not dog-worshipers? So he interpreted the lap-dog craze. Even burial of Christians with the clothes worn in life is supposed to have a religious purpose, and the firing of salutes at a soldier's funeral to be intended to drive away devils. The wearing of spectacles by so many foreigners has been mistaken for a badge of Christianity. An inquirer once asked for his spectacles after embracing the Christian faith.

One impression which the people have received is that drunkenness is permitted in a Christian, and is therefore not disgraceful. A story is told of an English captain whose ship touched at Bushire. The captain took a horseback ride through the city, but made such a poor display of horsemanship as to astonish and amuse the people. The next day a vendor of fruits came on board the ship and said to the captain, " I have made such an explanation as to free you from all reproach. There is no one who does not think that you are an expert rider, as becomes one of a nation of horsemen." " And how did you do that? " asked the captain. " I told them you were drunk "! As a part of his religion it was considered no disgrace.

The people acquire curious notions, too, of the missionaries, and of the means they are using to make converts. Sometimes they think they are working by a kind of magic. When a Jew, Rabbi Benjamin, of Mianduab, professed faith in Jesus, the Jews took him to the river-bank and ducked him to exorcize the evil spirit which they supposed had been cast into him. When some Jews in Hamadan accepted Christianity the report was spread abroad that the pastor had put some drug into the tea he gave them to drink, and had thus turned their heads.

Some are suspicious that they may be converted even by machinery. A story is told by a missionary of a woman who came to visit her and sat down in a rocking-chair. It rocked backward, so she drew her feet up under her. In doing so the chair tilted forward and she was pitched on the floor. She sprang up and ran out of the room, screaming, "Vy, vy! I have got into one of the converting-machines." Nothing could induce her to approach that Christian-making machine again.

Some of the people have the idea that money is the chief instrument used by missionaries. Help to the needy, food to the famished, and assistance to the persecuted are, it is supposed, given by missionaries, not as bribes, but as a loving ministry of charity. Orientals, with their mercenary ideas, often misunderstand such actions, and men come from unworthy motives to missionaries of all names and deceive them. One convert, after a time, requested money and was refused. He replied with indignation that he supposed, when he became a Christian, that whenever he asked for five hundred tomans he would receive them; and that as a brother he would be a sharer in the community of goods, as it was in the days of the apostles. How to fulfil the demands of Christian benevolence and yet avoid appealing to mercenary motives, is one of the difficult problems of missions.

Nor do Protestant missionaries aim to make converts by offers of political protection. Several English writers, especially some of ritualistic proclivities, have lately declared that the protection and aid rendered to the American Mission by British officials have helped to undermine the Nestorian Church, and have been, therefore, "mischievous" and "short-sighted." It is true that her Majesty's government graciously and ungrudgingly accorded the Americans protection during the half-century of the mission in which the United States was without diplomatic representation in Persia, and the American government and the missionaries have often expressed their appreciation of the favor.   It is strange now to read the words of these writers casting in the teeth of the recipients their obligation, and regretting that the favor was rendered.   But it is a pleasure to know that these complainers do not represent the spirit of Great Britain.   When Dr. Perkins and Dr. Grant established the mission, Sir Henry Ellis, British minister to Persia, requested them to apply to him for any assistance he might at any time be able to render them, and for British protection.   Once, in granting a passport, he wrote: " I feel confident that I act in accordance with the views of her Majesty's government, to whom the proposed introduction of the pure doctrine of the Reformed Church in the country cannot fail to be a matter of deep and serious interest. . . . I beg leave to assure you of my most anxious wishes for the success of your exertions. . . . Though a churchman myself, I bid God-speed to every pious Protestant engaged in this work."   Colonel C. E. Stewart, C.B., C.I.E., C.M.G., lately consul-general at Tabriz, wrote : " My daily prayer is that I may be of some assistance in furthering the kingdom of God."   As long as the history of the mission is read, the kindness and efficient help of a line of noble Britons, from Sir Henry Ellis and Sir John Campbell to Colonel Stewart, will be remembered with gratitude.   It has been the glory of Great Britain that she has been a bulwark to the evangelical church of Christ throughout the world ; and it would be lamentable indeed if the progress of ritualism had changed that attitude.

The same writers also make it a ground of accusation that Americans are known to some extent as English among the partially informed in Persia.   They even accuse the Americans of deception, and of trying to increase their influence by passing under the name of English.   The confusion in the popular mind would be sufficiently accounted for by the use of the English language, by being under English protection, and by the natural tendency of the people to use a familiar word rather than the term "American," which was almost unknown in Persia six decades ago. But there is a deeper reason. It is a universal Oriental mistake to confound racial and religious names. In Persia a Roman Catholic is popularly called a Frank (French), an Orthodox Catholic a Russ, and a Protestant an Inglees; that is, from the most conspicuous nation which represents each form of belief. This arises from an error of thought as well as expression, and is an injury to the progress of the truth. For instance, when an Armenian Gregorian in Persia accepts the Orthodox confession, people say he has become a Russian, and as a corollary think that he has ceased to be an Armenian, not being able to see that all the Armenians in Turkey and Persia might become Orthodox in ecclesiastical relation and not lose their race existence any more than the Bulgarians do, who are one with the Russians in religion. So Armenians and Nestorians who become Protestants are regarded popularly as Inglees. An Armenian Protestant refused to pay tribute to the Gregorian bishop, and gave the absurd reason, "I have become Inglees." The missionaries have made considerable effort to correct so false an idea, and to impress upon the people the fundamental distinction between race and religion. They wish their work completely separated from political names and issues. Those writers who hold that American missionaries, by some "deception," have originated this usage show their ignorance of Oriental modes of thought and expression. As a matter of fact, the doctrines of the Reformed Church as taught by the American missionaries represent more truly British Christianity and the English name than ritualism does. Neither need it be a matter of regret to our British friends if the ministry to the sick, the relief of the famished, the efforts for education and evangelization, and Christian lives have redounded to the credit of the English name before the Persian people.

At times the American Mission has been under the pro-

MISSION SCHOOL, TABRIZ.

tection of France. At other times it has received decided
help from Russian officials. When England was at war with
Persia, and it was proposed to mob the missionaries, Chevalier
Khanikoff made known to the Persian authorities that they
were under the protection of Russia, and harm was averted.
When the Jesuits had laid their plot to have the Protestants
expelled, the Russian ambassador, Count Medém, thwarted
their plans.

The strength of Protestant missionaries in Persia lies, then,
in the fact that they are known to have no political object.
They have no intrigues to engage in, nor civil policies to
antagonize or to promote. They have often been called upon
to appeal on behalf of the oppressed and persecuted, and have
been successful in securing relief, often by the assistance of
Christian diplomatists; but they have not made their friendly
aid contingent on the faith of the one in distress. Concerning this the Rev. B. Labaree, D.D., of the Armenian Mission,
writes: "Through the countenance and support of British officials in Persia the representations of the missionaries in behalf
of aggrieved Christians have often secured efficient redress.
Many a miscreant has been sent up to the capital or otherwise
punished who would have escaped free but for this interposi-
tion of the missionaries. Their very presence, and the general
belief that their truthful reports of outrages upon the Christians would echo back from the judgment-halls of Tabriz and
Teheran for the punishment of the guilty, have served in a
considerable degree as a check upon lawless Mohammedans.
It has been an irksome, unpleasant service. We have often
felt it an incubus upon our purely spiritual work. But duty
to the oppressed forbade our shirking the responsibility. That
this political influence has been abused for partizan ends I
boldly deny. From the most intimate acquaintance with the
facts I aver that it has been wielded by us in the interests of
justice and right alone; that all parties who have appealed to

it in need have shared impartially in its benefit; nor has it been exercised to weaken or tyrannize over the old church party in any form. It has been the principle of the Roman Catholic missionaries to help only such as belonged to or promised to join their communion. But the Presbyterian missionaries have never allowed any such rule of action. Did weeping parents flee to them with the tale of a daughter's forcible abduction; did a wife or a mother come to the mission with disheveled hair and outcries of grief, bringing the bloody clothes of a husband or a son ruthlessly murdered; did a body of priests and laymen from some oppressed village come telling of their landlord's rapacity or cruelty, it was never a question what was their creed. Jew or Christian, Protestant, Old Nestorian, or Armenian, if right and justice were clearly on their side, whatever aid was within the power of the American missionaries to bestow was freely given them. It was in the interest of an abducted Armenian girl, not a member of our congregation, that our missionary, Mr. Edward Breath, laid down his life, spending one night in her behalf in the cholera-infected city, and in twenty-four hours thereafter he was dead.

"Were any further statement needed to show the disinterested nature of this branch of our mission service it might be furnished from the 'Blue Book' of the English government, from the reports therein of British officials who have again and again testified to the truly philanthropic labors of the American missionaries."

Protestantism uses as instruments to make converts neither magic, money, machinery, nor ministers of state. The means on which it relies is the Word of God, translated, read, taught, preached, and made "quick and powerful" by the Spirit of God. To preach and translate the Word of God requires first of all, on the part of the missionaries, a thorough knowledge of the languages. In Persia each of the three great families of languages is represented, and the acquisition of more than one language is necessary for the best work. At Urumia the Syriac and Turkish are employed; at Mosul the Syriac and Arabic; at Tabriz and Salmas the Turkish and Armenian; at Teheran, Hamadan, and Ispahan the Persian and Armenian; at Bagdad the Arabic. Familiarity with the vernacular is expected of every missionary. No work is carried on by interpreters. Of all these languages Persian is the easiest and the sweetest. The acquisition of these languages is an arduous task, and ridiculous mistakes are at times made by missionaries when at first inadequately acquainted with the foreign tongues they use. A few examples of these may be cited. Wishing to order some meat (*at*), one said, "Bring me some *et*" (dog). Another, in preaching, wished to say, "He raised a load;" he said, "He burst himself." In the Armenian language a lady wished to ask, "Is the wife [*gen*] in the house?" The man quickly started and brought in wine (*gene*). Another, handing the slate to a girl whose problem was wrong, said, "Correct it!" She saw several of the girls smiling, and found she had said, "Oil it," using the word *yugher* for *ougher*. A minister, in prayer, instead of the term "pitiful God," said "pitiable God." An Armenian, in announcing in Turkish an offering for missions, and intending to say, "for the work of God in foreign lands," said, "for the work of the foreign God"!

One of the first aims of the missions has been to put the Bible into the languages of all the people. This has been largely accomplished. Henry Martyn's Persian version of the New Testament was followed by Dr. Green's version of the Old Testament. The whole has been lately revised by Dr. Bruce. The Bible in Turki for the Tartar Turks of northern Persia was translated by the Rev. Abraham Amirkhaniantz, of Tiflis, and revised by Dr. John N. Wright, of Salmas. The Armenian versions in Ararat and Constantinople dialects are both used. The modern Syriac version was prepared by Dr. Perkins, and has lately been revised by Dr. Benjamin Labaree. The Delitzsch Hebrew New Testament is used among the Jews, and the Arabic Bible by learned Mohammedans. The only work on this line remaining to be done is a Kurdish translation. In the preparation of these translations, as well as in their distribution, the British and Foreign and the American Bible societies have been both alike engaged. They have their agencies established in different parts of the country, and colporteurs itinerating through the outlying regions. A considerable number of religious works and text-books have been published in Syriac, and a few in Armenian, Persian, and Turki.

Medical work has been specially emphasized in the Persian missions. At each station both of the Presbyterian and the Church missions are physicians and dispensaries; while four American lady physicians and fully equipped hospitals are at Urumia and Teheran, with partially equipped ones at other stations. By these physicians tens of thousands of patients are treated annually in the dispensaries, a knowledge of true medical science is diffused, native physicians are trained, especially at Urumia, prejudices are dissipated, hearts opened to receive the truth, and many opportunities found for sowing the seed of the kingdom. The physicians are doing good work in maintaining cordial relations with the authorities, and thus are able to relieve the oppressed and persecuted, as well as to shield the mission from the machinations of its enemies. Lady physicians have been cordially welcomed by the Persians. A Persian fable relates that a queen at childbirth desired a doctor to be sent for. The king observed that a doctor was not necessary, for he had been out to the tent-dwellers and had seen the women give birth to children without the aid of a doctor. Afterward the queen, having commanded her people not to irrigate the garden, it withered, and the king scolded. She replied, "I have seen the forests grow without being watered; why cannot the garden do the same?" The lady physicians

will more and more be a boon and a blessing to suffering
womankind in Persia.

The Bible and medical work are beneficently directed
toward the whole population. The third great agency, education, is practically confined to the non-Moslems, on account
of the prohibition of the government. The American Mission
has one hundred and twenty schools, with thirty-four hundred
and seventy pupils. Eleven of these are schools of a high
grade, with one hundred and ninety-seven boys and two hundred and sixty-two girls as boarders. In Julfa, Ispahan, are
flourishing schools, with four hundred and twenty-five pupils in
attendance. Already some of their graduates have been enabled by a good knowledge of the English language to procure
lucrative positions. The educational work of Urumia station
is well organized. Its basis is an extended system of common
schools, reaching the villages on the plain and the hamlets in the
mountains. Several high schools occupy central localities,
while crowning the whole are the Fiske Seminary and the
college, with its academic, industrial, theological, and medical
departments. The spirit as well as the curriculum of these
schools, and of those in Tabriz, Teheran, Hamadan, Salmas,
and other places, is evangelistic. Thorough Bible instruction
prepares the hearts of the pupils for conversion by the Holy
Spirit, so that the schools are nurseries of the church as well as
training-institutions from which enlightened and well-equipped
evangelists, teachers, and preachers have gone forth with the
gospel in their lives and on their lips. One hundred and sixty
teachers and preachers have been graduated from the Urumia
College. An industrial school of carpentering and blacksmith-
ing is conducted in Urumia; and in Ispahan a woolen factory
is carried on. Industrial education is prosecuted with the object of furnishing the people with better means of self-support.

Turning now to the direct evangelistic work of the missions.

In this the missionaries are reinforced by about a hundred preachers and evangelists and ten Bible-women. This work has two stages—first, the pioneer work, and, secondly, the organized work. During the first stage an evangelist itinerates, or is stationed in a city or a village to reach the people by personal contact and conversation in their homes, in the bazaars, and at their various occupations. Results are often long delayed; at other times they are speedily manifested. Rev. Samuel A. Rhea once stopped at Hasan, a village in Kurdistan, where he entered into conversation with the Nestorian kand-khuda. The latter's earnest inquiry concerning truth was prolonged into the night, until finally his heart was convinced and he accepted evangelical doctrine. This conversion was the beginning of a flourishing church in that place.

The work among the Nestorians has a most interesting history and shows good results. It has been marked by manifestations of the Spirit's power and by times of refreshing, when deep conviction of sin, earnest seeking after salvation, and an intense joy of reconciliation with God characterized the converts. Some of them have reached a high plane of spiritual attainment.

A remarkable instance is that of Rabi Oshana, a young man upon whom the Spirit of God rested with special power. Early in his career he was awakened to his own personal need and the need of the church for greater consecration. He gave himself to the work of an evangelist, without salary, and organized a praying band of young men, who under his leadership went from village to village denouncing sin and calling the unconverted to repentance, and Christians especially to a higher degree of spiritual life. He was used as an instrument by God in bringing about some blessed revivals. His influence reached a wide circle, and his early death is lamented as a great loss to vital Christianity in Persia.

As another instance of the power of the gospel let me cite

the case of Hatoon of Degala. She had been a pupil in the seminary, but was dismissed for bad conduct. Afterward she kept a low grog-shop, where she sold liquor to Mussulmans. In the midst of a revival in Degala she was convicted of her sins, and their weight crushed her to the ground. With tears of penitence and humiliation she confessed, saying, "I am the crown of thorns that pierced my Saviour's brow; no one is like me." She became a reformed woman, and out of her deep experience began to tell others the story of her Saviour. Afterward she regained her former reputation and became one of the best teachers of the young of her sex in the village schools.

A spirit of dependence and lack of self-support has somewhat characterized these converts. The conduct of some in quickly changing back and forward between Nestorianism, Catholicism, Ritualism, and Protestantism has given them in some quarters the undeserved reputation of being time-servers. In the main, however, they are true and sincere. An example will manifest the character of some of them. Usta Pera, a carpenter of Urumia, was wicked and a drunkard. He was afterward converted and became a changed man, ever ready to suffer persecution for his faith. His reputation became such that it was said, "You will find this man true always, in all things." His only daughter, educated in the seminary, was accustomed to read the Bible to him, but she was stricken down with the cholera. He then made several attempts to learn to read, but found it difficult at his advanced age and gave it up. One day he noticed a little stream of water which, trickling down, had worn a course in the rock. He said to himself, " Perseverance can accomplish great things." He tried again, and in time became a good reader. Though he always continued to work at his trade, he became an elder, a teacher in the Sabbath-school, and an exhorter of considerable power. His shop was a place of testimony for the Saviour. At his funeral his Testament was shown, which he had read through twenty-five times. He was a liberal man and yearly supported two girls in the seminary. He lived next door to the Catholic Mission, the authorities of which offered him a large price for his property; but he left it by will to the gospel work. It was fitted up as a house of worship, and about the same time a company of Roman Catholics left that church and with some Protestants formed a congregation. Other converts have shown a like genuine spirit of liberality. A man in Charbash built a manse for the congregation, while a pastor left a legacy to the Board equal to two years' salary.

In steadfastness, too, these converts, when put to the test, have not been found wanting. Of one of these, Shedd narrates: "A girl of fourteen years, whose name was Hatoon, had learned to read of and love her Saviour, and, with other girls of her village, had formed a praying missionary band. She had a very bad mother, who had given two of her daughters to Mussulman husbands, and they have, in consequence, denied their faith. She resolved to do the same with this daughter. One morning, at family prayers, the village pastor heard a great disturbance in the street, and, going out, found the mother and some Mussulmans trying to compel Hatoon to go with them. He rescued her; but soon officers came, and she was carried before the prince governor. Here she was confined for four days, with access to no Christian, but only to her mother, and with every means used to induce her to consent to be a Mussulman. The Christians of her village gathered *en masse* and demanded possession of the girl, or that she be released. The governor called her to his presence, and permitted no one but her mother to be near. He allowed Shamasha Eleya and two others to be in the yard and in sight. He then tried to induce her to yield, but said he would not use force. She gave the most decided testimony—would not give up Christ; would give up her mother, her property, everything, but Christ never!   The prince had to confess that she was a Christian.   Then her mother tried to have her put again into her power, but she once more said that she would not deny her Saviour.   She could not stay with her mother, but fled and seized the skirts of her pastor, Shamasha Eleya. She is now with our school-girls."

These are but stray instances of the power of the gospel among the Nestorians.   The results of mission work among them cannot now be enlarged upon.   Any one who will compare the material, social, intellectual, moral, and spiritual condition of these people with what it was sixty years ago, and is aware of the large part the American Mission has had in bringing about this amelioration, will find reason to pronounce the work blessed.

Protestant mission work among the Armenians of Persia was begun about twenty-five years ago.   It encountered the prejudices and the hatred which had arisen against such work in Turkey, in addition to a newly aroused persecuting spirit, which had largely spent itself there some decades before. These difficulties cannot be detailed.   But notwithstanding the hindrances of priestly opposition, together with the skeptical tendencies, the worldliness, and the race prejudices that prevail, substantial progress, it will be seen, has been made in enlightening the Armenians in Urumia, Tabriz, Salmas, Hamadan, and Ispahan.   Converts have been made and churches organized.   At Ispahan there is a prosperous congregation of three hundred.   At Hamadan gospel truth has nearly leavened the Armenian community.   Services are no longer held in the old Gregorian church, which is crumbling to pieces.   All children of school age are now in the mission schools.   Evangelical truth has had a vital influence upon the Armenians throughout Persia, even upon those who have remained Gregorians. The acceptance of Reform doctrines is much wider than the

profession of Protestantism.   The missions, too, have spurred
the Armenians to open up good schools, and to improve their
condition in various ways.

One of the Armenian converts lately met a tragic death.
He was a merchant in Urumia, named Aga Jan Khan, with
a rank among the nobility, and was married to one of a
Georgian family in the shah's service, whose chief representative now is Persian minister to France.   His wife had been a
Catholic and he a Gregorian ; both had joined the evangelical
communion.   His store was frequently the place of religious
discussions, especially among Mohammedans, and because of
this he was hated by the mollas.   His apparent prosperity also
excited envy.   His enemies determined to accomplish his destruction, and laid a plot to effect this.   One morning, about
ten o'clock, a Mohammedan woman entered his store, where
some men also were present.   She had been negotiating with
him about the sale of a certain piece of land, on which he had
advanced a small sum.   They failed to strike a bargain, and
she left the store.   A sayid rapidly spread the report that she
had gone there for evil purposes.   This report was given out
in the Juma mosque and an attack was ordered.   Immediately an infuriated rabble of sayids, mollas, and looties rushed
upon Aga Jan, threw him out in the street, kicked and beat him,
and dragged him through the streets.   He was taken to the
mosque.   The chief molla, fearing he would be killed, put
him in the place of refuge and barred the door.   He then said
to him, "You are charged with adultery with a Mohammedan
woman ; whether true or false, you can save yourself only by
turning Mohammedan."   He refused, and promised the molla
five hundred dollars if he would save him.   The molla said,
"No; say the creed or they will kill you!"   Aga Jan fell on
his knees for a moment of prayer, while the mob, which now
filled all the courts and roofs and adjoining streets, was raging in fury for his blood.   Finally they broke down the door

and dragged him out.   After again offering him his life if he would deny his faith they thrust him through with thirty dagger wounds, and cursed his religion, while he ejaculated, " Eloi, Eloi, lama sabachthani? "   A rope was then tied around his neck, and his body, naked and beaten beyond recognition, was dragged through the streets and flung into a cesspool, and a dead dog thrown in beside him.

Great fear fell upon all the Christians, and several other murders occurred.   Afterward the shah's government paid an indemnity and granted a pension to the widow and orphans, with a title of nobility to the eldest son, in recognition of Aga Jan Khan's innocence, and as a reparation for the negligence of the government of Urumia in not rescuing him from the mob.

Mission work among the Jews is nominally permitted by the government, but often the local authorities hinder its prosecution.   Something has been done for their evangelization in Hamadan, Teheran, Urumia, Ispahan, and in the outstations of Tabriz and Salmas.   A church of converts from Judaism has been organized in Hamadan.   Much persecution has been endured by them.   Of their present condition Mr. Hawkes reports in 1895: "Among the Jews here there is now a remarkable spirit of inquiry.   It seemed to begin with a prominent Jewish doctor, who has been very friendly with Dr. Holmes from the day of his arrival, and has worked with him professionally.   Dr. Holmes utilized some of the opportunities which these occasions presented to ask him several pertinent questions about the coming of the Messiah, which led him to think about and investigate them, until he seems very near to the acceptance of Christ as his Saviour.   His thoughtfulness has been contagious, especially among his relatives and professional friends, and for several weeks quite a number of them have met the missionaries and Jewish Christians to discuss the claims of the Messiah.   These discussions have been carried on largely in a spirit of fairness quite unusual in my experience, and they have always resulted in the acceptance of the Christian interpretation of the Old Testament passages under discussion. The spirit of inquiry is becoming general, and the hand of God is evidently in the movement.

"It is too soon to look for results, or to prophesy whereunto this will grow; but it is already evident that those who have for a long time been convinced of the truth of Christianity, and have understood their duty, but have not had the courage to come out and make an open profession, are taking advantage of this movement to openly acknowledge Christ and thus relieve their consciences. This is especially true of several present and former pupils of the boys' school.

"Again, it is evident that the enforced acceptance of Islam by some, against their better judgment, which was accomplished by the Mullah Abdullah movement, is now reacting against a more general acceptance thereof, and is driving them, happily, to Christ."

This is encouraging testimony, and must be grateful to the well-wishers of missions in the Orient, as it is grateful to the workers and toilers in the field. Other signs are not wanting to attest the value of missionary labor in Persia and the faithfulness of the ministering work.

Summarizing the results of Protestant missions in Persia, there is first the Church Missionary Society, with two stations, four ordained, two medical, and six female missionaries, and two churches, with one hundred and thirty communicants. It is presided over by Bishop Stuart, formerly Bishop of New Zealand, who resigned that post to devote himself to work in Persia. A new station is projected at Yezd, where there are seven thousand Parsees and some hundreds of Jews in a large Mohammedan population.

The American Presbyterian Mission has five stations, eleven ordained, nine medical, one industrial, and thirty-eight female missionaries, thirty-eight churches, with twenty-eight hundred and thirty-eight communicants,* organized in three Presbyteries, with Boards of Missions, of Education, and of Jurisprudence.

There is also a congregation of Lutherans in Urumia, with other scattered communicants. The total number of Protestants in Persia is over three thousand communicants and about ten thousand adherents.

It is a trite criticism on missions to say that they do not pay. The Hon. George N. Curzon, in " Persia and the Persian Question," in speaking of the work of the Church Missionary Society at Ispahan, says, " Here, as in many parts of the East, the results do not, in my opinion, justify the expenditure both of labor and of money." It must be admitted that mission work in Persia is very difficult and encounters many obstacles, but the friends of missions have no reason to fear a comparison of missionary with commercial enterprise, as regards either economy or success. The missionaries may appear from a native standard to live in comfort and to have high salaries, but they are on the lowest scale paid to foreigners. The English artisans of the Mining Corporation had larger incomes than the missionaries. The manager of the branch of the Imperial Bank at Tabriz refused to continue his engagement, though he was receiving a salary equal to the expenditures of a whole mission station.

As to the results of the commercial enterprises, the conces-

* The progress of the Mission is seen in the following table:

	1873	1893
Churches	8	36
Congregations	70	119
Ordained natives	22	55
Other preachers	38	66
Received during year	53	294
Communicants	767	2,716
Attendants (average)	2,402	6,628
Sabbath-school scholars		5,440

sions for roads, railways, and artesian wells acquired and found unprofitable, merchant companies formed and dissolved, newspapers started and suspended, army drillers employed and dismissed, reforms projected and dying still-born, show that the promoters of civilization as distinct from religion have no reason to cast stones at the promoters of Christianity.

While rejoicing in the success of the telegraph, the banks, and everything that tends to progress, the missionary enterprise can show a good record of work accomplished. Thousands of children have been educated, orphans cared for, trades taught, the famished fed, the oppressed relieved, the sick ministered unto, and religious liberty and rights promoted. A knowledge of Reformed Christianity has been inculcated, resulting in an increased esteem for it, even among those who do not accept it ; a permanent basis of an evangelical literature has been laid in the translations of the Bible and religious books ; an impulse has been given to the Oriental churches to effect internal reforms ; and an aggressive evangelical community has been established. Of those who have taken part in this varied and beneficent work, or have been the recipients of its benefits, a goodly number have departed to join the glorious company of the redeemed. These benefits to the bodies, minds, and souls of people in Persia are above money value and cannot be measured by any mere commercial standard.

In Persia, when a fountain is to be opened, men go up into a valley, and with pick and shovel, bucket and windlass, put down wells and excavate underground channels, that the water may flow over the plains below. From the *chesma* or eye of this fountain a copious stream bursts forth, and soon there appears a scene of verdure—fertile fields, fruitful gardens and vineyards, and willows and poplars by the watercourses. Wherever the stream goes it manifests its fructifying, beautifying, purifying, refreshing, vivifying power, making what the Persians call a *fardus*—a veritable paradise.

So a fountain was opened in Jerusalem for sin and for uncleanness. Of old its streams flowed over these Eastern lands,
making them a garden of the Lord in spiritual beauty. But
the channels became filled up with superstitions, errors, and
evil practices, and the Oriental churches withered and decayed.
Now the servants of the Master-Husbandman are at work removing the debris, that the waters of life may again overflow
the waste places and reach even to new Mohammedan fields,
and the parched ground become a pool, and the thirsty land
streams of water.

Already in different parts of Persia we see little spiritual
oases. In the plains of Urumia and Salmas, among the
mountains of Kurdistan, through which Xenophon led his retreating ten thousand, along the banks of the Tigris, by the
ruins of ancient Nineveh, at Hamadan, hard by the tomb of
Esther and Mordecai, and in the cities of Tabriz, Teheran, and
Ispahan, we see the beginnings and look soon for the abundant fruits of Christian living.

As the streams become more copious and are led here and
there over the land, " the wilderness and the solitary place shall
be made glad, and the desert shall rejoice and blossom as the
rose."

APPENDIX

APPENDIX I

HISTORY OF TABRIZ

THE founding of Tabriz is lost in antiquity. It has sometimes been mistaken for the ancient Gaza, Ganzaca, or the northern Ecbatana. It probably received its name from Khosrau I. of Armenia, who, to revenge the death of his brother, attacked and defeated Ardashir, the first of the Sassanian dynasty, A.D. 246, and changed the name of the city from Shahistan to Ta-vrezh ("this revenge")—Tauris. It was retaken by Shapur, but was given by Galerius to Tiridates, with the province of Atropatene (Armenian, Aderbadagan; Persian, Azerbijan), after their successful war against Narsi. Tiridates made Tauris (Tabriz) his capital and beautified it. (Malcolm, i., 83.) Arshag Tiranus, of Armenia, assisted by the Huns and Alans, invaded Azerbijan A.D. 363, and defeated Shapur near Tabriz. (Gibbon, ii. 472.) Under the Sassanians it continued to be an important city.

A Persian legend says that, in the time of the caliphs, Zubaidah, the wife of Haroun-il-Raschid, was advised to travel for her health, and reaching this site, recovered, and then founded a city, which she named Tabriz on account of the salubrity of the climate. Tab-riz in Persian signifies "Fever-scatterer." The queen is said to have summoned Satah from Damascus to determine astrologically a fortunate time for founding a city. It is probable that she simply beautified and enlarged it. One of the fountains of the city is now called by her name. Others derive the name Tabriz from the Sanskrit *tab*, warm, and *riz*, to flow, from the warm springs in the neighboring mountain. There are none nearer than twenty miles. In 858 much destruction was wrought by a great earthquake, and Caliph Motavakkil rebuilt the city. In 1041 forty thousand people perished from the same cause. The warning of Abou Tahir, an astrologer of

323

Shiraz, who was at Tabriz, enabled many to escape. He also foretold
that there would be no more earthquakes for three hundred years.
(" Mirror of Cities," in Persian.) After the time of the Seljuks Tabriz
was for a brief period the capital of an independent principality, under the
Ata Begs of the Ilij-Guz family, whose power was overthrown by the sultan
of Khiva. As the capital of the Mongols Tabriz enjoyed a few decades
of great prosperity. Abaka Khan erected in it great buildings. The
bazaars in the time of Ghazan Khan (1295–1303) were said to make the
eyes swim. Finely dressed youths attracted customers by their beauty of
manner. The jewelry displayed was superb. Ghazan Khan, called Sham
(Syria) from his attempted conquest of Syria, built a combined palace,
school, and sepulchral monument, greater, according to Hamd-Ullah,
than any building in Persia. The ruins are now called Sham Ghazan,
consisting of cellars and mounds in the suburb, Hukmabad. Many of
the arches are being excavated, and the materials used for new buildings,
and the debris appropriated as fertilizers. Blue tiles can be picked up in
the ruins or obtained from the gardeners. The wall of the Mongol city
was thirty-five feet wide and fifteen thousand or twenty-five thousand
paces in length, with five main gates and eight smaller ones. Charanduab,
Sarkhab, and Beylan Kuh are within the walls. The population is said
to have been five hundred thousand. The mound of the wall can yet be
traced to the south of the city. Sham Ghazan's vizier built the Rub-i-
Rashidiah, which, though repaired by Shah Abbas, is now a shapeless
mound in Bagh-Meshed. The extent of Mongol influence may be seen in
the fact that Abaka Khan married a daughter of the Emperor Michael
Palæologus, and his successor married the daughter of the emperor of
China. Envoys from the pope visited their capital. A letter is extant
from Edward I. of England to Ghazan Khan.

We are informed by a native historian that in 1370 three hundred thousand died in Tabriz of the cholera; in 1384 Shah Shuja Muzaffari conquered it and spent four months in it; shortly afterward it was taken and
sacked by Tamerlane; yet in 1405 it had recovered and had two hundred
thousand inhabitants. During the fifteenth century it was ruled by the
Turkomans of the Black and White Sheep tribes. Of the former's
dominions it was the capital. Kara Yosef improved the city. Jehan
Shah, who was tributary to the Tartar shah, built the Blue Mosque.

Tabriz was favored as the seat of royalty by Shah Ismael, the founder
of the Safavian dynasty. When Ispahan became his capital the beglar-
begis governed Tabriz. The interest of this period (1500–1750) in the
story of Tabriz centers around the contests between the Osmanli sultans
and the Persians for the possession of Azerbijan. Here was the scene of

a long-fought and bloody contest of Sunni against Shiah, in which it was considered more meritorious to kill one Shiah than to have killed seventy Christians. Ismael, the holy sheik of the Persians, was called by the Turks the " slave of the devil." Selim I. defeated Shah Ismael at Khoi, took Tabriz, and sent away Armenian and Mussulman artisans to Constantinople. Sultan Suleiman besieged Tabriz, forced it to surrender, but soon abandoned it. Osman Pasha again took it, and the Osmanlis held it for eighteen years, until driven out by Shah Abbas. Some say that he sent five hundred soldiers into the city dressed as merchants, who seized the fort and prepared for his attack. After his death Murad Sultan captured the city, but again retreated. A terrible earthquake in 1725 destroyed a great part of the city and caused the death of eighty thousand people. Three years afterward, though without walls or cannon, the Persians destroyed an army of twenty-four thousand under the pasha of Van. When the sultan sent a greater army against them, they removed their women and children to Ghilan, and waged a bloody contest for days, in which thirty thousand men perished, and the remainder capitulated on condition of being allowed to retire to Ardebil. Tabriz was left without an inhabitant. (Malcolm, i., 458.) By an agreement between Turkey and Russia, northern Persia was to be divided between them, and Azerbijan was about to become a fixed part of the Turkish empire, when the magic prowess of Nadir Shah turned the tide of fortune and it became again Persian, and Persian, except during the Russian occupation of 1829, it has remained. But Tabriz's misfortunes were not yet at an end. In 1780 another earthquake ruined fifteen thousand houses and killed forty thousand people. During the period of confusion following Nadir Shah, Tabriz was ruled independently by the Dumbli khans, until the time of the Kajars, under whom this family have generally held the post of beglarbegi or mayor. The wall, three and a half miles long, around the old city, with the moat, was erected by the Dumbli khans. The eight gates are still the landmarks of the city. The Stamboul gate, with its blue tile pillars and ornamental decorations, is a handsome structure. It has a memorial stone with the name of Najef Guli Khan.

APPENDIX II

CALENDAR OF THE PERSIAN YEAR

Month	*Date*	*Event*
Muharram	1.	Beginning of mourning.
	10.	Ashura, the martyrdom of Imam Husain.
	12.	Death of Imam Zain-il-Abidin, A.H. 110.
Safar	1.	Battle between Ali and Muavia.
	3.	Birth of Imam Mohammed-Baghir.
	6.	Birth of Nazir-i-Din, Shah, A.H. 1247.
	7.	Birth of Imam Musa-Kazim.
	17.	Martyrdom of Imam Reza.*
Rabi-il-Avvel	5.	Birth of Imam Husain.*
	8.	Death of Imam Hasan-Askari.
	12.	Birth of Mohammed.
	14.	Abubekr becomes caliph, A.H. 11.
	15.	Death of Yezid.
Rabi-il-Akhir	4.	Birth of Imam Hasan-Askari, A.H. 232.
Jamadi-il-Avvel	4.	Death of Imam Hasan, A.H. 49.
	15.	Birth of Imam Zain-il-Abidin, A.H. 38.
Jamadi-il-Akhir	3.	Death of Fatima, A.H. 11.*
	20.	Birth of Fatima.*
Rajab	1.	Birth of Imam Mohammed-Baghir.*
	2.	Birth of Ali Nagi.
	13.	Birth of Ali.
	27.	Maraj (journey of Mohammed to heaven).
Shaban	3.	Birth of Imam Husain.*
	15.	Birth of Fatima.* / Birth of Mohammed Ibn Hasan.
Ramadan	1.	Month of fasting.
	2.	Death of Fatima.*
	15.	Births of Imam Hasan and Imam Mohammed-Tagi.
	18.	Smiting of Ali.
	21.	Death of Ali.
	24.	Martyrdom of Imam Reza.*
	27.	Execution of Ibn Mulzam.

* Some events are assigned two dates, according to different traditions.

Shavval	1. Fitr or Uruch Bairam.
	4. Disappearance of twelfth imam, A.H. 265.
	12. Smiting of the moon by Mohammed.
	25. Martyrdom of Imam Jafar-Sadik.
Zilgada	11. Birth of Imam Reza.
Zil Haja	10. Kurban Bairam.
	13. Accession of Ali to the caliphate.
	18. Mohammed declares Ali his successor.
	25. Feast of Khatam Bakhsh.
	26. Death of Omar.

APPENDIX III

MONETARY SYSTEM

Table of Denar System

5 denars	= 1 gazbeh
20 "	= 1 bisti
30 "	= 1 tanbal
50 "	= 1 shahi
100 "	= 1 yuzaltun
200 "	= 1 abbasi
500 "	= 1 penabad
1,000 "	= 1 kran
1,250 "	= 1 real
10,000 "	= 1 toman

The origin of these names is as follows: denar is from the Latin *denarius* (a penny); shahi from shah-king; abbasi from a coin struck by Shah Abbas at Tiflis; penabad from a coin struck at Shushan, which city is called also Pena-abad, from Pena Khan; kran is, in full, sahib-kran ("lord of a generation"), and was first struck by a shah to commemorate the thirtieth year of his reign; real is from a Spanish coin of a like value; toman means ten thousand, and was used for a division of the old Tartar army, and is retained in the title Amir-i-Toman.

WEIGHTS AND MEASURES

Table of Weights		*Urumia Weights*	
4 grains	= 1 nokhud	100 miskals	= 1 dirham
6 nokhuds	= 1 dang	4 dirhams	= 1 hefta
4 dangs	= 1 miskal	8 heftas	= 1 batman
640 miskals	= 1 sagat batman	10 batmans	= 1 load
800 "	= 1 meeskar "	20 "	= 1 dewan load
1,000 "	= 1 rasta " (Tabriz)	25 "	= 1 bazaar load
1,280 "	= 1 batman-i-shah		
2,560 "	= 1 rhé batman		
3,200 "	= 1 Urumia batman		
100 "	= 1 kharvar		

The unit of length is the arshîn (Tabriz), dry (Urumia), or zar (Teheran). It is 44 inches in the former and 42½ inches in the two latter places. The farsakh (parasang) or agach is 6000 arshîns. For land measure the term "batman" is also used in Tabriz. There are three kinds, called the yuzaltun, eke-shahi-yarum, and bir-abbasi batmans, which contain respectively 100, 125, and 200 square arshîns. The second is commonly used.

INDEX

A MAP
OF
NORTHWESTERN PERSIA
TO ACCOMPANY
WILSON'S PERSIAN LIFE AND
CUSTOMS

Scale

- - - - - - Boundaries
·············· Journeys of Author
——————— Mission Stations

Important New Books.

Rambles in Japan. By Rev. Canon H. B. Tristram, D.D. Indexed. With many illustrations by E. Whymper, and a map. Large 8vo cloth.................................. ....$2.00

"Canon Tristram has been prompted to publish these pages from his journal by the new zest for all things Japanese....He always writes pleasantly, freshly, and intelligently; and he has a veteran naturalist's eye for the flora and fauna of the land of the rising sun....He did a good deal of traveling and had an excellent guide and interpreter in his daughter, who has spent several years at mission work in the country."—*The British Weekly.*

Persian Life and Customs. With Incidents of Residence and Travel in the Land of the Lion and the Sun. By the Rev. S. G. Wilson, M.A., for fifteen years a missionary in Persia. Well indexed. With map and other illustration. 8vo, cloth........ 1.75

Mr. Wilson tells in bright, terse sentences of his experience as a resident of Tabriz and a traveler through different parts of Persia, thus giving a vivid idea of life in that ancient country.

From Far Formosa. The Island, its People and Missions. By Rev. G. L. Mackay, D.D. Well indexed. With many illustrations from photographs by the author, and several maps. 8vo, cloth.................................. ....$2.00

Dr. Mackay has lived in Formosa for twenty-two years, being the first missionary to establish a permanent station there. The physical features of the island, its minerals, animal and vegetable life, and its inhabitants, are among the subjects treated at length. Space is also given to the author's experience as a missionary.

The Life of John Livingston Nevius, for Forty Years a Missionary in China. By his wife, Helen S. C. Nevius. Map and other illustrations. 8vo, cloth..... .... 2.00

Dr. Nevius stood in the front rank of modern missionaries as organizer, pastor, educator, and as a translator of Christian literature into a Pagan tongue.

"Ought to be and is sure to be widely read. As interesting as it is valuable."—*The Evangelist.*

The Personal Life of David Livingstone. Chiefly from his unpublished journals and correspondence in the possession of his family. By W. Garden Blackie, D.D., LL.D. With portrait. New cheap edition. 508 pages, 8vo, cloth................... 1.50

This is not a new life of Livingstone, but the republication of the standard work, which has been out of print for some years.

A Maker of the New Japan. The Life of Joseph Hardy Neesima, founder of Doshisha University, Japan. By Rev. J. D. Davis, D.D., Professor in Doshisha. With 16 original illustrations. 12mo, cloth................................. .... 1.00

"The life is admirably and spiritedly written, and its hero stands forth as one of the most romantic and inspiring figures of modern times."—*The Examiner.*

Pioneering in New Guinea, 1877-1894. By Rev. James Chalmers, the Pioneer Missionary to New Guinea. With 43 original illustrations. 12mo, cloth.......... .... 1.50

Important New Books.

The Pilgrim Fathers of New England. And their Puritan Successors. By John Brown. D.D., author of "John Bunyan, His Life, Times and Work." Introduction by Rev. A. E. Dunning, Editor of *The Congregationalist.* Illustrated. 8vo, cloth, gilt top... 2.50
     This is an elaborate and comprehensive sketch, by an acknowledged authority, of the history and influence upon both sides of the Atlantic of the religious movement initiated by the Pilgrim Fathers.

The Shepherd Psalm. A new holiday edition of the Rev. F. B. Meyer's famous work. With illustrations by Mary A. Lathbury on every page. 12mo, richly ornamented cloth covers, boxed. 1.25
     A devotional exposition of the Twenty-third Psalm printed in two colors.

Gifts for the Day. A set containing "A Gift of Love" (Morning Hour) and "A Gift of Peace (Evening Hour). 2 vols., long 18mo, decorated buckram cloth, gilt top, boxed 2.50

Successward. A Young Man's Book for Young Men. By Edward W. Bok, Editor of *The Ladies' Home Journal.* 16mo, cloth 1,00
     "There has long been need of just such a plain, practical, common-sense volume as this. It is founded upon personal experience. Mr. Bok speaks many a true word in this guide to conduct "—*Boston Beacon.*
     "Full of common sense. For young men it is unquestionably the book of the day."—*Commercial Advertiser.*
     "Earnest, sincere and practical....It will not last simply for a day, but will be read again and again."—*Boston Journal.*
     "Every young man will believe that Mr. Bok is talking directly and solely to him."—*Mail and Express.*

Questions of Modern Inquiry. A Series of Discussions. By Rev. Henry A. Stimson, D.D., Pastor Broadway Tabernacle, N. Y. 12mo, cloth.. 1.25
     "The strength of the authors method lies in its good sense."—*The Independent.*

The Diary of a Japanese Convert. By Kanzo Uchimura. 12mo, cloth.. 1.00
     Written in English by a native Japanese, it is probably the first attempt of a "heathen" convert to record the growth and development of an awakened mind. His comments on the accepted beliefs of Christiandom are very interesting.

Madagascar of Today. By W. E. Cousins, for twenty-two years a missionary in Madagascar. Illustrated, 12mo, cloth...... 1.00
     "Completely successful in its purpose to set forth in brief the main facts as to the country, its people and its history."—*Nation.*

The Missionary Pastor. By Rev. J. E. Adams. Helps for developing the Missionary Life. Edited from the material of the educational department of the Student Volunteer Movement for Foreign Missions. With 57 full page charts prepared by R. J. Kellogg. 16mo, cloth.................................. .75
     "A useful and. should be an inspiring manual."—*The Independent.*

Travel and Exploration.

Reality versus Romance in South Central Africa. Being an Account of a Journey Across the African Continent, from Benguella on the West Coast, to the mouth of the Zambesi. By James Johnston, M.D. With 51 full-page photogravure reproductions of photographs by the author, and a map. Royal 8vo, cloth, boxed...... ....$4.00

"Dr. Johnston has the courage of his opinions gained by what he has seen. . . . The merits of this volume are incontestable. The photogravures are as novel as they are excellent."—*The New York Times.*

Chinese Characteristics. By Arthur H. Smith. *Second Edition, Revised.* With 16 illustrations from original photographs. 8vo, cloth 2.00

"Cannot be praised too highly."—*The Independent* (N. Y.)

"Not only one of the ablest analyses and portrayals of the Chinese character, but on the whole one of the most judicial. Twenty-two years' residence among the people, with command of their language, has enabled Mr. Smith to see them as they are."—*The Nation.*

"A completely trustworthy study."—*The Advance.*

"Combines rare insight into facts with clear and forcible forms of expression. Most delightful reading."—*Rev. A. T. Pierson, D. D.*

The Chronicles of the Sid; or, The Life and Travels of Adelia Gates. By Adela E. Orpen. With many illustrations. 8vo, cloth 1.50

"If Miss Gates is not the great American traveler, it would be hard to find anyone who has a better right to the title. . . . Her life is well worth the telling."—*The New York Evangelist.*

Among the Tibetans. By Isabella Bird Bishop, author of "Unbeaten Tracks in Japan," etc. Illustrations by Whymper. 12mo, cloth... 1.00

Paper...... .... .35

"This volume is as fresh and striking as was Miss Isabella Bird's first notable venture, the much appreciated 'Unbeaten Tracks in Japan.' "—*The N. Y. Times.*

Ten Years Digging in Egypt, 1881-1891. By W. M. Flinders Petrie. With a map and 116 illustrations. *Second Edition.* 12mo, cloth..... .... 1.50

"The increase of our knowledge of the history of ancient Egypt, made during the last decade has been largely due to the brilliant conjectures and subsequent sagacious investigations of Mr. Petrie."—*The Outlook.*

The Ainu of Japan. The Religion, Superstitions and General History of the Hairy Aborigines of Japan. By Rev. John Batchelor. With 80 illustrations. 8vo, cloth............... 1.50

A Winter in North China. By Rev. T. M. Morris. With a map. 12mo, cloth.. 1.50

*** See also *Pen and Pencil Series, By-Paths of Bible Knowledge, and Missions.*

www.ingramcontent.com/pod-product-compliance
Lightning Source LLC
Chambersburg PA
CBHW020240290326
41929CB00045B/844